Karen —

Glad to have the
opportunity to work with
you and the GRC team!

All the best —

Perry

FIXED-INCOME SYNTHETIC ASSETS

FIXED-INCOME SYNTHETIC ASSETS

Packaging, Pricing, and Trading Strategies for Financial Professionals

Perry H. Beaumont

John Wiley & Sons, Inc.

New York • Chichester • Brisbane • Toronto • Singapore

To my mother and father

In recognition of the importance of preserving what has been
written, it is a policy of John Wiley & Sons, Inc., to have
books of enduring value published in the United States
printed on acid-free paper, and we exert our best efforts
to that end.

Library of Congress Cataloging-in-Publication Data

Beaumont, Perry H., 1961–
    Fixed-income synthetic assets : packaging, pricing, and trading
strategies for financial professionals / by Perry H. Beaumont.
        p.   cm.—(Wiley finance editions)
    Includes index.
    ISBN 0-471-55162-7 (cloth : acid-free paper) :
    1. Financial engineering.   2. Fixed-income securities.   I. Title.
II. Series.
HG176.7.B43   1992
332.63′2—dc20   92-10373

Printed in the United States of America

10 9 8 7 6 5 4 3 2 1

Foreword

Financial markets have witnessed phenomenal expansion worldwide. While many new products appear to be increasingly complex, any fixed-income strategy may be evaluated as a creative combination of fundamental building blocks.

As investors and issuers create new instruments with a vast array of securities in an ever-evolving marketplace, the only limit to growth will be our own imagination.

From A-tranche collateralized mortgage obligations to zero coupon bonds, *Fixed-Income Synthetic Assets* guides the novice and professional through a variety of innovative structures. Using the nuts and bolts of financial engineering, Perry H. Beaumont provides a variety of techniques for packaging, pricing, and managing financial products for the markets of today and the future.

As the first sourcebook of its kind, *Fixed-Income Synthetic Assets* will undoubtedly prove to be an invaluable desktop reference that you will consult time and again.

JOHN G. WIDMER
Senior Vice-President
Swiss Bank Corporation

Preface

In the process of writing this book, I have had the good fortune of corraborating with several helpful individuals. Deserving of a very special recognition is Gilbert Benz of Swiss Bank Corporation. Gil reviewed every chapter and offered many useful suggestions. The book is stronger because of his influence. Jack Malvey of Kidder, Peabody, John Tierney of Lehman Brothers, and Thomas J. Hickey and Michael Sigman of Swiss Bank Corporation also provided many helpful suggestions. Molly E. Kenefick of Swiss Bank Corporation shared her sharp editing skills.

I would also like to thank Swiss Bank Corporation generally for both supporting and encouraging this book along the way. In particular, I wish to thank Forrest Collier.

Finally, while every effort has been made to ensure that data, charts, and text are accurate and true, any errors are my responsibility alone.

PERRY H. BEAUMONT

Brooklyn, New York
July 1992

Contents

Appendices

Glossary   292

Index   303

Introduction

Innovative financial products are entering the marketplace at a dizzying pace. These products are increasingly complex, and it is essential that the fixed-income professional understand the basic structure of these securities.

Fixed-Income Synthetic Assets provides a cookbook approach to financial engineering. The reader is provided with an overview of the tools and techniques for creating synthetic assets as well as an explanation of how to identify fair market value.

Simply defined, a synthetic asset is any product created with other securities. For example, a synthetic asset may be designed to replicate the risk/return profile of an existing security. In this instance, the motivation for the trade may be that the net cost for creating the synthetic asset is below that of the security being replicated. Another motivation may be that a desired risk/return profile is not available for any existing security.

There are generally three reasons investors and issuers should be knowledgeable about synthetic assets. First, issuers and investors may create a security that is more desirable than the asset being replicated. Second, understanding the structure of synthetic assets will allow issuers and investors to better identify value among complex financial products. Third, issuers and investors may want to tailor a security with cashflows and market sensitivities that are not available among assets currently in the marketplace.

Fixed-Income Synthetic Assets is more concerned with practical applications than theory, yet financial theory is explained when it facilitates an intuitive understanding of financial strategies. For example, since covered interest rate parity plays an essential role in the way forward rates are determined in the foreign exchange market, this theory is reviewed when we consider international opportunities.

Finally, it is hoped that *Fixed-Income Synthetic Assets* will encourage the reader to approach the fixed-income market in a new way. To put it simply, any fixed-income security can be reduced to an interest-rate-sensitive asset with cashflows. And with the variety of fixed-income securities available, including Treasury issues, STRIPS, futures, options, futures options, floating rate notes, mortgage-backed securities, and many others, an almost infinite combination of assets may be created to capture a desired interest rate sensitivity for any particular pattern of cashflows. Traditional securities are increasingly viewed as the building blocks of innovative assets, and not just investment vehicles in and of themselves. *Fixed-Income Synthetic Assets* will help prepare the fixed-income professional for the marketplace of the future.

Part One provides an overview of the building blocks required to create synthetic assets. In Part Two, we consider a variety of synthetic structures among money market assets. In Part Three, we move further along the yield curve and evaluate synthetic strategies for notes and bonds. Part Four explores portfolio implications of synthetic structures. Finally, in Part Five, we review a variety of the more innovative structures in the marketplace including commodity- and equity-linked products.

PART ONE
THE BUILDING BLOCKS OF SYNTHETIC ASSETS

In Part One, we explore the various ways fixed-income securities are valued. This part provides the reader with a toolbox for evaluating the strategies presented throughout this text. If you are already comfortable with the concepts of present value, compound interest, total returns, forward rates, spot rates, duration, and convexity, you may want to proceed to Part Two.

1
Present Value, Compound Interest, and Total Returns

PRESENT VALUE

Among cash fixed-income securities, an asset's present value is its price. Cash fixed-income securities would include such products as U.S. government-issued Treasury Bills, and Treasury Notes and Bonds.

Various pricing conventions exist among cash fixed-income securities, and the methodology used to calculate the present value of one asset may not be the appropriate methodology to determine the present value of another asset. Throughout this chapter, we will make a point of showing not only how to calculate a particular cash security's present value, but how to compare an asset's present value calculation with conventions used to price other securities.

A present value formula tells us today's dollar price for a security with one or more future cashflows. For example, a Treasury Bill has one future cashflow, and that cashflow is received when the Treasury Bill matures. To calculate a Treasury Bill's present value, we simply need the number of days from the settlement date to the maturity date, the rate of discount, and the face value.

Among U.S. Treasury securities, "cash settlement" requires a payment or receipt of funds on the day a trade is made. "Regular settlement" requires a payment or receipt of funds on the first business day following a trade date, and "skip settlement" requires a payment or receipt of funds two business days following the trade date. Settlement dates beyond two business days can be arranged. Treasury Bills generally settle as "regular."

On May 4, 1990, the Treasury Bill of 8/16/90 traded at a 7.810% rate of discount; its price is calculated as follows:*

$$P = \frac{F(360 - Tsm \cdot D)}{360} \tag{1.1}$$

$$97.8089 = \frac{100(360 - 101 \cdot 0.0781)}{360}$$

where: Settlement date is 5/7/90, the date when funds are actually paid or received for the purchase or sale of a security

Maturity date is 8/16/90, the date when Treasury Bill matures and is worth full face value

Tsm = Time in days from settlement to maturity: 101 days

D = Rate of discount: 7.810%
Time value of money over investment period, or equivalently, rate earned on Treasury Bill if held until maturity.

F = Face amount: $1,000,000
Dollar value of Treasury Bill at maturity

Treasury Bills trade in minimum face value denominations of $10,000, and in multiples of $5,000 above this minimum

P = Price
Dollar value or, equivalently, present value of Treasury Bill

Thus, the present value—the dollar price—for the above Treasury Bill on May 4, 1990, was $978,089 per $1,000,000 face value purchased. With some simple algebraic operations, it is possible to rearrange Equation 1.1 to solve for D if P is known.

---

* This calculation and most others throughout the text are available on the Bloomberg. The Bloomberg is a market service product with analytical tools and other items of interest to analysts.

$$D = \left(\frac{F - P}{F}\right)\left(\frac{360}{Tsm}\right) \qquad (1.1a)$$

$$7.810\% = \left(\frac{100 - 97.8089}{100}\right)\left(\frac{360}{101}\right)$$

Notice that 360 appears in the numerator and denominator of Equation 1.1, and in the numerator of the second term of Equation 1.1a. All measures of return among fixed-income securities are expressed on an *annualized* basis. However, what may differ across fixed-income securities is the *way* in which a measure of return is annualized. For Treasury Bills, the convention is to annualize returns on the basis of a 360-day year. To use the jargon of the marketplace, Treasury Bill values are calculated using an Actual/360 day-count basis. "Actual" refers to the number of days between settlement and maturity dates (Tsm). Differences in day-count conventions across fixed-income securities are one reason a present value calculation for one security is not necessarily the appropriate calculation to use for another security.

To better visualize what a present value calculation attempts to quantify, Figure 1.1 shows differences in cashflows among various Treasury issues. In particular, the figure shows cashflows for a Treasury Bill and two Treasury coupon securities. The latter consist of Treasury Notes and Treasury Bonds. A Treasury Note is defined as an issue having an original term-to-maturity between 2 and 10 years. A Treasury Bond is defined as an issue having an original term-to-maturity of more than 10 years.

Figures 1.1a and b highlight a striking similarity in cashflows between a Treasury Bill and a coupon security with one remaining coupon (so-called short coupon issues). Specifically, a Treasury Bill and a short coupon have only two cashflows: the up-front payment for the security, and the payoff at maturity. Since things get a little complicated when calculating present value for a security with coupon payments between settlement and maturity, let's ease our way into the realm of present value calculations for coupon securities with a short coupon example. Not surprisingly, the present value calculation is similar to that for a Treasury Bill.

On May 4, 1990, the 8.625% Treasury Note of 8/31/90 traded at a 8.189% bond-equivalent yield; its price is calculated as follows:

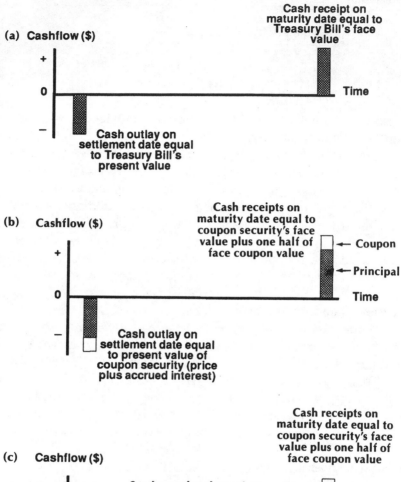

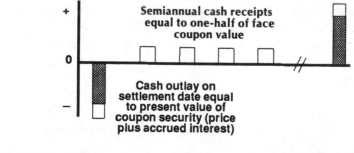

FIGURE 1.1 Cashflow of a Treasury Bill and Coupon Securities: (a) cashflows for a Treasury Bill; (b) cashflows for a Treasury coupon security with one remaining coupon; (c) cashflows for a Treasury Coupon Security with more than one coupon.

$$P = \frac{F(1+C/2)}{(1+Y/2)^{Tsm/Tc}} \qquad (1.2)$$

$$101.7066 = \frac{100(1+0.08625/2)}{(1+0.08189/2)^{116/184}}$$

where: Settlement date is 5/7/90; Treasury Notes and Bonds generally settle "regular," also known as "next day"

Maturity date is 8/31/90

Tsm = Time in days from settlement to maturity: 116 days

Y = Bond-equivalent yield: 8.189%

F = Face amount: $1,000,000
Treasury Notes and Bonds trade in minimum face value denominations of $1,000

C = Coupon: 8.625%

Tc = Time between last coupon paid and next coupon to be paid: 184 days

P = Price

Thus, the present value for this Treasury Note on May 4, 1990, was $1,017,066 per $1,000,000 face value.

The careful reader will observe that the trade was evaluated on May 4 for settlement on May 7. If Treasury Notes and Bonds tend to settle next day, why the three days between May 4 and May 7? May 5, 1990, was a Saturday, so Monday May 7 was the first "next day" business day.

There is an important difference between a present value calculation for a Treasury Bill (Equation 1.1) and a short coupon (Equation 1.2). A Treasury Bill calculation assumes a 360-day year, while all Treasury coupon calculations use the actual number of days in a given coupon period. For Treasury coupon security calculations, variables are broken down into half-year or semiannual terms because coupons are paid semiannually. Coupon and bond-equivalent yield are divided by two in a Treasury coupon's present value equation so as to express these values in semiannual terms. This method of calculation is known as an Actual/Actual day-count basis. A yield calculated with an Actual/Actual day-count basis is known as a bond-equivalent yield.

In the marketplace, the value of P in Equation 1.2 is known as a security's "dirty" price; that is, the price that includes accrued interest. A dirty price may also be called a full price. Accrued interest is calculated as follows:

$$\left(\frac{F \cdot C}{2}\right)\left(\frac{Tc - Tsc}{Tc}\right)$$

where: F = Face amount
          C = Coupon
          Tc = Time in days from last coupon payment to next coupon to be paid
          Tsc = Time in days from settlement to coupon payment

To appreciate the significance of accrued interest, consider Figure 1.2. When a Treasury coupon security is purchased, the buyer effectively owns the right to receive all future cashflows. Accordingly, when an investor purchases a Treasury coupon security prior to a coupon payment (as shown in Figure 1.2) he or she will be expected to pay the *accrued* value of the coupon up to the settlement date. This accrual payment is required since the investor will receive the *entire* coupon payment on the next (in this case, the last) coupon payment date. Hence, if a Treasury coupon security is purchased on the day a coupon payment is made, then Tc − Tsc = 0, and no accrued interest payment is required. An accrued

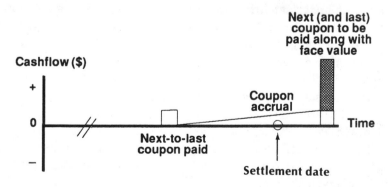

FIGURE 1.2   Coupon accrual.

interest payment is not required because the full coupon is paid to the security's previous owner.

If accrued interest were subtracted from P in Equation 1.2, this would give a security's "clean" price; that is, the price that does *not* include accrued interest. When a price is quoted, it is usually the clean price. Further, it is convention to quote a Treasury security's clean price in 32nds. If P is a price in decimal of 100.25, then its price in 32nds becomes 100-08 (0.25 = 8/32). Many times a Treasury coupon security will trade at a price expressed in 64s. For example, if a price is quoted "at the plus," this means the security trades at the price quoted plus 1/64.

Henceforth, we denote a clean price as Pc and a dirty price as Pd.

Since we've reviewed the differences in bond-equivalent yield and rate of discount calculations, let's see what these equations have in common. Table 1.1 shows prices for given levels in the rate of discount and bond-equivalent yield.

In Table 1.1 there is an *inverse* relationship between price and respective measures of return. Since the purpose of a present value calculation is to discount future cashflows to today's market value, the higher the value at which future cashflows are discounted, the lower the present value. This is intuitively consistent with the notion that the lower a present value for fixed and known future cashflows, the higher the expected return from those future cashflows.

If a security looks like a Treasury Bill, behaves like a Treasury Bill, and can be substituted for a Treasury Bill, is it a Treasury Bill?

Since Treasury Bills and short coupons exhibit comparable cashflows, it may be appropriate to view these assets as substitutes. However, if we are going to evaluate these securities as substitutes, it is necessary to do so on an apples-to-apples basis. In other words, we will need to convert the

Table 1.1 Prices for Given Levels in the Rate of Discount and Bond-Equivalent Yield

Rate of Discount/Price (360 days from settlement to maturity)	Bond-Equivalent Yield/Price 8% Coupon Priced at Par (1-year from settlement to maturity)
4% / 96.00	4% / 103-28
8% / 92.00	8% / 100-00
12% / 88.00	12% / 96-11

Treasury Bill's rate of discount into a bond-equivalent yield, convert the short coupon's bond-equivalent yield into a rate of discount, or something in between. When comparing Treasury Bills and short coupons, the most common practice is to calculate respective simple interest values. Simple interest, also known as a "cash-in, cash-out" calculation, is a measure of annualized return. It is the annualized difference in a security's value between settlement and maturity dates.

Equation 1.3 solves for simple interest on the 8.625% Treasury Note of 8/31/90. Notice that in Equation 1.3 we use 101.6875 for a dirty price instead of the 101.7066 that we calculated in Equation 1.2. The slight differences in price can be explained by the fact that different price expressions are used. Equation 1.2 solves for price in decimal, and the convention for quoting a Treasury's clean price is to use 32nds. If we add a price of 100-03 to 68 days worth of accrued interest, we get a price in decimal of 101.6875:

$$S = \left(\frac{\overset{\text{cash out} \quad \text{cash in}}{F(1+C/2) - \quad Pd}}{Pd} \right) \left(\frac{365}{Tsm} \right) \tag{1.3}$$

$$8.123\% = \left(\frac{104.3125 - 101.6875}{101.6875} \right) \left(\frac{365}{116} \right)$$

where: S = Simple interest
          Tsm = Time in days from settlement to maturity
          F = Face amount
          C = Coupon
          Pd = Dirty price

The reader may question the 8.123% simple interest value since we earlier identified this Treasury Note's bond-equivalent yield as 8.189%. The explanation is that bond-equivalent yield is calculated with an Actual/Actual day-count basis, and the above simple interest calculation uses an Actual/365 day-count basis. Since there were 184 days in the semiannual period between when the last coupon was paid and when the final coupon was to be paid, using a 368-day year (184 · 2) instead of a true 365-day year does indeed generate a simple interest value of exactly 8.189%. The reader can prove this by replacing 365 with 368 in Equation 1.3. Although we use a 365-day year in Equation 1.3, a 360-day year or any other annualization value of interest can be used. There really is no convention for a particular day-count basis with simple interest, except perhaps for Actual/360.

How is it possible that simple interest and bond-equivalent yield values match since the former assumes that cashflows are discounted on a daily basis, whereas the latter assumes that cashflows are discounted on an Actual/Actual basis. The explanation is that unless a Treasury coupon security is purchased on the day that the next-to-last coupon is paid, a fractional period assumption is required. By "fractional period assumption," we mean a fraction of one semiannual coupon period.

Since a fractional period is the number of *days* between settlement and maturity dates divided by the number of *days* between the last coupon paid and the next coupon to be paid, cashflows are discounted on a *daily* (not semiannual) basis. Since simple interest discounts on a daily basis, simple interest values will match bond-equivalent yield values *if* the Treasury coupon security has one coupon payment to go, *and* if the assumed number of days in a year is equal to twice the number of days over the final coupon period.

Thus, although Treasury coupon securities are valued on an Actual/Actual day-count basis, Treasury coupon cashflows are not always discounted on a semiannual basis. As the preceding example demonstrates, Treasury coupon cashflows may be discounted on a daily basis or with a mix of daily and semiannual day-count bases.

As future creators of synthetic assets, we will want to account for every basis point of a given trade. It is essential to appreciate the nuances of respective valuation methodologies since these tools will be used to build our strategies.

Equation 1.3a solves for simple interest on the Treasury Bill of 8/16/90 using an Actual/360 day-count basis:

$$S = \left(\frac{F - P}{P}\right)\left(\frac{360}{Tsm}\right) \qquad (1.3a)$$

$$7.985\% = \left(\frac{100 - 97.8089}{97.8089}\right)\left(\frac{360}{101}\right)$$

where: S = Simple interest
Tsm = Time in days from settlement to maturity
F = Face amount
P = Price

Recall that we previously calculated a rate of discount for this Treasury Bill as 7.810%. Although an Actual/360 day-count basis is used for both the simple interest calculation and our earlier rate of discount calculation, we get different answers. This difference is explained by the fact that "P" appears in the denominator of Equation 1.3a, and an "F" appears in the denominator of the rate of discount formula in Equation 1.1a. Again, these not-so-subtle differences across price calculations make it important to understand not only how various equations differ from one another, but the implications of these differences as well. For example, the Treasury Bill simple interest calculation shown here is also known as a money market yield. A money market yield is nothing more than a simple interest calculation with an Actual/360 day-count basis. A money market yield will *always* be greater than a rate of discount, and simple interest calculated with an Actual/365 day-count basis will *always* be greater than a money market yield.

At this point we have the requisite tools to identify an investment opportunity that may exist among short-term U.S. Treasury securities. Appendix A provides a case study that makes use of the material presented thus far.

To complete this section on present value, we consider the case where a Treasury coupon security has more than one coupon payment between settlement and maturity. The equation for this present value calculation is written as

$$Pd = \frac{F \cdot C/2}{(1 + Y/2)^{Tsc/Tc}} + \frac{F \cdot C/2}{(1 + Y/2)^{1 + Tsc/Tc}} + \cdots \frac{F(1 + C/2)}{(1 + Y/2)^{N + Tsc/Tc}} \quad (1.4)$$

where: Tsc = Time from settlement to first coupon
Y = Bond-equivalent yield
F = Face amount
C = Coupon
Tc = Time in days between last coupon payment (or issue date) and next coupon payment
Pd = Dirty price
N = Number of whole coupon periods

Let's examine Equation 1.4 term by term. The first term on the right side calculates the present value of the first coupon payment, the second term determines the present value of the second coupon payment, and so forth until we come to the last term, which determines the present value of the last coupon payment and face value at maturity.

What distinguishes Equation 1.4 from our Treasury Bill and short coupon calculations is the presence of cashflows between settlement and maturity dates. With a Treasury Bill or short coupon, there is one cashflow up front when the security is purchased and a second cashflow at maturity when the security pays off. That's it. And because these two cashflows are known, it is possible to state with *certainty* at the time of investment what our return will be if the Treasury Bill or short coupon is held to maturity. Conversely, for a coupon security with cashflows between settlement and maturity dates, it is *not* possible to state with certainty at the time of investment what our total return will be if the security is held until maturity. An investor will, presumably, want to invest any cashflows received between settlement and maturity dates. However, it is not possible to know at the time of investment what those future investment rates will be. Equation 1.4 attempts to address this problem by assuming that all future cashflows are invested at the same bond-equivalent yield.

Equation 1.4 discounts (determines the present value of) each cashflow at the *same* rate. This is equivalent to assuming a flat yield curve. Every cashflow between settlement and maturity dates, regardless of when the cashflow is paid, is valued at the same yield. Thus, at a minimum, an investor purchasing a coupon security with more than one remaining coupon can expect to earn the stated bond-equivalent yield if the security is held until maturity and if interim cashflows are invested at the same yield. Beyond that, however, an assumption is required as to expected future yield levels if an investor wants an indication of expected total returns. If yields rise and coupon cashflows are invested at yields above the bond-equivalent yield at the time of purchase, then a higher effective return will be earned relative to that implied by the bond-equivalent yield. Conversely, if yields fall and coupon cashflows are invested at yields below the bond-equivalent yield at the time of purchase, then a lower effective return will be earned relative to that implied by the bond-equivalent yield.

On March 11, 1991, the 6.75% Treasury Note of 2/28/93 was priced at 99-13 which corresponds to a 7.076% bond-equivalent yield. The Treasury Note's dirty price is calculated as follows:

$$99.6087 = \frac{100\,(0.0675/2)}{(1+0.07076/2)^{173/184}} + \frac{100\,(0.0675/2)}{(1+0.07076/2)^{1+173/184}}$$

$$\frac{100\,(0.0675/2)}{(1+0.07076/2)^{2+173/184}} + \frac{100\,(1+0.0675/2)}{(1+0.07076/2)^{3+173/184}}$$

where: Settlement date is 3/11/91
Maturity date is 2/28/93
Tsc = Time in days from settlement to first coupon: 173 days
Y = Bond-equivalent yield: 7.076%
F = Face amount: $1,000,000
C = Coupon: 6.75%
Tc = Time in days between last coupon payment (or issue date) and next coupon payment: 2/28/91 to 8/31/91, 184 days
Pd = Dirty price: 99.6087
N = Number of whole coupon periods: 3

The exponent in the denominator of the first term on the right side is 173/184. The exponent in the denominator of the second term is 1 + 173/184, the exponent in the denominator of the third term is 2 + 173/184, and so on. Thus, while the first coupon payment is discounted using a fraction of one coupon period, subsequent coupon periods are discounted using a combination of the first coupon's fractional period *and* following whole coupon periods.

As stated earlier, using a fraction of one coupon period is consistent with a daily discount assumption. Since the cashflows are discounted with a fraction of one period and whole numbers for later periods, present value is calculated with a mix of daily and semiannual discounting assumptions. Thus, while it is often said that Treasury coupon securities are discounted on a semiannual basis, this might not always be precisely correct. If a Treasury coupon security settles on the issue date or the date that a coupon is paid, then there will not be a fractional coupon period.

Since Treasury coupon securities pay coupons on a semiannual basis, it is a simple matter to identify coupon payment dates by keying-off the stated maturity date. Thus, a security with an 8/15/93 maturity generally pays a coupon on the 15th of every February and August up to and including the maturity date. If the 15th should happen to fall on a weekend or holiday, then funds will be made available on the first business day following the 15th. And if a coupon security's stated maturity is, say,

12/31/93, then June coupon payments will be targeted for the 30th; that is, the last day of the month in June.

In Table 1.2, we calculate present value using Equation 1.4 across a variety of coupons, maturities, and yield levels. Table 1.2 suggests there is an inverse relationship between yield level and price for any given coupon. What may be less obvious (though easily proved with a few simple

Table 1.2 Present Value across Coupons,
Maturities, and Yield Levels

Bond-Equivalent Yield (%)	2-Year Treasury Coupons		
	2%	8%	14%
14	79-22	89-27	100-00
12	82-22	93-02	103-15
10	85-27	96-15	107-03
8	89-04	100-00	110-28
6	92-18	103-23	114-27
4	96-06	107-19	119-00
2	100-00	111-22	123-12

Bond-Equivalent Yield (%)	10-Year Treasury Coupons		
	2%	8%	14%
14	36-14	68-07	100-00
12	42-21	77-02	111-15
10	50-05	87-17	124-29
8	59-08	100-00	140-24
6	70-08	114-28	159-16
4	83-21	132-22	181-24
2	100-00	154-04	208-08

Bond-Equivalent Yield (%)	30-Year Treasury Coupons		
	2%	8%	14%
14	15-24	57-28	100-00
12	19-06	67-22	116-05
10	24-09	81-02	137-27
8	32-04	100-00	167-28
6	44-21	127-22	210-22
4	65-08	169-17	273-25
2	100-00	234-27	369-23

calculations) is that for a given change in yield level, the percentage change in price is greater when yields fall. Further, for a given change in yield level, the percentage change in price is greater among longer-dated and lower coupon securities. By keeping these basic tenets in mind, investors may be able to better structure assets and capitalize on investment options among securities.*

Let's now review the salient points of this section.

Present Value Summary

- An asset's present value is its price.
- Various pricing conventions exist among cash fixed-income securities.
- When comparing two securities with six months or less to maturity, a common practice is to calculate money market yields. When comparing two securities with six months or more to maturity, a common practice is to calculate respective bond-equivalent yields.
- A security's day-count basis is one factor that affects a present value calculation. A Treasury Bill's day-count basis is Actual/360, and the day-count basis for a Treasury coupon security is Actual/Actual.
- Rate of discount and bond-equivalent yield have an inverse relationship to price.
- Treasury Bills and short coupons may be considered to be substitutes since they exhibit similar cashflows. However, it is important to evaluate these securities on an apples-to-apples basis, and money market yield is a useful way to do this.
- For coupon securities with more than one coupon to maturity, all cashflows are discounted at the same rate; that is, the bond-equivalent yield. The present value formula for coupon securities assumes that any cashflows are invested at the bond-equivalent yield.
- Among coupon-bearing securities, there is an inverse relationship between yield level and price for any given coupon.
- For a given change in yield level: (a) prices change by a greater percentage when yields fall relative to when yields rise, (b) prices change

---

* For more detail on price/yield dynamics and other fundamental fixed-income relationships, *Yield Curve Analysis* by Livingston G. Douglas, CFA (New York: New York Institute of Finance Corp., 1988) provides a solid overview.

by a greater percentage among longer-dated securities, and (c) prices change by a greater percentage among lower coupon securities.

COMPOUND INTEREST

If a portfolio manager wants to invest in Treasury Bills over a 3-month horizon, would it be more advantageous to buy 3-month Treasury Bills or 1-month Treasury Bills over three 1-month intervals?

If 3-month Treasury Bills are purchased and held until maturity, then at the time of investment the investor would know the rate of return with certainty. However, there may be an opportunity cost to the investor's "locking in" funds for three months if rates should become more attractive down the road. Successive Treasury Bill purchases could allow an investor to capture higher returns as they evolved. Furthermore, buying 3-month Treasury Bills does not allow an investor to earn compound interest.

A compound interest formula allows one to calculate the effect of *invested* income. For example, successive proceeds earned on rolling 1-month Treasury Bills can be invested over time.

To calculate the potential return from compounding if a security is rolled over an entire 360-day period, we solve for

$$Mc = (1 + M/N)^N - 1 \qquad\qquad (1.5)$$

where: Mc = Compounded money market yield
M = Money market yield
N = Number of compounding periods

To calculate the return potential from compounding when compounding over a period less than 360 days, we use Equation 1.6:

$$Mc = [(1 + M/(360/Tsm_1))^N - 1]\ 360/Th \qquad\qquad (1.6)$$

where: Mc = Compounded money market yield
M = Money market yield
Tsm_1 = Time in days from settlement to maturity for first security
Th = Time in days over investment horizon
N = Number of compounding periods

For our 3-month Treasury Bills versus rolling 1-month Treasury-Bills scenario, assume that a 30-day Treasury Bill has a money market yield of 7.684%. We would calculate the value for Mc as

$$7.733\% = [(1 + 0.07684/(360/30))^3 - 1]\ 360/90.$$

In this instance, compounding 30-day Treasury Bills over a 3-month investment horizon could add 4.9 basis points to the 30-day money market yield (7.733% vs. 7.684%). Is it worth it? If the 90-day Treasury Bill is yielding more than 7.733%, it may not be worth it to purchase successive 1-month Treasury Bills, especially if the investor believes that short-term rates may fall over the near term. If short-term rates were to decline, 30-day Treasury Bills would be rolled into successively lower rates of return.

It is important to recognize that the compounding formula imposes some rather restrictive assumptions. First, Equations 1.5 and 1.6 assume that each successive security will be purchased at the same money market yield. This assertion is not unlike the constant bond-equivalent yield assumption we encountered with Treasury coupon securities. Second, as a practical matter, it is unlikely that an investor will find securities that exactly correspond to his or her desired cashflow and investment horizon. In calculating a compounded money market yield of 7.733%, it is assumed we could find three successive 1-month Treasury Bills each with 30 days to maturity and that our compounded yield could be evaluated against an existing 90-day Treasury Bill.

On May 4, 1990, the following Treasury Bills were available:

Treasury Bill	Days from Settlement to Maturity	Money Market Yield
6/7/90	31	7.684%
	28 days	24 basis points
7/5/90	59	7.928%
	28 days	16 basis points
8/2/90	87	8.092%

As an alternative to buying the Treasury Bill of 8/2/90, an investor could have purchased The Treasury Bill of 6/7/90 to be rolled over into the Treasury Bills of 7/5/90 and 8/2/90, successively. To calculate the potential return of this compounding strategy, we make the simplifying assumption that all 1-month Treasury Bills are purchased at a 7.684% money market yield. We use 29 days since this was the average maturity of the Treasury Bills on respective rollover dates:

$(31+28+28)/3 = 29$

Hence,

$7.732\% = [(1 + 0.07684/(360/29))^3 - 1]\ 360/87$

Although 7.732% would have represented a pickup of 4.8 basis points over the Treasury Bill of 6/7/90 (7.732% vs. 7.684%), 7.732% was 36 basis points expensive to the Treasury Bill of 8/2/90 (7.732% vs. 8.092%). This analysis suggests that it may not have been worthwhile to purchase three successive 1-month Treasury Bills in place of simply buying the 3-month Treasury Bill. However, since the compounding formula assumes that each 1-month Treasury Bill is purchased at the same yield, the compound formula will *understate* potential returns if proceeds are actually invested at progressively higher yields. Conversely, the compound formula will *overstate* potential returns if proceeds are actually invested at progressively lower yields. To adjust for the limitation imposed by a single yield input required by the compound formula, an investor may use a "best guess" yield for the investment horizon.

In sum, to benefit from the effect of compounding, a rollover strategy is most likely to be successful when investments are made at rates that exceed prevailing longer-term yields. Figure 1.3 helps to show why this is the case.

While the compounding formula has certain limitations, it is important to appreciate what useful information it can convey. Table 1.3 shows compound interest values across a variety of securities. The following list highlights some observations from Table 1.3.

Compound Interest Summary

- The spread between compounded and noncompounded yields varies directly with yield levels.
- Compounded yield levels vary directly with the compounding frequencies.

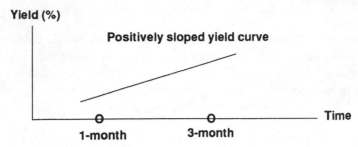

Since the 3-month yield clearly dominates the 1-month yield, it is doubtful that a roll-over strategy would be appropriate. An investor may be better off buying a 3-month Treasury Bill instead of three successive 1-month Treasury Bills.

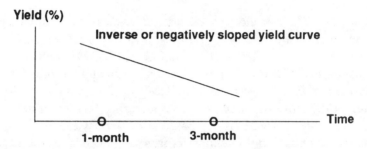

Since the 1-month yield clearly dominates the 3-month yield, it is probable that a roll-over strategy would be appropriate. An investor may be better off buying three successive 1-month Treasury Bills instead of a 3-month Treasury Bill.

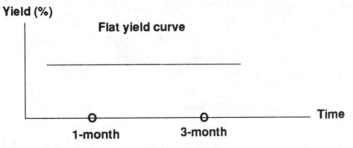

At first glance, an investor might be indifferent to earning either the 1-month or 3-month yields, but the potential for compound income makes a roll-over strategy worth consideration.

The above three scenarios do not allow for the fact that an investor may have a view of future market dynamics. An investor's expectations of the yield curve for a future flattening, steepening, or whatever, could well alter the strategies presented above.

FIGURE 1.3 Slopes of the yield curve and the benefits of compounding.

Table 1.3   Compound Interest Values across a Variety of Securities

Treasury Bills

Maturity	Compounding Frequency*	Money Market Yield (%) Compound Yield (%)		
30 days	12	4/4.07	8/8.30	12/12.68
90 days	4	4/4.06	8/8.24	12/12.55
180 days	2	4/4.04	8/8.16	12/12.36
360 days	1	4/4	8/8	12/12

* Compounding assumed to occur over a 360-day period.

8% Treasury Bond, 20-Year Maturity, Price of 100

Total Coupon Income* ($10,000)	Reinvestment Rate (%)	Interest on Interest ($10,000)	Contribution of Interest on Interest to Total Returns (%)	Compound Yield (%)
1600	2	355.45	12.03	5.492
1600	4	816.08	23.89	6.238
1600	6	1,416.05	35.26	7.074
1600	8	2,201.02	45.84	8.000
1600	10	3,231.99	55.42	9.014
1600	12	4,590.48	63.84	10.111
1600	14	6,385.40	71.06	11.285

* $1 million face value.

- The incremental yield from compounding declines as compounding frequencies rise.
- Compounding can make a significant contribution to a security's total return. Among longer-dated coupon securities, this contribution can account for nearly two thirds of a security's total return.

TOTAL RETURNS

Thus far, we have assumed that securities are held to maturity once purchased. Among Treasury Bills and short coupons, assuming that these securities are held to maturity allows the investor to know the future return with certainty at the time of investment. The return can be known with certainty since the only two cashflows involved are the up-front payment to purchase the security and the security's payoff at maturity.

Liberating the hold-to-maturity assumption has several important consequences. One obvious implication is that a security's future price is no longer known with certainty. Although fixed-income securities mature at par, prices may deviate from par in a significant way up until the maturity date draws near. Interest rates, and by definition prices, fluctuate on a daily basis.

To calculate an expected return on a Treasury Bill with six months or less to maturity, Equation 1.7 may be used. Equation 1.7 expresses the return as a money market yield:

$$M = \left(\frac{Ps - Pp}{Pp}\right)\left(\frac{360}{T_1 - T_2}\right) \tag{1.7}$$

where: M = Money market yield
Pp = Price at purchase
Ps = Price at sale
T_1 = Time in days from settlement to maturity
T_2 = Time in days from sale to maturity

Equation 1.7 may be rewritten so that the future rate of discount can be estimated in place of the future price:

$$M = \left(\frac{1 - \dfrac{Ds \cdot T_2}{360}}{1 - \dfrac{Dp \cdot T_1}{360}} - 1\right)\left(\frac{360}{T_1 - T_2}\right) \tag{1.7a}$$

where: Dp = Rate of discount at purchase
Ds = Rate of discount at sale

To solve for the expected return on a short coupon security or for a coupon security that is held for less than six months with no coupons paid, Equation 1.8 expresses the return as a money market yield:

$$M = \left(\frac{Pds - Pdp}{Pdp}\right)\left(\frac{360}{T_1 - T_2}\right) \tag{1.8}$$

where: Pdp = Dirty price at purchase
Pds = Dirty price at sale

Aside from using Equations 1.7, 1.7a, and 1.8 to calculate expected returns, they may also be used to solve for *actual* returns when securities are sold prior to maturity.

To determine the expected or actual total return on a Treasury coupon security that pays a coupon over the holding period, the calculation is more complex. The expected return on a coupon security that (a) pays a coupon over the holding period, (b) has more than six months to maturity, and (c) is held for less than six months, may be calculated with Equation 1.9:

$$M = \frac{Pds + (F \cdot C/2)(1 + Y/2)^{Tch/Tc} - Pdp}{Pdp} \tag{1.9}$$

where: Tch = Time from coupon payment in holding period to sale of security

Tc = Time between coupon received and next coupon to be paid

The term $(F \cdot C/2)(1 + Y/2)^{Tch/Tc}$ accounts for the interest income earned on the coupon from the time the coupon is paid until the security is sold.

To calculate an expected return on a coupon security where more than one coupon is paid, we need to break out returns into one of three categories: new price and accrued interest, coupon payments, and invested coupon payments. The equation to calculate coupon income—coupon payments plus interest earned on coupon payments—is:

$$Ic = F \cdot C_1(1 + Y/2)^{N + Tlh/Tlc} + F \cdot C_2(1 + Y/2)^{N - 1 + Tlh/Tlc}$$
$$+ \, . \, . \, F \cdot C_N(1 + Y/2)^{Tlh/Tlc} \tag{1.10}$$

where: Ic = Coupon income

Tlh = Time from last coupon payment in holding period to sale of security

Tlc = Time between last coupon received in holding period and next coupon to be paid

In words, coupon income is equal to coupon payments plus the value of invested coupon payments compounded from when the coupon is paid until the security is sold. The total value of a security at the time the security is sold can be written as:

$$Vs = Pds + Ic \tag{1.11}$$

where: Vs = Total value at sale

And to calculate a total return for an entire holding period:

$$Pdp = \frac{Vs}{(1 + R/2)^{N + Tlh/Tlc}} \tag{1.12}$$

where: R = Total return

Equation 1.12 assumes an Actual/Actual compounding of the return, and this is consistent with the day-count basis of a bond-equivalent yield calculation. If the security involved were a noncoupon-paying security with more than six months to maturity, Equation 1.12 would simplify to:

$$Pdp = \frac{Pds}{(1 + R/2)^{N + Tth/Ttc}} \tag{1.13}$$

where: Tth = Time from last theoretical coupon payment in holding
        period to sale of security
        Ttc = Time over last theoretical coupon period

Total Returns Summary

- To calculate the total return on a security sold prior to maturity, an assumption must be made as to expected price or yield levels.
- To calculate expected or realized total returns on Treasury Bills or short coupons with six months or less to maturity, a simple interest cash-in/cash-out methodology will suffice. A variation of the simple interest formula may be used to calculate the expected or realized total return on a coupon security held for six months or less when a coupon is paid. In this way, accrued interest from the coupon payment is considered.
- To determine expected or realized total returns on a Treasury coupon security or non-coupon-paying security held longer than six months, a calculation is required that expresses the return on an Actual/Actual day-count basis.

2

Forward Rates and Spot Rates

FORWARD RATES

We have already encountered a few instances where it would have been nice to gaze into a crystal ball to structure the optimal strategy. And while there are market gurus galore with claims that their market model pegs the best investment opportunities, there is no market forecast quite like the market's forecast. This is not at all to say that the market's forecast is always accurate. It isn't. Yet a security's price—at any given point in time—embodies a supply-and-demand equilibrium driven by investors worldwide. It's tough to argue, therefore, that one model is somehow wiser than the collective wisdom of an entire marketplace. The market continuously provides an implicit forecast of yield levels. These are easily derived from prevailing market prices and are called forward rates.

Several studies have evaluated a variety of forecasting methodologies. Technical analysis can be as simple as charting historical data, and elaborate systems have been structured around various interest rate relationships as defined by multisector economic models, time series analysis, and the Fisher equation, among others. Broadly speaking, empirical evidence related to forward rates suggests that short-term forecasts tend to be more reliable than longer-term forecasts, and short-term forecasts of short-term rates tend to be more reliable than short-term forecasts of

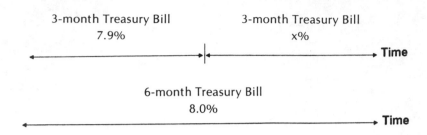

FIGURE 2.1   Solving for forward rates.

longer-term rates. However, forward rates may be no more or less valid an *a priori* predictor of future interest rates than the most elaborate quantitative models.

If a portfolio manager wants to invest in Treasury Bills over the next six months, would it be more advantageous to buy 6-month Treasury Bills, or 3-month Treasury Bills to be rolled over three months hence? If 3-month and 6-month Treasury Bills are offered at rates of discount at 7.9% and 8.0%, respectively, it may be instructive to know the market's implicit forecast for 3-month Treasury Bills three months forward. Figure 2.1 helps to show the problem we want to solve.

A naive approach would be to solve for the missing link with a simple average calculation, namely (7.9% + X%) / 2 = 8.0%. While this technique probably provides a good guess, we can be more precise.

To get right down to it, what we really want to solve for is a *break-even* rate. In short, what rate must we earn on the second 3-month Treasury Bill to be indifferent between owning two successive 3-month securities or one 6-month security? The rate that makes us indifferent to these two strategies is the forward rate, and Equation 2.1 allows us to calculate that break-even rate:

$$W = \left(1 - \frac{P_1}{P_2}\right)\left(\frac{360}{Tsm_1 - Tsm_2}\right) \tag{2.1}$$

where: W = Forward rate
             P_1 = Price of 6-month Treasury Bill
             P_2 = Price of first 3-month Treasury Bill
       $Tsm_{1,2}$ = Time in days from settlement to maturity for the 6-month
                and 3-month Treasury Bills

Substituting numbers for the symbols, we have

$$8.263\% = \left(1 - \frac{96.000}{98.025}\right)\left(\frac{360}{180 - 90}\right)$$

Thus, in three months' time, a 3-month Treasury Bill rate would have to be 8.263% for an investor to be indifferent between buying a 6-month Treasury Bill or two successive 3-month Treasury Bills. If the investor believes the market's implicit forecast of 8.263%, then he or she should be indifferent between the 6-month and 3-month Treasury Bill strategies. If the investor believes that the market's implicit forecast fails to consider a near-term ease in monetary policy (arguing for lower interest rates) or tightening in monetary policy (arguing for higher interest rates) then the forward rate may still be of value to the extent that it reflects current market expectations. However, the investor would no longer be indifferent to the two different strategies if the Treasury Bills are held to maturity. A near-term unexpected ease in monetary policy would argue for locking-in at the 6-month rate of discount while an unexpected tightening would argue for buying two successive 3-month Treasury Bills.

The theory underlying the preceding forward rate calculation is known as *expectations theory.* Its main tenets are as follows:

Investors are risk-neutral. Risk-neutrality means that investors are neither risk-prone nor risk-averse. In actuality, investors tend to be risk-averse and demand premiums for any additional risk (real or perceived) that is borne.

Investors and issuers are neutral as to maturity preference. In reality, there is evidence that different classes of investors prefer different segments of the yield curve. Indeed, the market segmentation theory posits that the yield curve can be broken down into a smattering of maturity sectors, and sector-specific players dominate respective maturity structures. In support of this theory, numerous investment funds distinguish among short-, mid-, and longer-term fixed-income products.

Investors are predisposed toward securities that allow for the recovery of principal in fairly short order. The liquidity preference theory postulates that longer-dated securities should trade at higher yields than shorter-dated securities since the latter pay off earlier.

The market consensus forecast of interest rates is unbiased. The forecast neither over- nor underreacts to news. This assumption is difficult to accept in all situations since the market is traded by human beings likely to bring an emotional bias to the market place.

There are no transaction costs. Transaction costs do exist as reflected in bid/ask spreads. This is discussed in detail in Appendix A.

In sum, while expectations theory does not allow for a perfect bridge between theory and practice, it is widely accepted as a good foundation for building a forward rate term structure. Moreover, once constructed, adjustments can be made to a forward curve to better reflect transactions costs, liquidity, and so forth.

SPOT RATES

When we calculated the forward rate for our Treasury Bill example, we did not have to fuss over intervening cashflows between settlement and maturity dates of respective securities. As is the case with all Treasury Bills, the only cashflow other than the initial up-front payment is the payoff received at maturity. Because of this single cashflow characteristic, a Treasury Bill's rate of discount is also called a "spot rate." A spot rate can be defined as the interest rate earned on a *single* cashflow paid at a security's maturity. In the strictest sense, a forward rate is the future interest rate implied by the shape of a spot rate curve.

Now then, if we are to continue to identify forward rate values for maturity dates beyond Treasury Bill maturities, where can we find a good spot curve? The answer to this question is not as easy as it may appear to be at first glance.

If a spot rate is nothing more than the interest rate earned on a single cashflow at maturity, why not just round up all existing Treasury zero coupon securities (called STRIPS, for Separate Trading of Registered Interest and Principal Securities)? After all, a Treasury STRIPS has no intervening cashflows between settlement and maturity dates, and maturities range from less than 1 year to more than 29 years. The problem with using the Treasury STRIPS curve as a representative spot rate curve is perhaps best shown in Figure 2.2.

As Figure 2.2 shows, the Treasury STRIPS curve dips below the Treasury coupon curve as terms-to-maturity lengthen. This phenomenon is

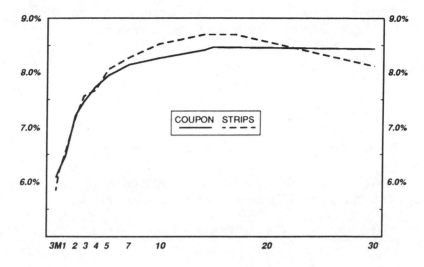

FIGURE 2.2   Treasury coupon curve versus Treasury STRIPS curve.

not so much attributable to the theoretical relationship between the coupon and STRIPS curves as it is explained by supply and demand imbalances among Treasury STRIPS. On the supply side, Treasury STRIPS can only be created from a limited universe of eligible Treasury securities. In Part Three, we examine the process by which Treasury STRIPS are created and reconstituted. On the demand side, as we will see in the next section, Treasury STRIPS possess some rather unique properties among fixed-income securities. The net effect of these supply/demand factors is that a STRIPS curve is a less-than-ideal spot rate curve.

So where are we going to find our spot rate curve? Why not build our own?

Building a Spot Rate Curve

If we are to build our spot rate curve by 6-month increments (to correspond to semiannual cashflows), then we can start with Treasury Bills. And since Treasury Bill rates are also spot rates, all we need to do is convert rates of discount to bond-equivalent yields. By calculating our spot rates on a bond-equivalent basis, we can make direct comparisons between Treasury coupon and Treasury spot yield curves.

To convert a rate of discount into a bond-equivalent yield on a Treasury Bill with six months or less to maturity, we solve for

$$Y = \frac{365 \cdot D}{360 - D \cdot Tsm} \tag{2.2}$$

where: Y = Bond-equivalent yield
          D = Rate of discount
          Tsm = Time in days from settlement to maturity

To convert a rate of discount into a bond-equivalent yield on a Treasury Bill with more than six months to maturity, we solve for

$$Y = \frac{-2 \cdot Tsm/365 + 2 \cdot ((Tsm/365)^2 - (2 \cdot Tsm/365 - 1)(1 - F/P))^{1/2}}{2 \cdot Tsm/365 - 1} \tag{2.3}$$

On March 6, 1991, the Treasury Bill of 9/5/91 had 182 days from settlement to maturity and a rate of discount of 6.01%. Its bond-equivalent yield was

$$6.284\% = \frac{365 \cdot 0.0601}{360 - 0.0601 \cdot 182}$$

On the same date the Treasury Bill of 2/13/92 had 343 days to maturity and a rate of discount of 6.07%. Its bond-equivalent yield was

$$6.435\% = \frac{-2 \cdot 343/365 + 2 \cdot [(343/365)^2 - (2 \cdot 343/365 - 1) \cdot (1 - 1/0.94216639)]^{1/2}}{2 \cdot 343/365 - 1}$$

To continue to plot our spot curve at 6-month intervals, we now require an 18-month Treasury security. Since the maximum potential maturity of a Treasury Bill is 366 days, we must use a Treasury coupon security. But if a spot curve is to be constructed with securities having a single cashflow, how do we justify the use of coupon security? One way to address this issue is to limit our search to 18-month Treasury securities trading at or close to par. To appreciate the desirability of this qualification, let's consider the present value equation for an 18-month Treasury coupon security, as shown with Equation 1.4 from Chapter 1:

$$P = \frac{F \cdot C/2}{(1 + Y/2)^{Tsc/Tc}} + \frac{F \cdot C/2}{(1 + Y/2)^{1 + Tsc/Tc}} + \frac{F(1 + C/2)}{(1 + Y/2)^{2 + Tsc/Tc}} \qquad (2.4)$$

where: F = Face value
            C = Coupon
            Y = Bond-equivalent yield
      Tsc = Time in days from settlement to coupon payment
       Tc = Time in days from last coupon payment (or issue date) to next
                coupon payment

As shown in Table 1.2, in Chapter 1, a Treasury coupon security's bond-equivalent yield will equal its coupon rate when the security trades at par. Further, since Treasury securities mature at par, price will equal a Treasury security's face value when the bond-equivalent yield equals the coupon rate. Accordingly, if we let C = Y, P = F, and multiply 1/F through Equation 2.4,* we get

$$1 = \frac{Y/2}{(1 + Y/2)} + \frac{Y/2}{(1 + Y/2)^2} + \frac{(1 + Y/2)}{(1 + Y/2)^3} \qquad (2.4a)$$

An accrued interest term does not appear in Equation 2.4a since it is assumed that a coupon is paid on the date that the spot rate curve is calculated. We now have an equation where cashflows between settlement and maturity dates have "disappeared" with some simple algebraic substitutions.

But hold on a minute! On any given day, what is the likelihood of finding an 18-month Treasury coupon security trading at or near par? In actuality, the probability isn't great, and many innovations have been proposed to address this issue.** A crude but popular technique is to build a spot rate curve using the on-the-run Treasury yield curve. "On-the-run" refers to the most recently auctioned Treasury securities.

---

*Multiplying 1/F through Equation 2.4 is permissible by the distributive property of multiplication.
** A rigorous methodology for calculating spot rates is provided in "Term Structure Modeling Using Exponential Splines," by O. A. Vasicek and H. G. Fong, *The Journal of Finance,* May 1982. Vasicek and Fong outline a procedure that derives the spot curve with regression analysis and a cubic spline fitting technique. The model is popular in that it tends to fit the data reasonably well and generally provides a smooth term structure.

When a new Treasury coupon issue comes to the market, the security's bond-equivalent yield determines its coupon, and its coupon will always be equal to or slightly less than the bond-equivalent yield. Treasury coupons are expressed in units of 1/8. At the time a Treasury security is auctioned, its price will always be equal to or slightly less than par. Since Treasury auctions occur with some frequency—Treasury Bills are auctioned weekly, 2- and 5-year Treasury Notes are auctioned monthly, and 7-, 10-, and 30-year Treasury securities are auctioned quarterly—the on-the-run yield curve generally represents a liquid universe of securities trading close to par.

Equation 2.4b shows a modified version of Equation 2.4a that we can use to derive an 18-month spot rate:

$$1 = \frac{C/2}{(1 + Y_1/2)} + \frac{C/2}{(1 + Y_2/2)^2} + \frac{1 + C/2}{(1 + Y_3/2)^3} \qquad (2.4b)$$

where: C = Coupon of 18-month Treasury security
        Y_1 = Yield-to-maturity for 6-month Treasury Bill
        Y_2 = Yield-to-maturity for 12-month Treasury Bill
        Y_3 = Yield-to-maturity for 18-month Treasury Note

On March 6, 1991, the 6.75% Treasury Note of 2/28/93—the on-the-run 2-year Treasury—had a bond-equivalent yield of 7.100%. Since we need a coupon value for an 18-month Treasury, we interpolate between the bond-equivalent yield of the 12-month Treasury Bill (7.039%) and the bond-equivalent yield of the 2-year Treasury Note (7.100%) to derive an estimated 18-month coupon of 7.0695% ((7.039% + 7.100%)/2). Substituting symbols for values, we solve for Y_3:

$$1 = \frac{0.070695/2}{(1 + 0.06284/2)} + \frac{0.070695/2}{(1 + 0.06435/2)^2} + \frac{1 + 0.070695/2}{(1 + Y_3/2)^3}$$

$Y_3 = 7.094\%$

If we continue adding to this equation and solve for successive spot rate values, we will build an entire spot curve.

Aside from using spot rates to calculate forward rates, many investors use the spot rate curve to calculate theoretical note and bond prices.

Theoretical prices are calculated by substituting individual spot rate values for constant bond-equivalent yield values at respective cashflow dates. If the spot curve suggests that various securities are trading rich or cheap with the market's value, then investment opportunities may arise. Theoretical note and bond values generated using the spot curve *will converge* to a security's market value at maturity.

Now that we've described how the spot curve can be derived, let's complete this section by building a forward rate curve. Since we have our spot rates, calculating forward rates is quite simple.

Building a Forward Rate Curve

Since a forward rate is a marginal yield—a yield on the margin between two successive spot rates—the forward rate between the 12-month and 18-month semiannual spot rates can be calculated as

$$W_{12,18} = \left(\frac{(1 + Y_3/2)^3}{(1 + Y_2/2)^2} - 1\right) \cdot 2 \qquad (2.5)$$

$$= \left(\frac{(1 + 0.07094/2)^3}{(1 + 0.06435/2)^2} - 1\right) \cdot 2$$

$$= 8.418\%$$

Table 2.1 shows hypothetical spot and forward rate curves. In sum, forward rates trade above spot rates when the spot rate curve is normal or

Table 2.1   Forward Rates under Various Spot Rate Scenarios

	Scenario A*		Scenario B**		Scenario C†	
	Spot	Forward	Spot	Forward	Spot	Forward
6-Month	8.00	8.00	8.00	8.00	8.00	8.00
12-Month	8.25	8.50	7.75	7.50	8.00	8.00
18-Month	8.50	9.00	7.50	7.00	8.00	8.00
24-Month	8.75	9.50	7.25	6.50	8.00	8.00
30-Month	9.00	10.00	7.00	6.00	8.00	8.00

 * Normal slope spot curve.
** Inverted slope spot curve.
 † Flat spot curve.

upward sloping, forward rates trade below spot rates when the spot rate curve is inverted, and the spot rate curve is equal to the forward curve when the spot rate curve is flat.

Forward Rate and Spot Rate Summary

- It is often useful to have a forecast of future yield levels, and market prices embody implicit market forecasts known as forward rates.
- Forward rates are derived from spot rates, and spot rates can be derived in a variety of ways.
- Spot rates can be used to generate theoretical market values, and trading strategies can be structured around differences between theoretical and market values.
- Forward rates trade above spot rates when the spot rate curve is normal or upward sloping, forward rates trade below spot rates when the spot rate curve is inverted, and the spot rate curve is equal to the forward curve when the spot rate curve is flat.
- Although forward rates provide an implicit market forecast, a fixed-income investor is well advised to consider other market-moving phenomena including near-term Federal Reserve monetary policy.

3
Duration and Convexity

Table 3.1 provides total return calculations for three Treasury securities. Using a 3-month investment horizon, it is clear that return profiles are markedly different across securities.

The 30-year Treasury STRIPS offers the greatest potential return if yields fall. However, at the same time, the 30-year Treasury STRIPS could well suffer a drastic loss if yields rise. At the other end of the spectrum, the 6-month Treasury Bill provides the lowest potential return if yields fall, yet offers the greatest amount of protection if yields rise. In an attempt to quantify these different risk/return profiles, many fixed-income investors evaluate the duration of respective securities.

Table 3.1 Total Return Calculations for Three Treasury Securities on a Bond-Equivalent Basis, 3-Month Horizon (Settlement Date, 3/13/91)

Change in Yield Level (basis points)	Treasury Bill of 2/13/92 (%)	7.75% Treasury Note of 2/15/2001 (%)	Treasury STRIPS of 2/15/2021 (%)
−100	8.943	36.800	75.040
−50	7.580	21.870	39.100
0	6.229	8.030	7.920
+50	4.883	−4.820	−19.130
+100	3.545	−16.750	−42.610

DURATION

Duration is a measure of a fixed-income security's price sensitivity to a given change in yield. The larger a security's duration, the more sensitive that security's price will be to a change in yield. A desirable quality of duration is that it serves to standardize yield sensitivities across all cash fixed-income securities. This can be of particular value when attempting to quantify differences across varying maturity dates, coupon values, and yields. The duration of a 3-month Treasury Bill, for example, can be evaluated on an apples-to-apples basis against a 30-year Treasury STRIPS or any other Treasury security.

The equations below provide duration calculations for a variety of securities.

To calculate duration for a Treasury Bill:

$$\text{Duration} = \left(\frac{P}{P}\right)\left(\frac{\text{Tsm}}{365}\right) \tag{3.1}$$

where: P = Price
          Tsm = Time in days from settlement to maturity

The denominator of the second term is 365 in Equation 3.1 because it is the market's convention to express duration on a bond-equivalent basis.

To calculate duration for a Treasury STRIPS:

$$\text{Duration} = \left(\frac{P}{P}\right)\left(\text{Tsm}\right) \tag{3.2}$$

where: Tsm = Time from settlement to maturity in *years*

It is a little more complex to calculate duration for a coupon security. One popular method is to solve for the first derivative of the price/yield equation with respect to yield using a Taylor series expansion. We repeat the price/yield equation as follows:

$$Pd = \frac{F \cdot C/2}{(1 + Y/2)^{Tsc/Tc}} + \frac{F \cdot C/2}{(1 + Y/2)^{1 + Tsc/Tc}} + \cdots \frac{F(1 + C/2)}{(1 + Y/2)^{N - 1 + Tsc/Tc}}$$

where: Pd = Dirty price
          F = Face value
          C = Coupon payments
          Y = Bond-equivalent yield
       Tsc = Time in days from settlement to coupon payment
        Tc = Time in days from last coupon payment (or issue date) to
            next coupon payment

The solution for duration using calculus may be written as $(dP'/dy)/P'$, where P' is dirty price. This method was first proposed by J. R. Hicks in 1939.

The price/yield equation can be greatly simplified with the greek symbol sigma, Σ, which means summation. Rewriting the price/yield equation using sigma, we have

$$Pd = \sum_{t=1}^{T} \frac{C't}{(1 + Y/2)^t}$$

where: Pd = Dirty price
        Σ = Summation
        T = Total number of cashflows in the life of the security
       C'_t = Cashflows over the life of the security
            Cashflows include coupons up to maturity, and coupons
            plus principal at maturity
        Y = Bond-equivalent yield
        t = Time in days security is owned from one coupon period to
            the next divided by time in days from last coupon paid (or
            issue date) to next coupon date

Using sigma, another way to calculate duration is to solve for

$$\frac{\displaystyle\sum_{t=1}^{T} \frac{C'_t \cdot t}{(1 + Y/2)^t}}{\displaystyle\sum_{t=1}^{T} \frac{C'_t}{(1 + Y/2)^t}} \tag{3.3}$$

There is but a subtle difference between the formula for duration and the price/yield formula. In particular, the numerator of the duration formula is the same as the price/yield formula except that cashflows are a product of time (t). The denominator of the duration formula is exactly the same as the price/yield formula. Thus, we may say that duration is a time-weighted average value of cashflows.

The calculation in Equation 3.3 was first proposed by Frederick Macaulay in 1938. Macaulay's duration assumes continuous compounding while Treasury coupon securities are generally compounded on an Actual/Actual (or discrete) basis. To adjust Macaulay's duration to allow for discrete compounding, we solve for

$$\text{Dmod} = \frac{\text{Dmac}}{(1 + Y/2)} \qquad (3.4)$$

where: Dmod = Modified duration
　　　　Dmac = Macaulay duration
　　　　　Y = Bond-equivalent yield

The above measure of duration is known as *modified duration* and is generally what is used in the marketplace. Hick's method to calculate duration is consistent with the properties of modified duration. Our bias in this text is to use modified duration.

In Table 3.2 we calculate duration for the 7.625% Treasury Note of 5/31/96 using Macaulay's methodology. We find that the modified duration of this 5-year security is 4.0503.

In sum, for Treasury Bills and Treasury STRIPS, Macaulay's duration is nothing more than time in years from settlement to maturity dates. For coupon securities, Macaulay's duration is the product of cashflows and time divided by cashflows where cashflows are in present value terms.

Using Equations 3.1, 3.2, and 3.3, we calculate Macaulay durations for the securities in Table 3.1 as follows:

Treasury Bill of 2/13/92, 0.9205

7.75% Treasury Note of 2/15/2001, 7.032

Treasury STRIPS of 2/15/21, 29.925

Modified durations on our three Treasury securities are as follows:

Treasury Bill, 0.8927
Treasury Note, 6.761
Treasury STRIPS, 28.786

Table 3.2 Calculating Duration

(A) C'_t	(B) t	(C) $C'_t/(1+Y/2)^t$	(D) (B) · (C)
3.8125	0.9344	3.6763	3.4352
3.8125	1.9344	3.5359	6.8399
3.8125	2.9344	3.4009	9.9796
3.8125	3.9344	3.2710	12.8694
3.8125	4.9344	3.1461	15.5240
3.8125	5.9344	3.0259	17.9571
3.8125	6.9344	2.9104	20.1817
3.8125	7.9344	2.7992	22.2102
3.8125	8.9344	2.6923	24.0544
103.8125	9.9344	70.5111	700.4868
Totals		98.9690	833.5384

Notes:

C'_t = Cashflows over the life of the security. Since this Treasury Note has a coupon of 7.625%, semi-annual coupons are equal to 7.625/2=3.8125.

t = Time in days defined as the number of days the Treasury Note is held in a coupon period divided by the number of days from the last coupon paid (or issue date) to the next coupon payment. Since this Treasury Note was purchased 11 days after it was issued, the first coupon is discounted with t = 171/183 = 0.9344.

$C'_t/(1+Y/2)^t$ = Present value of a cashflow.

Y = Bond-equivalent yield; 7.941%

The summation of column (D) gives us the value for the numerator of the duration formula, and the summation of column (C) gives us the value for the denominator of the duration formula. Note that the summation of column (C) is also the dirty price of this Treasury Note.

Dmac = 833.5384/98.9690 = 8.4222 in half years
= 8.4222/2 = 4.2111 in years

The convention is to express duration in years.

Dmod = Dmac/(1+Y/2)
= 4.2111/(1+0.039705)
= 4.0503

Modified duration values increase as we go from Treasury Bill to Treasury Note to Treasury STRIPS, and this is consistent with our total returns analysis in Table 3.1. That is, if duration is a measure of risk, it is not surprising that the Treasury Bill has the lowest duration and the better relative performance when yields rise.

Now that we have an idea of what modified duration is, how can we use it?

Many times a fixed-income investor will want to know the dollar value of a one-basis-point change in a security's yield. This measure of price sensitivity is called a DV01, and can be estimated using

$$DV01 = Pd \cdot Dmod / 10{,}000 \tag{3.5}$$

Similarly, if a fixed-income investor wants to know the basis point value of a 1/32 price change, we can estimate a BPV01 (or BP01) using

$$BV01 = ((100/Dmod) \cdot 1/32) / 100 \tag{3.6}$$

DV01s and BV01s are calculated for our three Treasury securities.

	DV01	*BP01*
Treasury Bill	0.008927	0.033949
Treasury Note	0.067600	0.004623
Treasury STRIPS	0.028160	0.001086

The larger DV01 values are associated with the longer modified duration securities, while the larger BV01 values are associated with the shorter modified duration securities. This inverse relationship is explained by the inverse relationship between price and yield.

Just as modified duration can be used to estimate DV01 or BP01, it can be used to estimate a security's price for a given change in its yield. When using modified duration to estimate price, it is assumed that yields change instantaneously. Further, it is assumed that the entire yield curve shifts by the same number of basis points as the change in yield for the particular security involved. If we recall the similarity between equations for present value and modified duration, modified duration's parallel shift in the yield curve assumption is consistent with present value's constant investment rate assumption.

Table 3.3 contrasts "true" price values generated by the present value formula (Equation 1.4) against estimated price values when modified duration is used as in Equation 3.7:

$$P^e = Pd \cdot (1 + Dmod \cdot \Delta Y) \tag{3.7}$$

where: P^e = Price estimate
Pd = Dirty price
Dmod = Modified duration
ΔY = Change in yield (100 basis points is written as 1.0)

Price differences widen between present value and modified duration calculations as changes in yield become more pronounced. Modified duration provides a less accurate price estimate as yield scenarios move further away from the current market yield. Figure 3.1 highlights the differences between true and estimated prices.

While the price/yield relationship traced out by modified duration appears to be linear—and indeed it is—the price/yield relationship traced out by present value appears to be curvilinear. Table 1.3, in Chapter 1, shows that prices do not change by a constant amount as yields change by fixed

Table 3.3   "True" versus Estimated Price Values Generated by
Present Value and Modified Duration
7.75% Treasury Note of 2/15/2021
(Settlement Date, 3/13/91)

Change in Yield Level (basis points)	Price plus Accrued Interest, Present Value Equation	Price plus Accrued Interest, Duration Equation	Difference
+400	76.1448	71.5735	4.5713
+300	81.0724	78.2050	2.8674
+200	86.4398	84.8365	1.6033
+100	92.2917	91.4681	0.8236
0	98.0996	98.0996	0.0000
−100	105.6525	104.7311	0.9214
−200	113.2777	111.3227	1.9550
−300	121.6210	117.9942	3.6268
−400	130.7582	124.6257	6.1325

intervals. Furthermore, the modified duration line is tangent to the present value line where there is zero change in yield. What this may suggest to the more mathematically inclined reader is that modified duration can be derived from a present value equation by solving for the derivative of price with respect to yield.

In sum, because modified duration posits a linear price/yield relationship while the true price/yield relationship of a fixed-income security is curvilinear, modified duration provides an inexact estimate of price for a given change in yield. This estimate is less accurate as we move further away from current market levels.

Figure 3.2 shows price/yield relationships implied by modified duration for two of our three Treasury securities.

While the slope of Treasury Bill's modified duration function is relatively flat, the slope of the Treasury STRIPS is relatively steep. As the reader may confirm by visual inspection, an equal change in yield for the Treasury Bill and Treasury STRIPS will suggest very different changes in price. The price of the Treasury STRIPS will change by more, and this is because the STRIPS has a greater modified duration. The STRIPS has a greater price sensitivity for a given change in yield.

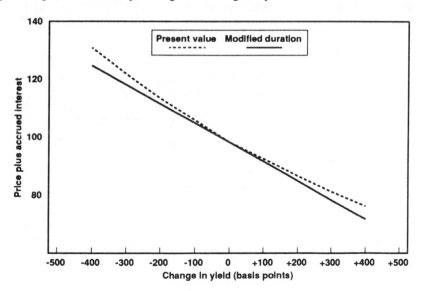

FIGURE 3.1 "True" versus estimated price values: present value versus modified duration values.

How then can we better approximate a security's price if modified duration is of limited value? Or to put it differently, how can we better approximate the price/yield property of a fixed-income security as implied by the present value formula? With *convexity.*

CONVEXITY

To solve for convexity, we could go a step further with either Hick's or Macaulay's methodologies. To proceed using Hick's method we would solve for the second derivative of the price/yield equation with respect to yield using a Taylor series expansion. This is expressed mathematically as $(d^2P'/dY^2)/P'$, where P' is the dirty price.

To proceed using Macaulay's methodology, we would solve for

$$\frac{\sum_{t=1}^{T} \dfrac{C'_{t \cdot t}}{(1 + Y/2)^t} \cdot t + 1}{\sum_{t=1}^{T} \dfrac{C'_t}{(1 + Y/2)^t} \cdot 4 \cdot (1 + Y/2)^2} \tag{3.8}$$

In Table 3.4 we calculate convexity for the 7.625% Treasury Note of 5/31/96. We calculate convexity to be 20.1036.

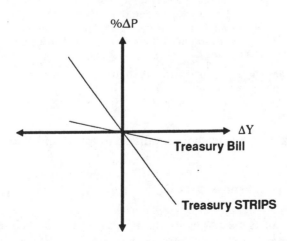

FIGURE 3.2 Price/yield relationships implied by modified duration.

Table 3.4   Calculating Convexity

(A) C'_t	(B) t	(C) $C'_t/(1+Y/2)^t$	(D) (B) · (C)	(E) (C) · (B)²	(F) (D) · (B)$_{t+1}$
3.8125	0.9344	3.6763	3.4352	3.2100	6.6452
3.8125	1.9344	3.5359	6.8399	13.2313	20.0712
3.8125	2.9344	3.4009	9.9796	29.2843	39.2638
3.8125	3.9344	3.2710	12.8694	50.6338	63.5033
3.8125	4.9344	3.1461	15.5240	76.6022	92.1263
3.8125	5.9344	3.0259	17.9571	106.5652	124.5223
3.8125	6.9344	2.9104	20.1817	139.9487	160.1304
3.8125	7.9344	2.7992	22.2102	176.2255	198.4357
3.8125	8.9344	2.6923	24.0544	214.9121	238.9665
103.8125	9.9344	70.5111	700.4868	6958.9345	7659.4031
Totals		98.9690	833.5384	7769.5475	8603.0678

Notes:

    C' = Cashflows over the life of the security.

    Since this Treasury Note has a coupon of 7.625%, semi-annual coupons are equal to 7.625/2=3.8125.

    t = Time in days defined as the number of days the Treasury Note is held in a coupon period divided by the number of days from the last coupon paid (or issue date) to the next coupon payment.

    Since this Treasury Note was purchased 11 days after it was issued, the first coupon is discounted with t = 171/183 = 0.9344.

$C'_t/(1+Y/2)^t$ = Present value of a cashflow.

    Y = Bond-equivalent yield; 7.941%.

The reader will notice that columns (A) through (D) are exactly the same as in Table 3.2 where we calculated this Treasury Note's duration.

The summation of column (F) gives us the numerator for our convexity formula. The denominator of our convexity formula is obtained by calculating the product of column (C) and 4 · $(1+Y/2)^2$. Thus,

Convexity = 8603.0678 / (98.9690 · 4 · $(1+0.039705)^2$)
         = 20.1036

To estimate price using both modified duration and convexity requires solving for

$$P^e = Pd + Pd (Dmod · \Delta Y + Convexity · \Delta Y^2/2) \tag{3.9}$$

Equation 3.8 is used to estimate prices in Table 3.5. Note how "true" versus estimated price differences are significantly reduced relative to Table 3.3. Residual price differences between "true" and estimated

Table 3.5 "True" versus Estimated Price Values Generated by
Present Value and Modified Duration/Convexity
7.75% Treasury Note of 2/15/2021
(Settlement Date, 3/13/91)

Change in Yield Level (basis points)	Price plus Accrued Interest, Present Value Equation	Price plus Accrued Interest, Duration/Convexity Equation	Difference
+400	76.1448	76.2541	(0.1090)
+300	81.0724	80.8378	0.2350
+200	86.4398	86.0067	0.4330
+100	92.2917	91.7606	0.5311
0	98.0996	98.0996	0.0000
−100	105.6525	105.0237	0.6290
−200	113.2777	112.5328	0.7449
−300	121.6210	120.6270	0.9440
−400	130.7582	129.3063	1.4519

values could be reduced even further by incorporating derivatives of a higher order beyond duration and convexity.

Figure 3.3 highlights the difference between estimated price/yield relationships using modified duration alone and modified duration with convexity.

Figure 3.3 helps to show that convexity is a desirable property. Convexity means that prices fall by *less* than that implied by modified duration when yields *rise*, and that prices rise by *more* than that implied by modified duration when yields *fall*.

We will return to the concepts of modified duration and convexity time and again. These are perhaps among the most fundamental properties to be replicated when creating a synthetic security.

Duration and Convexity Summary

- Duration is a measure of a fixed-income security's price sensitivity to a given change in yield.
- Duration is of limited value when estimating price/yield dynamics since it posits a linear price/yield relationship.
- Duration has an inverse relationship to yield levels and coupons.

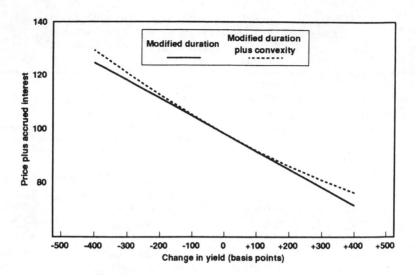

FIGURE 3.3   Modified duration versus modified duration plus convexity.

- Modified duration is equal to Macaulay's duration divided by $(1 + Y/2)$. Modified duration adjusts Macaulay's duration to allow for discrete compounding.
- Convexity means that prices fall by less than that implied by duration when yields rise. Convexity also means that prices rise by more than that implied by duration when yields fall.

PART TWO
SYNTHETIC MONEY MARKET SECURITIES

Simply defined, a money market security is a cash fixed-income product with one year or less from original issue to maturity.

At any given point in time, the dollar value of outstanding money market securities greatly exceeds the dollar value of outstanding securities of any other sector of the yield curve. Money market derivative products such as Treasury Bill futures and Eurodollar futures are among the most actively traded of all financial futures.

Although money market securities may appear to be simple securities, they can be a real challenge to manage effectively. From an economic perspective, money market yields are particularly sensitive to monetary policy as dictated by the Federal Reserve. Thus, an active money market investor will generally have an outlook on near-term economic fundamentals when determining how to structure his/her money market portfolio.

In this part, we consider a variety of strategies that may be used to create synthetic money market assets.

4
A Survey of Cash Money Market Securities

Although Treasury Bills are perhaps the best-known money market securities, other products include Certificates of Deposit, Commercial paper, Bankers' acceptances, Agencies, and Municipals.

CERTIFICATES OF DEPOSIT

A Certificate of Deposit (CD) is a money market security issued by banks to help fund loans. A CD is generally sold in units of $1 million, and typically has a maturity of one to three months. CD calculations require an Actual/360 day-count basis, and a simple interest pricing convention is used. CD products include Domestic CDs, Eurodollar CDs, Yankee CDs, and Variable-rate CDs.

Domestic CDs are dollar-denominated securities issued by U.S. banks in the United States. Domestic CDs tend to trade cheap to Treasury Bills since the former are less liquid and carry a credit risk. That is, Domestic CDs tend to trade at higher yields relative to Treasury Bills. Domestic CDs are generally sold directly by banks to investors, though some issues pass through dealers who also make a secondary market in these securities.

When a *Eurodollar CD* is issued, a Eurodollar deposit is created. A Eurodollar deposit is a deposit denominated in dollars in a bank or bank branch outside the United States. While the "Euro" in Eurodollar suggests that the bank or bank branch is somewhere in Europe, it could be located anywhere outside the United States. Banks that participate in the Eurodollar market actively borrow and lend Eurodollars among themselves just as U.S. banks borrow and lend Federal Funds. Federal Funds are monies lent and borrowed among banks in the United States. However, while Federal Funds tend to be lent and borrowed on an overnight basis, Eurodollar deposits tend to be longer term. Eurodollar CDs tend to be priced cheaper than Domestic CDs. Eurodollar CDs are less liquid relative to Domestic CDs, and many investors perceive Eurodollar CDs as bearing extra risk since they are issued outside the United States.

Yankee CDs are dollar-denominated CDs issued by non-U.S. banks through respective bank branches. Yankees CDs tend to trade at money market yields close to Eurodollar CDs.

As the name implies, *Variable-rate CDs* pay varying rates of interest over the life of a security. A Variable-rate CD is something like a coupon-bearing security since it generates cashflows between the time of issue and maturity. It's also something like a money market security since the variable-rate is linked to an index such as the 3-month Eurodollar rate or 3-month Treasury Bill rate. Variable-rate CDs are generally not as liquid as other CD products.

Commercial paper (CP) is an unsecured promissory note issued by corporations including industrial, manufacturing, and finance companies. A firm may find it more attractive to borrow with a CP program than to take out a short-term loan with a bank. Although CP cannot have a maturity in excess of 270 days, most CP issues have a maturity of 30 days or less. The 270-day maturity limit is mandated by the Securities and Exchange Commission. However, many CP issuers will simply roll over an issue when it matures and will continue to do so until funds are no longer required.

BANKERS' ACCEPTANCES

Bankers' acceptances (BAs) are among the more creative of money market securities. Perhaps the best way to describe a BA is to give an example. Suppose a U.S.-based importer wants to buy a shipment of Swiss-made chocolates but won't have the money to pay for the chocolates until after the chocolates are sold. If our importer is too small or not well-known enough to issue CP, he or she may decide to have his or her bank write a letter of credit for the cost of the chocolates. This letter of credit would be sent to the Swiss exporter, and the exporter would use this letter to draw a time draft on the importer's U.S. bank. Once the time draft is obtained, the exporter would discount the time draft at his or her local bank and thus obtain immediate payment for the chocolates. The exporter's Swiss bank would, in turn, send the time draft to the U.S. importer's bank. Upon receiving the time draft, the importer's bank would stamp the time draft as "accepted," and an acceptance would thus be created. At this point, the time draft becomes an irrevocable primary obligation of the importer's bank. If the Swiss bank were to demand immediate payment, the importer's bank would have to honor that demand. If cash weren't immediately required by the Swiss bank, the exporter's bank might send the acceptance to the Swiss bank for it to hold to maturity or sell to an investor. In any case, it is the importer's responsibility to provide its bank with required payment(s), in a timely manner. If the importer should fail to do this, his or her bank would ultimately be responsible to pay off the acceptance at maturity.

Although the preceding example considers how a BA is created by an import transaction, BAs may also arise in connection with export sales, trades among third parties, domestic shipments of goods, and domestic or foreign storage of goods. Most BAs are created by foreign trade transactions.

Finally, since BAs most closely resemble CP, they are often compared against CP yields. However, CP is guaranteed only by the issuing company, and a BA is backed by the issuer's pledge to pay, the goods being financed, and the guarantee of the accepting bank. Thus, BAs may trade slightly rich to CP. That is, BAs may trade at lower yields relative to CP.

AGENCY SECURITIES

Agency securities are issued by various agencies of the U.S. government. Agencies that issue money market securities include (but are not limited to) the Federal Farm Credit Bank (FFCB), Federal Home Loan Bank (FHLB), Federal National Mortgage Association (FNMA), and Student Loan Marketing Association (SLMA). Agency money market securities tend to trade cheap to Treasury Bills and rich to CDs, BAs, and CP. Unlike most money market securities, Agencies trade with a 30/360 day-count basis. The 30 in the numerator assumes 30-day months (even though there may actually be more or fewer days), and the 360 in the denominator assumes a 360-day year.

MUNICIPAL SECURITIES

Several *Municipal* money market securities (also called Municipal notes) are issued every year, and these include a mix of coupon- and noncoupon-bearing securities. Municipal securities trade rich to Treasury Bills because the former are exempt from federal income taxes and are usually exempt from state and local taxes within the state of issue. Treasury Bills are exempt from only state and local taxes.

Municipal note yields are also influenced by how the collected funds will be used. For example, a municipal security sold in anticipation of future tax receipts may have a lower yield relative to a security sold in anticipation of revenues on a city project. With a general obligation security (or GO), payment of principal and interest is secured by the issuer's pledge of its full faith, credit, and taxing power. With a revenue obligation security, payment of principal and interest is made from revenues derived from those who use the facility being financed. Examples of municipal securities include (but are not limited to) Tax anticipation notes (TANs), Revenue anticipation notes (RANs), Bond anticipation notes (BANs), and Project notes (PNs). There is no single day-count convention among Municipal securities, so it is important for an investor to know if a given security is quoted using a day-count basis of Actual/360, Actual/Actual, or 30/360.

Cash Money Market Securities Summary

There are a variety of cash money market securities, and we will consider strategies involving these and related products in the following chapters. In Appendix C, we provide an overview of commonly traded money market securities, and highlight differences that may better allow investors to identify relative value.

5

Repos, Reverse Repos, and Dollar Rolls

THE REPO MARKET

The repo market, it may be argued, plays the role of a "community bank" in the financial markets. A community bank takes in deposits from individuals with cash, and in turn lends cash to persons who want to borrow. When a bank lends cash, its collateral is often tied to the asset being purchased. For example, the collateral for a home mortgage is usually the home being financed. And when a community bank takes in deposits, the depositor's "collateral" is the strength of the bank itself. If the bank is insured by the Federal Deposit Insurance Corporation, then a depositor is also covered by this agency's pledge to guarantee deposits of up to $100,000. The bank earns money on the difference between what is paid (deposit rates) and what is received (loan rates) plus any fees.

Similarly, a firm's repo desk takes in cash and fixed-income securities from investors, and in turn lends cash and fixed-income securities to investors. When an investor lends cash, this is called a reverse repo (short for "reverse repurchase agreement"), and fixed-income securities serve as collateral. When a investor lends fixed-income securities, this is called a repo (short for "repurchase agreement"), and cash serves as collateral. Since many repo desks try to run a "matched book" where the dollar value of cash and securities lent is matched against the dollar value of cash and securities borrowed, the desk earns money on respective bid/offer spreads.

So why would an investor place his or her cash in the repo market instead of buying Treasury Bills or other money market securities? Generally because the repo market affords a flexibility that is unmatched by *any* money market security. The repo market can accommodate a variety of investment horizons from overnight out to three months or more. When a given transaction is for a fixed period of time, it is called a "term repo."

For an investor who has funds to put to work over a short but otherwise uncertain time span, the repo market can provide an attractive alternative to traditional fixed-income securities. For example, funds can be rolled-over indefinitely in the overnight repo market. Conversely, purchasing a money market security exposes the investor to the risk that the asset may have to be sold prior to maturity and at an unattractive yield. The repo market is particularly active with trafficking short-term trades and can be a much more liquid and viable market relative to cash money market securities.

And why would an investor lend his or her securities in the repo market? One reason may be to use the repo proceeds to finance a security's purchase price. An incentive also exists for an investor to loan securities in exchange for cash when a short-term cash position is desirable. For example, if a buy-and-hold investor has securities to loan for one month, the cash received in exchange for the loan can be invested in short-term money market assets. This repo is generally of limited interest to active investors since loaning their securities precludes any trading in these securities over the term of the reverse repo. Let's look at some examples.

On April 24, 1991, the overnight rate in the repo market was 5.90%/5.95%. Thus, a repo desk would have paid 5.90% for cash and would have paid 5.95% for "general collateral." General collateral is market jargon for U.S. Treasury securities that are not trading on special. "On special" is a term that identifies a particular security with a repo rate substantially *below* prevailing general collateral rates. A security may trade on special as an inducement to bring scarce securities into the marketplace.

For an investor with an idle overnight cash reserve, the repo market would be an attractive place to put the funds to work. For an overnight cash reserve of $10 million, an overnight repo at a rate of 5.90% would have paid $1,638.89:

$$\$1,638.89 = \$10,000,000 \cdot 0.059 \cdot 1/360$$

Repo rates are calculated using an Actual/360 day-count basis.

For an investor who expects to have a significant cash position over a longer period of time, say one week, some options emerge. Among other things, the investor could roll over the cash position in the repo market on a day-to-day basis, could buy a money market security, or could deposit the money in a bank account. The pros and cons of each of these strategies are summarized in Table 5.1.

As to the risks of placing funds in the repo market versus buying a money market security, both entail interest rate risk. The interest rate risk with a rolling day-to-day repo strategy is that the repo rate can fluctuate. The rate risk with a money market security is that the security may have to be sold prior to maturity, possibly at an unattractive yield.

In the following equation, we calculate the daily compounded money market yield for a repo that is rolled over seven days. Recall that a

Table 5.1 Evaluating Cash Investments over a Short but Unknown Horizon

Strategy	Pros	Cons
Roll over funds in repo market	A natural market for daily investments Opportunity to earn daily compound interest	The daily rate paid for cash can vary from day-to-day
Buy a money market security	If held until maturity, a money market security may yield more than the repo strategy	Short-term money market securities tend not to be very liquid, and the investor could suffer a minimal return or loss if the security is sold prior to maturity
Deposit funds in a bank	A natural market for daily investments Opportunity to earn daily compound interest	Bank deposit rates tend not to be competitive with money market or repo market rates

compounding calculation generally assumes that successive trades are reinvested at the same rate; that is, 5.90%.

$$5.903\% = [(1 + 0.059 / (360/1))^7 - 1] \, 360/7$$

On that day in April 1991 when the overnight repo rate was 5.90%, the money market yield on the May 2 Treasury Bill with seven days to maturity was 5.616%. In this instance, we see that a rolling repo might have outperformed a 7-day Treasury Bill by more than 28 basis points (5.903% vs. 5.616%).

Just as it is possible to invest cash in the repo market on a day-to-day basis, it is possible to invest cash for terms of a week, month, quarter, or longer. However, investors ought to be aware that although there is no secondary market for term repos, it may be possible to get out of a term repo prior to its expiration with the consent of the respective dealer. Further, a second offsetting trade might be executed.

Term repo rates sometimes have a special significance because of the day on which they expire. For example, many term repo rates are linked to the expiration date of a futures contract. When a term repo is said to be priced to "the Board" or "the Board date," this means that the repo matures on the day that the respective nearby (front-month) futures contract expires.

And just as it is possible to construct a yield curve using Treasury securities, it is possible to construct a term structure for the repo market. The term structure of general collateral rates can be normal (upward sloping), inverted, or flat. When the term structure is inverted, there is a strong incentive to roll over funds on a daily basis instead of locking-in at lower longer-term rates. In this instance, an outlook on near-term monetary policy could be an important consideration. If the Federal Reserve is expected to ease monetary policy, the repo curve can be expected to steepen, and term repos may look more attractive. If the Federal Reserve is expected to tighten monetary policy, the repo curve can be expected to flatten, and daily rollovers may look more attractive.

There is a repo strategy by the name of "flex repo," and its profitability for a repo desk is very much dependent on the repo term structure. Flex repos are particularly popular among bond issuers. If a bond issuer does not require the proceeds from a bond sale all at once, there is an incentive to put the cash to work until it's needed. One way to keep the cash invested is to place it in the repo market. Accordingly, the issuer may draw up a schedule of its anticipated cash requirements over the life of a project and will ask a sampling of repo desks to quote a rate that they will pay on this cash over an anticipated horizon. Since varying amounts of cash will be required at different times (hence, flex repo), the pool of funds will shrink as cash is used.

A flex repo may be most attractive to a repo desk when the repo curve is inverted. In this instance, it is possible to generate the highest effective repo rate with a daily rollover, and the repo desk is not compelled to lock-in cash for term. The repo desk does not want to be in a position where it will have to provide immediate cash when the bulk of the cash position is in term repo. When the repo curve has a normal shape, a flex repo may not be as attractive to a repo desk. There is a trade-off between the lower rate earned from daily rollovers, and higher rates earned on less liquid term repos.

On the same day that the repo market was paying 5.90%/5.95% on overnight transactions, the repo market was paying 3.625%/4.0% "to date" for the on-the-run 10-year Treasury Note. To date means to the settlement date of the Treasury issue that is to become the *new* on-the-run security in postauction trading. The on-the-run 10-year Treasury Note on April 24 was the 7.75%/2-15-2001, and the new on-the-run 10-year Treasury Note was to settle on May 15, 1991.

Thus, an investor holding $100 million of the 7.75% Treasury Note of 2-15-2001 with no immediate plans to sell the security could have loaned the security in the repo market in exchange for cash. The amount of cash received would have been $99,367,800:

$$Cr = Pd - H \tag{5.1}$$

$$99.3678 = 99.4928 - 0.1250$$

$$\$99,367,800 = \$100,000,000 \cdot 99.3678 / 100$$

where: Cr = Cash received
        Pd = Dirty price, bid-side
        H = Haircut

"Haircut" is market lingo for a repo desk's fee in executing a reverse repo transaction. In this instance the haircut was 0.125, or "an eighth" in the market vernacular. A haircut is a fee only in the sense that the repo desk pays out a rate of 4.0% on something *less than 100%* of the security's full value; that is, the dirty price *less* an eighth. The rationale for a haircut is that the repo desk is lending the more liquid asset: cash. Thus, a haircut might be thought of as having to post margin. Margin is a deposit of cash and/or securities to help ensure an investor's good faith and credit to make good on a given trade. By the same token, many investors who lend cash to a repo desk will often demand a "102% repo." A 102% repo requires that the cash loan be backed by collateral valued at 102% of the cash position.

The amount of cash to be paid back on May 15 would have been $99,588,600:

$$(Pd - H)(1 + R \cdot Tsd / 360) \tag{5.2}$$
$$99.5886 = (99.4928 - 0.1250)(1 + 0.04 \cdot 20 / 360)$$
$$\$99,588,600 = \$100,000,000 \cdot 99.5886 / 100$$

where: R = Term repo rate
Tsd = Time in days of the reverse repo

Now then, what could our reverse repo investor have done with $99,367,800 to date? For one thing, he or she could have rolled the cash in the overnight repo market, perhaps to earn $99,694,002:

$$5.909\% = [(1 + 0.059 / (360 / 1))^{20} - 1] 360 / 20$$
$$\$99,694,002 = \$99,367,800 (1 + 0.05909 \cdot 20 / 360)$$

The difference between what might have been earned in the repo market versus what would have to be paid back on May 15 would have been $105,402:

$$\$105,402 = \$99,694,002 - \$99,588,600$$

In sum, an investor could have lent the 7.75% Treasury Note of 2/15/2001 over 20 days to pick up $105,402. The DV01 of the Treasury Note was 0.06613, and this translates into 1.59 basis points. Thus, this repo transaction may have added nearly two basis points to the 10-year's bond-equivalent yield:

$$1.59 \text{ basis points} = \$105,402 / \$100,000,000 \cdot 0.06613 / 100$$

Instead of lending cash in the overnight repo market, our reverse repo investor could have purchased a money market security. The challenge would have been to find a money market security maturing on May 15. If the money market security were to mature *prior* to May 15, then funds might be left idle. However, presumably the funds could be placed in overnight repo from the time the money market security matured until May 15. If the money market security were to mature *after* May 15, then the security might have to be sold at an unattractive yield.

On April 24 there was an outstanding Treasury Bill maturing on May 16. Although the Treasury Bill would have to be sold prior to maturity, it is unlikely that its price would be substantially below par. Since the money market yield on the Treasury Bill was 5.608%, an investor would have had to make a judgment call. Would the effective compounded overnight repo rate fall from 5.909% to below 5.608%? If no, the rolling overnight repo strategy might be most appropriate. If yes, the Treasury Bill might be the more appropriate investment vehicle. The Federal Funds rate was trading at 6.0% at the time, and the Federal Reserve had eased monetary policy just one week earlier when the Federal Funds rate was trading at 6.25%. And although economic data suggested the economy was sluggish (arguing for a further ease and a lower repo rate), Federal Reserve Chairman Greenspan had made comments that inflationary pressures were a problem (arguing for no further ease and a stable repo rate). In hindsight, the Federal Reserve eased monetary policy on April 30 with a cut in the discount rate and a lower Federal Funds rate. The overnight repo rate fell by only 15 basis points, so the overnight repo strategy would have outperformed the Treasury Bill.

Aside from lending securities in the repo market to enhance yield, an investor may use the repo market to build a strategy around a particular interest rate outlook. For example, an investor may purchase a 90-day Treasury Bill and immediately turn around and loan it in the repo market for a term of 30 days. An incentive for doing this is that the investor is able to use the repo market to "finance" his or her Treasury Bill position with the cash received in exchange for the securities loaned. Another incentive for doing the trade may be that the investor believes he or she can create a *future* security that can be sold at a profit. The success of the strategy depends on the spread relationship between Treasury Bills and Federal Funds, and the spread relationship between 60- and 90-day Treasury Bills. To see exactly how this would work, let's consider an example.

Assume that the following rates prevail on a given day (all rates expressed on a money market yield basis):

Federal Funds: 8.0%
90-day Treasury Bill: 7.90% (offer)
30-day term repo: 7.75% (bid)

If an investor were to buy the 90-day Treasury Bill and finance it with a 30-day term repo, he or she would enjoy a positive carry equal to 15 basis points:

15 basis points = 7.90% − 7.75%

By positive carry, we mean a positive yield spread between the rate earned on the cash security and the rate charged in the repo market to finance that security.

By engaging in the above transactions, our investor may create a future 60-day Treasury Bill. The 60-day Treasury Bill is created by the unfinanced portion (or tail) of the repo transaction. If we think of the positive carry as raising the effective yield at which our investor purchases the future security, then the effective yield becomes 7.975%:

7.975% = 7.90% + 0.15% / 2

We divide our positive carry by two since the 15 basis points are earned over 30 days while the future Treasury Bill will have 60 days to maturity.

Thus, it would be inviting to do the repo and create a 60-day Treasury Bill *if* our investor believes he or she can sell that future Treasury Bill at a money market yield of 7.975% or lower.

If the yield spreads were to remain constant over the horizon of the term repo, then the following rates would prevail 30 days hence:

Fed Funds: 8.15%
90-day Treasury Bill: 8.05%

In sum, if our investor does not believe that the Federal Reserve will tighten monetary policy, which would serve to push up the Federal Funds rate, then the trade would look attractive.

Table 5.2 Where Fixed-Income Products Trade in the
Repo Market Relative to Federal Funds

Fixed-income products that tend to trade in the repo market above Federal funds	Whole loan products
	Segmented MBSs
	Deliverable MBSs
	Segmented money market products
	Segmented MBSs
	Segmented Agencies
	Segmented Treasuries

Federal Funds

Fixed-income products that tend to trade in the repo market below Federal funds	Deliverable money market products
	Tri-party MBSs (wireable only)
	Tri-party Agencies
	Tri-party Treasuries
	Deliverable generic MBSs
	Deliverable general Agencies
	Deliverable general Treasuries
	Deliverable general specials, Agencies, or Treasuries
	Deliverable regular specials, Agencies, or Treasuries
	Deliverable special specials, Agencies, or Treasuries

Definitions:

Whole loan products: An individual mortgage in which an investor has a full participation interest.

Segmented: Repo collateral is held in a segregated account in the name of the firm lending the money. Use with repos only.

MBSs: Mortgage-backed securities. A large and diverse group of securities including pass-through securities, CMOs, IOs, POs, and others.

Deliverable: Repo collateral is delivered to the customer against the money lent to the repo desk, and vice versa. Most common type of repo or reverse repo.

Tri-party: Repo collateral is held in custody by a third party. Custodian acts as fiduciary for customer. Use with repos only.

Wireable: Securities that are book-entry; delivery of securities not required.

Generic: Not special

General: Securities not specifically requested for a given transaction, and not in strong demand.

General specials: Securities specifically requested for a given transaction, and not in strong demand.

Regular specials: Securities specifically requested for a given transaction, and in strong demand.

Special specials: Securities specifically requested for a given transaction, and in particularly strong demand.

Table 5.2 provides a schematic diagram of where repo and reverse repo rates might trade in relation to the securities involved and in relation to the Federal Funds (Fed Funds) rate.

Table 5.2 puts Fed Funds at the center of attention. It is commonly held that all money market rates trade in relation to the Fed Funds rate. Simply defined, the Fed Funds rate is the rate of interest banks charge one another to borrow money to satisfy cash reserve requirements imposed by government banking regulations. The reason repo rates tend to trade below the Fed Funds rate is that the former are tied to "collateralized loans." That is, when cash is lent in the repo market, it is backed by fixed-income securities. Fed Funds are backed by the good faith and credit of respective banks.

Another observation worth making about Table 5.2 is that a variety of fixed-income securities may pass through the repo market, not just Treasury securities. Agencies, BAs, CP, and other securities may be used in the repo market. Not surprisingly, the further away the securities get from Treasuries in terms of credit quality, the higher the respective repo rates.

Finally, a type of overnight repo is an open repo. With an open repo, an investor agrees to lend cash for an unspecified period, and the agreement can be terminated by either the investor or dealer at any time. Further, the dealer may have the right of substitution where securities serving as collateral may be different over time. The rate on open repos may be slightly above overnight repo rates, and only one compound period is used in contrast to daily compounding with true overnight repos.

Repo Market Summary

- The repo market is one of the more accommodative investment vehicles.
- Lending cash in the repo market is known as a reverse repo, and cash may be loaned for periods as short as overnight, or as long as a quarter or more. Lending cash in the repo market may prove to be an attractive alternative to money market securities, particularly if the time span of the investment horizon is not known with certainty.
- When securities are loaned instead of cash, this is called a repo. Repos can offer buy-and-hold investors an opportunity to enhance total returns. Repos may also be used to create future securities that may prove to be attractive investments.

DOLLAR ROLLS

A dollar roll is a specialized reverse repo transaction found in the mortgage-backed securities (MBSs) market. Dollar rolls differ from regular reverse repos in that the investor is unlikely to receive the same securities that were initially delivered. On the other hand, the investor can potentially borrow funds at a rate well below the repo rate.

The reason for these features lies in the purpose of the dollar roll transaction. The MBS market differs from most other fixed-income sectors in two important respects. First, settlement of security trades occurs once a month. Second, there is a highly developed and liquid forward market, a result of mortgage bankers selling anticipated production of new mortgages. Dollar rolls allow dealers to manage their positions more efficiently. If a dealer agreed to sell securities but did not have the required securities on settlement day, he or she can "borrow" them through the dollar roll market and agree to return substantially similar securities. The dealer is willing to pay for this privilege in the form of a favorable borrowing rate up to the cost of failing to make timely delivery, which is the accrued interest between the scheduled and actual settlement date. The liquidity of the dollar roll market is enhanced by the active forward market, which assures that the dealer will be able to obtain securities to close out the roll transaction.

MORTGAGE-BACKED SECURITIES

Since MBSs are unlike the fixed-income products reviewed thus far, these unique assets are deserving of a comment or two. Part Three provides even more detail on these unique assets.

To put it simply, the principal of a pass-through MBS is paid out over the life of the asset, not at the maturity of the asset. Further, these principal cashflows are paid on a monthly basis along with interest payments.

To understand the nature of monthly pass-through MBS cashflows, it is important to appreciate how a pass-through MBS is put together. A pass-through MBS embodies a pool of individual fixed-rate mortgages. When monthly mortgage payments are made, these are passed along to holders of pass-through MBSs in the form of amortized principal and coupon cashflows. In addition to paying these standard monthly cashflows, an MBS may also generate cashflows related to the early payoff of mortgages within a pool. These cashflows are called prepayments.

When an individual takes out a mortgage at a fixed rate, he or she has the right to refinance that mortgage at a more attractive rate of interest if interest rates should fall. In this way a person with a mortgage has an implicit call option on interest rates; the value of refinancing increases as interest rates fall. Conversely, an investor holding a pass-through MBS is short an implicit call; the value of the pass-through MBS rises at a slower rate as interest rates fall.

In Part One, we stated that there is an inverse relationship between yield and price. As yield levels rise, price levels fall, and vice versa. In Chapter 3, we also stated that convexity serves to enhance price appreciation when yields fall and to moderate price depreciation when yields rise. How is convexity affected when an asset is characterized by a combination of a traditional coupon-bearing fixed-income asset and an embedded short call? We will discuss options in detail in Part Three, but for now, Figure 5.1 helps to demonstrate how an embedded short call affects duration and convexity.

As shown in Figure 5.1, the price/yield relationship tends to "bend back" when there is an embedded short call with a traditional coupon-bearing fixed-income security. This bending back of the price/yield relationship is also known as "price compression" or "negative convexity." Price increases as yield levels decline, but the price appreciation becomes dampened at ever-lower yields.

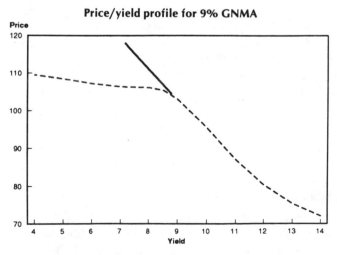

FIGURE 5.1   The effect of an embedded short call on
duration and convexity.

EXAMPLE OF A DOLLAR ROLL

Assume that a fixed-income investor is holding some pass-through MBSs and would like to restructure a portion of assets and add to portfolio total returns. To restructure a portion of his or her pass-through MBS holdings, our investor can engage in a dollar roll whereby securities are exchanged for cash. At the end of the dollar roll an investor is not guaranteed to receive the same security he or she originally exchanged for cash. The only guidelines that must be followed as to the security returned are that the security must (a) be of the same type issued by the same agency, (b) be collateralized by similar mortgages, (c) have the same original term to maturity, (d) have the same coupon, and (e) satisfy rules of good delivery (i.e., aggregate principal amounts of the securities delivered and received must be within 2.5% of face value of transaction).

An investor may insist that the securities that are returned must meet certain criteria, although this may serve to reduce the amount of up-front cash an investor receives to invest over the length of the dollar roll.

To add to portfolio returns, the cash received on the dollar roll can be placed in the repo market or invested in a money market security.

When determining the maximum amount of cash a dealer will want to pay for a dollar roll, he or she will want to consider the minimum repurchase price that would make him or her indifferent between (a) doing a dollar roll to meet a delivery requirement, or (b) paying the accrued interest associated with delayed delivery. By delivery we mean the dealer's obligation to return bonds to the investor at the end of the dollar roll. Market lingo for the difference between the MBS's price at the start of the roll and the minimum repurchase price is the "drop." Conversely, when determining the minimum amount of cash a customer will want to receive on a dollar roll, he or she will want to consider the maximum repurchase price that would make him or her indifferent between the dollar roll and an alternative money market type investment. To put this differently, the customer will want to evaluate the cost of borrowing, as implied by the repurchase price, and compare this cost with the potential return and risks of the trade. Figure 5.2 shows the relationship between an implied cost of borrowing and the drop.

As shown in Figure 5.2, there is an inverse relationship between the price drop and the implied roll rate. Intuitively, this suggests that the better the price an investor can get on the MBS at the end of a roll, the more attractive the implied roll rate.

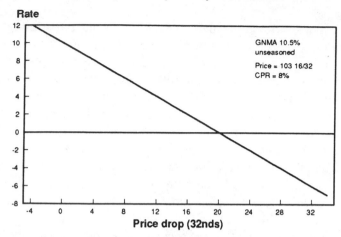

FIGURE 5.2   The effect of the drop on the implied cost of funds.

In Figures 5.3 and 5.4, we show how prepayments affect the implied roll rate. Prepayments are stated in terms of a constant prepayment rate, or CPR. For example, if a CPR is said to be 15%, then it is assumed that prepayment of principal is at a constant rate of 15% over the life of the MBS. The MBSs used to generate Figure 5.3 and 5.4 are unseasoned securities. That is, neither security has yet experienced any prepayments.

In Figure 5.3, we see that there is a direct relationship between the CPR and implied roll rate. As the CPR increases, so too does the implied roll rate. This occurs because the MBS in Figure 5.3 is a discount MBS, and as prepayments on a discount MBS increase, its yield rises because the discount MBS is amortized more rapidly. Thus, if an investor rolls a rapidly prepaying discount MBS, he or she forgoes the favorable yield behavior of that security. This opportunity loss is reflected in a higher implied roll rate.

Figure 5.4 illustrates the indirect relationship between the CPR and implied roll rate. As the CPR increases, the implied roll rate decreases because the MBS in Figure 5.4 is a premium MBS; and as prepayments on a premium MBS increase, its yield falls. This happens because slower prepayments enhance the yield performance of a premium MBS. Thus, if an investor rolls a slow-prepaying premium MBS, he or she forgoes the favorable

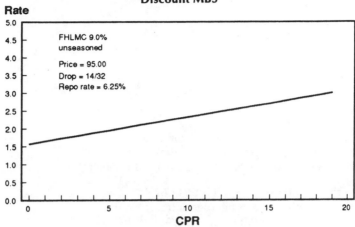

FIGURE 5.3   The effect of prepayments on the implied roll rate for a discount MBS.

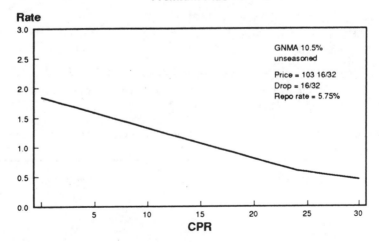

FIGURE 5.4   The effect of prepayments on the implied roll rate for a premium MBS.

Table 5.3   Calculating an Implied Roll Rate

Security: FHLMC PC 9%
Initial roll date: 6/26/89
Closing roll date: 7/17/89
Open price: 95-00
Drop: 14/32
Closing price: 94-18
Face value: $1.0 million

Step 1: Price at start of dollar roll is $956,250
$956,250 = Open price plus accrued interest
$\quad\quad\quad\quad = \$950,000 + (0.09/12) \cdot (25/30) \cdot \$1,000,000$

Step 2: Price at end of dollar roll is $949,625
$949,625 = Close price plus accrued interest
$\quad\quad\quad\quad = \$945,625 + (0.09/12) \cdot (16/30) \cdot \$1,000,000$

Step 3: Price spread is $6,625
$6,625 = Step 1 minus Step 2
$\quad\quad\quad = \$956,250 - \$949,625$

Step 4: Interest payment and interest income foregone by rolling is $7,520.83
$7,520.83 = Interest payment + Interest income
$\quad\quad\quad\quad = (0.09/12) \cdot \$1,000,000$
$\quad\quad\quad\quad\quad + (0.09/12) \cdot \$1,000,000 \cdot 0.0625 \cdot (16/360)$

Step 5: Financing cost is $895.83
$895.83 = Step 4 minus Step 3
$\quad\quad\quad = \$7,520.83 - \$6,625.00$

Step 6: Effective annual financing rate is 1.605%
1.606% = (Financing cost/Open price) $\cdot$ (360/Time in days of roll)
$\quad\quad\quad = (\$895.83/\$956,250) \cdot (360/21)$

Conclusion: Funds can be borrowed at an effective rate below 2.0% and invested at a rate 400 basis points higher.

yield behavior of that security. This opportunity loss is reflected in a higher implied repo rate.

Table 5.3 shows a step-by-step overview of a dollar roll trade. The effective annual financing cost of the dollar roll is 1.605%. Since the cash received on the dollar roll could have been put into daily repo trades at a rate of, say 6.0%, our investor may have been able to earn a return of more than 400 basis points (6.0% vs. 1.605%).

Finally, there may be tax incentives for doing a dollar roll. In short, a dollar roll may be consummated without accounting for it as a sale and subsequent repurchase of securities. This provides a significant tax advantage on pass-through MBSs with book values significantly different from market values.

Dollar Roll Summary

- A dollar roll allows an investor the opportunity to enhance returns by selling his or her MBSs for a subsequent repurchase of comparable MBSs.
- The difference between the price at the beginning of a dollar roll and the price at the end of a dollar roll is known as the drop. The smaller the drop, the lower the implied roll rate. The lower the implied roll rate, the lower the effective annual cost of funds over the horizon of the dollar roll. And the lower the effective annual cost of funds, the greater the basis point spread between the cost of funds and the return earned by putting those funds to work in the repo market or elsewhere.
- The value of an MBS is significantly affected by prepayments. A slow prepaying premium MBS will tend to have a high implied roll rate, as will a fast prepaying discount MBS. An MBS's implied roll rate varies in a direct relationship with its yield.
- There are risks with a dollar roll. For example, the securities sold to an investor at the end of a dollar roll may not be the securities an investor was hoping to receive. However, this risk may be an opportunity. That is, an investor may choose to sell undesirable MBSs with a dollar roll in hopes of receiving better MBSs at the other end.

6
Treasury Bill Futures

A Treasury Bill futures contract began trading in January 1976 on the International Monetary Market, or IMM. The IMM is now a part of the Chicago Mercantile Exchange, or CME.

One Treasury Bill Futures contract represents $1 million face amount of a Treasury Bill. One Treasury Bill futures contract matures each quarter, and there are eight Treasury Bill futures contracts that trade at any given time. Thus, when a new Treasury Bill future is first introduced, there is a span of 24 months from the first trade date of the new contract to the maturity date of the last (eighth) contract.

An investor who buys a Treasury Bill future and holds the position until the future expires is required to "take delivery" on a Treasury Bill. Take delivery means that the investor is required to purchase a Treasury Bill at the offer-side rate of discount where the Treasury Bill future expires. Conversely, an investor who sells a Treasury Bill future and holds the position until the future expires is required to "make delivery" with a Treasury Bill. Make delivery means that the investor is required to sell a Treasury Bill at the bid-side rate of discount where the Treasury Bill future expires. The Treasury Bill must have a face value of $1 million and mature 90, 91, or 92 days from the future's date of expiration. Generally, there will only be one Treasury Bill with 90, 91, or 92 days to maturity at the time a given Treasury Bill future expires.

When a Treasury Bill future is purchased or sold, an investor does not pay or receive the future's price as when purchasing a Treasury Bill. Rather, he or she pays commissions and makes a so-called margin deposit. A margin deposit is generally posted in the form of cash, Treasury Bills, or short coupon Treasuries. A margin deposit is often thought of as collateral to ensure that an investor has set aside at least some funds should the futures position move against him or her over time. As of April 1991, the margin deposit requirement is $200 per futures contract for spread trades and $500 per futures contract for speculative trades. An example of a spread trade would be to purchase a Treasury Bill future maturing in three months and simultaneously sell a Treasury Bill future maturing in six months. An example of a speculative trade would be to short Treasury Bill futures.

Because a Treasury Bill futures contract is not "purchased" in the same way as a Treasury Bill, investors will often say that they are "going long" the futures contract. And since a Treasury Bill futures contract is not "sold short" in the same way as a Treasury Bill, investors will often say that they are "going short" futures contracts.

If a Treasury Bill futures contract is not purchased or sold like Treasury Bills, how are profits or losses determined? Profits or losses are determined with a daily debiting or crediting of the margin account by a process known as "marking-to-market." If the market rallies and the investor is long Treasury Bill futures, then the futures account earns a credit at the end of the day. Conversely, if the market declines, a long futures account is debited at the end of the day. Table 6.1 shows an actual profit and loss profile for the June 1991 Treasury Bill future.

So how does an investor identify a Treasury Bill future's fair market value? As straightforward as this question may appear to be, it has generated quite a controversy among academicians and practitioners alike. One

Table 6.1 Profit/Loss Profile for the
June 1991 Treasury Bill Future
$10,000,000 Face Value Treasury Bill Futures

Date	Price	Change*	Cumulative Profit/Loss
04/08/91	94.47		
04/09/91	94.44	−0.03	−$750
04/10/91	94.41	−0.03	−$1,500
04/11/91	94.45	+0.04	−$500
04/12/91	94.51	+0.06	+$1,000

* A 0.01 change in price is worth $25 and is called a "tick."

school of thought argues that a futures contract is analogous to a forward contract, and this is the view taken in this book. Let's examine this line of reasoning.

Because a long Treasury Bill futures contract is deliverable against a 3-month Treasury Bill at some future date, the Treasury Bill future may be said to obligate the investor to a *delayed* purchase or sale of a Treasury Bill. Thus, prior to a Treasury Bill future's expiration, the difference in price between the Treasury Bill future and the deliverable Treasury Bill may be explained by the delayed payment for/delivery of the deliverable Treasury Bill. The price difference between a Treasury Bill future and a deliverable Treasury Bill may be quantified and termed a forward rate.

The notion of a forward rate embodied in a future's price does not sit well with many who have studied futures markets. For example, it is argued that while futures contracts are marked-to-market on a daily basis, a true forward contract requires delivery and payment only at the expiration of the contract. It is this daily mark-to-market requirement that leads many to argue that a futures contract is better valued as something other than a forward contract. The daily mark-to-market requirement leads many investors to view a futures contract as a string (or strip) of *daily* forward contracts. For our purposes now, the difference between future and forward valuation methodologies is negligible.

Assume that an investor holds a deliverable 9-month Treasury Bill and wants to evaluate the merits of selling the Treasury Bill today or in six months' time. Further, assume that the rate of discount on the deliverable Treasury Bill is 8.25% and that the 6-month term repo rate is 8.0%.

The investor selling his or her deliverable Treasury Bill today would receive \$93.8125:

$$\$93.8125 = \frac{100\,(360 - 270 \cdot 0.0825)}{360}$$

If the \$93.8125 is invested in an 8.0% six-month term repo, a total of \$97.5650 would be received at the repo's expiration:

$$\$97.5650 = \$93.8125\,(1 + 0.08\,(180\,/\,360))$$

Alternatively, our investor could take a short position in the deliverable Treasury Bill's futures contract and make delivery with his or her

Treasury Bill in six months' time. This strategy of delaying the sale of the deliverable Treasury Bill would not be attractive unless our investor could sell the future at a price of $97.5650 or higher. Our investor could earn $97.5650 if the Treasury Bill were sold today with proceeds invested in a 6-month term repo.

Now assume that another investor wants to evaluate the merits of *buying* a deliverable 9-month Treasury Bill today, or *taking delivery* on the deliverable Treasury Bill in six months' time. If our investor buys his or her deliverable Treasury Bill today, he or she would pay $93.8125. Alternatively, this investor could take a long position in the deliverable Treasury Bill's futures contract and take delivery on the deliverable Treasury Bill in six months' time. And since the purchase of the deliverable Treasury Bill would be a delayed purchase, funds that would have been used to buy the Treasury Bill today could instead be invested in a 6-month term repo at 8.0% to earn a total of $97.5650. This strategy of delaying the purchase of the deliverable Treasury Bill would not be attractive unless this investor could buy the future at a price of $97.5650 or lower.

Thus, whether an investor is considering a delayed *sale* or delayed *purchase* of the deliverable Treasury Bill, the futures price works out to be $97.5650.

In actuality, we would not expect the futures price for a delayed purchase to be *exactly* equal to the futures price for a delayed sale. We would expect a bid/ask spread to prevail, and this would be influenced by bid/ask spreads on the respective repo and Treasury Bill transactions. The bid/ask spread on a Treasury Bill future is generally one "tick." A tick is the smallest unit of change in price on a Treasury Bill futures contract and is equal to $25.

Further, while theory suggests that the Treasury Bill futures' price ought to converge to the deliverable Treasury Bill's price at delivery, this may not happen. Over the last few days of its life, the Treasury Bill future may trade at an implied yield that is a few basis points higher than the yield on the deliverable Treasury Bill. This phenomenon can be explained by the commissions and other transactions costs associated with futures contracts. Commissions on a Treasury Bill futures contract may range from $9 to $20 per contract for a round-turn. A round-turn is the purchase and subsequent sale of a futures contract.

It is now an easy matter to quantify a Treasury Bill future's fair market value. It is defined as

$$Pf = Pb \, (1 + R \cdot Tsd \, / \, 360) \tag{6.1}$$

where: Pf = Futures price
          Pb = Deliverable Treasury Bill price
          R = Term repo rate
          Tsd = Time from settlement to delivery

It is somewhat misleading to say that Equation 6.1 gives us the theoretical futures price. It is misleading because the futures price in Equation 6.1 is quoted in terms of how a *cash* Treasury Bill price is quoted. The price of a Treasury Bill *future* is quoted as par minus a rate of discount. To see the difference between conventions of quoting the price of a Treasury Bill futures versus a cash Treasury Bill, consider the following. For a cash 3-month Treasury Bill with a rate of discount equal to 6.0%, its price is 98.4833. If we were to follow the methodology for pricing a Treasury Bill future, the price of the cash Treasury Bill would be quoted as $100 - 6 = 94.00$. Clearly, the difference between a "price" of 98.4833 and 94.00 is significant.

It is a simple matter to convert the futures price generated by Equation 6.1 into a price consistent with the convention for Treasury Bill futures. Just calculate the rate of discount implied by the futures price generated by Equation 6.1, and subtract that value from 100. To calculate the implied rate of discount, the standard Treasury Bill formula may be used with two modifications: (a) Substitute the number of days from settlement to maturity for the number of days from the delivery date of the futures contract to the maturity date of the deliverable cash Treasury Bill, and (b) use the forward price of the Treasury Bill.

The role of the repo rate, R, in Equation 6.1 is to proxy a fair rate of return. That is, R is assumed to be the rate at which an investor can put funds to work. Why a repo rate instead of a Treasury Bill rate or any other interest rate? Market convention. And why is it market convention? For one thing, the repo market is the only money market vehicle with the flexibility to accommodate futures contracts' trading cycles. Further, even when a future's price is being calculated for a period of more than one day, an overnight repo rate is generally used instead of a term repo rate. The rationale for this convention may be that a future's position is more likely to be reversed prior to expiration than held to expiration.

Rearranging Equation 6.1 to solve for R we get

$$Ri = ((Pf / Pb) - 1)\ 360 / Tsd \qquad\qquad (6.1a)$$

When Equation 6.1 is solved for R, the value for R is commonly referred to as an "implied repo rate" (Ri). The implied repo rate is an important measure for fixed-income investors.

Although referred to as an implied repo rate, it is perhaps more instructive to view Ri as a *breakeven* term repo rate. For example, if the true term repo rate were ever less than the breakeven term repo rate, it would be desirable for an investor to execute an arbitrage strategy. If the true term repo rate were less than the breakeven repo rate, an investor would (a) buy the deliverable Treasury Bill, (b) go short an equal face amount of Treasury Bill futures, and (c) finance the deliverable Treasury Bill position in the repo market. Since the deliverable Treasury Bill can be financed at the true repo rate for *less* than the implied repo rate, the return earned on this "cash-and-carry" trade is a leveraged, arbitraged profit. Steps *a* and *b* constitute a cash-and-carry trade, while steps *a, b,* and *c* constitute a leveraged cash-and-carry trade.

The arbitraged profit from the financed cash-and-carry trade is equal to the spread between the true term repo rate and the implied term repo rate. The term "arbitrage" means a riskless position. Here's how it works.

Equation 6.1a posits a direct relationship between the price of a future and the implied term repo rate. Thus, if the term repo rate implied by Equation 6.1a is greater than the true term repo rate, then the futures' price may be said to be "overvalued." It is overvalued because it is trading at a price higher than suggested by the repo market. To put this differently, the Treasury Bill future is pricing the forward value of the deliverable Treasury Bill "richer" than the repo market.

Borrowing from our earlier example, assume that the implied term repo rate is 8.25% while the true term repo rate is 8.20%. The price of the Treasury Bill future generated by a term repo rate of 8.25% is 97.6823, and the price generated by a term repo rate of 8.20% is 97.6588. Since the price of the Treasury Bill future will converge to the price of the deliverable Treasury Bill, it would be attractive to go short the "rich" Treasury Bill futures and make delivery with Treasury Bills financed in the repo market. The profit earned would be the difference in spread between the rate *earned* on the *"rich"* implied repo rate and the rate *paid* on the *"cheap"* true repo financing.

Aside from alerting investors to arbitrage opportunities, the implied repo rate can help an investor determine if he or she would be better off buying futures or Treasury Bills on any given day. When the implied term repo rate is greater than the true term repo rate, an investor is better off buying the deliverable Treasury Bill (also called the deliverable cash Bill, or cash) instead of going long Treasury Bill futures and investing in term repo. When the implied term repo rate is greater than the true term repo rate, then we may say that futures are trading rich to cash.

Conversely, when the implied term repo rate is less than the true term repo rate, an investor is better off going long Treasury Bill futures and investing in term repo instead of buying Treasury Bills. In this instance, we may say that futures are trading cheap to cash.

In sum, futures contracts can be used as vehicles to create future products and to create products to evaluate against current market opportunities. For example, to create a 3-month Treasury Bill to be purchased in six months' time, the investor simply goes long a Treasury Bill future with six months to expiration and takes delivery on the deliverable cash bill when the future expires. And to evaluate futures against other investment opportunities in the current market environment, the investor need only compare the implied repo rate against the money market yield of a security with a comparable maturity and credit risk. An implied repo rate is the return an investor will earn with certainty on a cash-and carry trade held to a futures' expiration.

Treasury Bill Futures Summary

- An investor who buys and holds a Treasury Bill future to expiration is required to take delivery. That is, purchase the deliverable cash bill at the Treasury Bill future's offer-side rate of discount at delivery. An investor who goes short a Treasury Bill future and holds the position to expiration is required to make delivery. That is, sell the deliverable cash bill at the Treasury Bill future's bid-side rate of discount at delivery.
- Although there is some debate as to how a Treasury Bill future ought to be priced, the market convention is to value it as a forward contract.

- Aside from using Treasury Bills to speculate on market direction—going long Treasury Bill futures in anticipation that Treasury Bill rates will fall, or going short Treasury Bill futures in anticipation that Treasury Bill rates will rise—Treasury Bill futures can be used to create future products and to capture current market opportunities.
- When a Treasury Bill future's implied term repo rate is *greater* than the true term repo rate, an investor is better off buying the deliverable Treasury Bill instead of going long Treasury Bill futures and investing in term repo. When the implied term repo rate is *less* than the true term repo rate, an investor is better off going long Treasury Bill futures and investing in term repo instead of buying deliverable Treasury Bills.
- The implied repo rate is the return an investor will earn with certainty on a cash-and-carry trade held to a future's expiration.

7

Eurodollar Futures and International Money Markets

In the previous chapter we created money market strategies using futures contracts with cash-and-carry trades. A cash-and-carry trade is executed by going long cash securities and shorting futures contracts against that position. We showed that it may be possible to earn a holding period return in excess of prevailing yields on cash securities.

In this chapter, we create money market strategies with long positions in *both* cash securities *and* futures contracts. Again, we show that it may be possible to earn a holding period return in excess of prevailing yields on cash securities.

EURODOLLAR STRIPS

On June 17, 1991, 1-year Libor was trading at 6.875%. In this context it should be noted that Libor is nothing more than a benchmark. Although Libor is defined as the London interbank offer rate, "interbank" does not refer to any one bank or a particular group of banks. Libor is a generic rate that is generally recognized as a fair market yield for an AA/Aa-rated bank security.

At any given point in time, the market's sentiment on the credit risk of a given security may be reflected in that security's yield spread to Libor. For example, an AAA/Aaa-rated bank may be able to issue 1-year Eurodollar CDs at a yield *below* Libor, while a lesser-rated bank may not be able to issue 1-year Eurodollar CDs for anything less than Libor *plus* 50 basis points. For purposes of this chapter, we assume that Eurodollar products trade at Libor. That is, we do not adjust Libor one way or another to reflect any particular credit risk.

Table 7.1 Creating a Synthetic 1-Year Eurodollar CD

Product	Price	Yield (%)
3-month Eurodollar CD (3-month Libor rate)		6.125
September 1991 Eurodollar future	93.46	6.540
December 1991 Eurodollar future	92.90	7.100
March 1992 Eurodollar future	92.75	7.250

A step-by-step procedure to create a synthetic 1-year Eurodollar CD with a strip of Eurodollar futures contracts is provided below.

Step 1: Buy \$1.0 million market value of the 3-month Eurodollar CD at a yield of 6.125% to earn \$1,015,482.64

$\$1,000,000 \cdot (1 + 0.06125 \cdot 91/360) = \$1,015,482.64$

Step 2: Go long \$1,015,482.64 face amount of September 1991 Eurodollar futures contracts at 6.540% to earn \$1,032,270.26

$\$1,015,482.64 \cdot (1 + 0.06540 \cdot 91/360) = \$1,032,270.26$

Step 3: Go long \$1,032,270.26 face amount of December 1991 Eurodollar futures contracts at 7.100% to earn \$1,050,796.64

$\$1,032,270.26 \cdot (1 + 0.07100 \cdot 91/360) = \$1,050,796.64$

Step 4: Go long \$1,050,796.64 face amount of March 1992 Eurodollar futures contracts at 7.250% to earn \$1,070,053.96

$\$1,050,796.64 \cdot (1 + 0.07250 \cdot 91/360) = \$1,070,053.95$

Conclusion: A return of \$70,053.95 on an investment of \$1,000,000 (\$1,070,053.95 versus \$1,000,000) represents a yield of 7.005% on this synthetic 1-year Eurodollar CD. A yield of 7.005% is *13 basis points above* what would have been earned on a *true 1-year Eurodollar CD* at 1-year Libor (7.005% versus 6.875%). A conservative estimate of transactions costs might lower the synthetic return by less than 0.5 basis point.

Assume that an investor is faced with the choice of investing in a 1-year Eurodollar CD at 6.875%, or creating a synthetic 1-year Eurodollar CD with a 3-month Eurodollar CD and a strip of three successive Eurodollar contracts. Table 7.1 shows prices and yields for each piece of the synthetic strategy and presents a step-by-step procedure to calculate a holding period return.

In sum, we see from Table 7.1 that our 1-year synthetic Eurodollar CD outperforms a true 1-year Eurodollar CD by 13 basis points. Thus, if an investor views the credit risk of the synthetic strategy as equivalent to a cash security yielding the 1-year Libor rate of 6.875%, then there appears to be an incentive to purchase the synthetic in place of the cash. However, if an investor views the credit risk of the synthetic strategy as something worse than a cash security yielding the 1-year Libor rate, then purchasing the synthetic may or may not be an appropriate investment.

The above example demonstrates how it is possible to move from one maturity sector of the yield curve to another using futures contracts. In short, we took a 3-month cash position in a Eurodollar CD and a strip of Eurodollar futures and synthetically created a 1-year Eurodollar CD. This methodology may also be applied to floating rate notes.

For example, assume that an investor has a choice between a Eurodollar floating rate note (FRN) that pays 3-month Libor plus 100 basis points and a 1-year Eurodollar FRN that pays 1-year Libor plus 50 basis points. We evaluate FRNs in some detail in the next chapter. If the Libor yield curve suggests that the spread between 3-month and 1-year Libor ought to be 25 basis points, which security has the greatest value?

At first glance it may appear that 100 basis points over the 3-month Libor is comparable to 75 basis points over 1-year Libor:

75 basis points = 100 − 25

where: 100 = Spread over 3-month Libor
        25 = Spread between 3-month Libor and 1-year Libor

Thus, an investor would presumably choose the FRN paying 3-month Libor since it is 25 basis points (25 basis points = 75 basis points − 50 basis points) more attractive than the FRN paying 1-year Libor.

However, what if our investor could create a synthetic one-year Eurodollar FRN paying 100 basis points over 1-year Libor? Such a product would certainly be superior to either a Eurodollar FRN paying 3-month Libor plus 100 basis points or a Eurodollar FRN paying 1-year Libor plus 50 basis points. To create such a product, an investor might simply purchase the 3-month Eurodollar FRN and a strip of three successive Eurodollar futures contracts. If the synthetic 1-year Eurodollar rate compares favorably with the true 1-year Eurodollar rate on the 1-year Eurodollar FRN, then the synthetic may be preferable to the true. That is, if the yield on the synthetic is greater than the true, then the synthetic may make for an attractive investment opportunity.

Eurodollar Summary

- It may be possible to create a synthetic Eurodollar cash instrument with a combination of cash and futures securities. In the example provided in this section, we created a synthetic 1-year Eurodollar CD that outperforms a true 1-year Eurodollar CD by more than 10 basis points.

INTERNATIONAL MONEY MARKET SECURITIES

The U.S. marketplace is not the only source of money market securities. Indeed, Canada and the United Kingdom have well-developed money markets. The depth and breadth of money market products are growing in Japan, New Zealand, and Australia as well. Table 7.2 shows money market yields for various nondollar Treasury Bills. It shows money market yields because local conventions for pricing Treasury Bills differ among these countries.

Table 7.2 Money Market Yields across Treasury Bill Markets
Offer-Side Quotes on May 3, 1991

| | Money Market Yields (%) | | |
Country	3-Month	6-Month	12-Month
United States	5.520	5.716	6.071
Canada	8.867	8.877	9.100
United Kindgom*	11.280	11.721	

* As of this writing, the United Kingdom does not have a liquid market for 12-month Treasury Bills.

Although money market yields have been significantly higher in Canada, the United Kingdom, and Australia relative to the United States, a U.S.-based investor may not have been eager to invest in these overseas markets. Why? Exchange rate risk.

If a U.S.-based investor buys Canadian Treasury Bills denominated in Canadian dollars, the Canadian dollar might depreciate against the U.S. dollar over the investment horizon. If the depreciation of the Canadian dollar is significant, it is possible that the yield advantage of investing in Canadian Treasury Bills can disappear completely. An investor's total return could even become negative. Equations 7.1 and 7.1a help to show how this could happen.

Equation 7.1 shows a traditional money market yield calculation, and Equation 7.1a shows a money market yield calculation that incorporates exchange rates.

$$\left(\frac{F-P}{P}\right)\left(\frac{360}{Tsm}\right) \tag{7.1}$$

$$\left(\frac{F/Em - P/Ep}{P/Ep}\right)\left(\frac{360}{Tsm}\right) \tag{7.1a}$$

where: Em = Exchange rate at maturity
         Ep = Exchange rate at purchase

The U.S. dollar/Canadian dollar exchange rate was 1.1512 on May 3, 1991. This means that $1.00 U.S. could have been exchanged for $1.1512 Canadian (offer-side). Conversely, $1.00 Canadian could have been exchanged for $0.8687 U.S. Note that $0.8687 is simply the inverse of $1.1512. Thus, if a U.S.-based investor bought $1 million Canadian face value of 3-month Canadian Treasury Bills at a money market yield of 8.867%, he or she would have spent $979,020.97 Canadian, or $850,435.17 U.S.

If we want to calculate a projected rate of return assuming that the 3-month Canadian Treasury Bill is held to maturity, we need an estimate for what the U.S. dollar/Canadian dollar exchange rate will be at the maturity of the Canadian Treasury Bill. We might assume, for example, that the exchange rate at maturity will be identical to the exchange rate prevailing at the time the Treasury Bill is purchased. Is that a realistic assumption? Probably not. However, if the exchange rate were unchanged at maturity, the return would be 8.867%—exactly equal to the Canadian Treasury Bill's money market yield at the time of purchase.

The fact of the matter is that the Canadian dollar is likely either to appreciate (strengthen) or depreciate (weaken) against the U.S. dollar over a given investment horizon. Thus, if a U.S.-based investor places funds in Canadian securities, it can be important to have a view of the Canadian dollar's near-term direction. A strengthening Canadian dollar will mean returns in excess of a Canadian Treasury Bill's money market yield. A weakening Canadian dollar will mean returns less than a Canadian Treasury Bill's money market yield. At the very least, an investor ought to know the exchange rate at which he or she will break even relative to investing in a comparable maturity U.S. Treasury Bill. We can identify the break-even exchange rate, Em, by rearranging Equation 7.1a.

$$Em = 360 \cdot F / ((B \cdot Tsm \cdot P / Ep) + 360 \cdot P / Ep) \qquad (7.1b)$$

$$1.1604 = 360 \cdot 100 / ((0.0552 \cdot 87 \cdot 97.90 / 1.1512) + 360 \cdot 97.90 / 1.1512)$$

where: Em = Exchange rate at maturity
      F = Face amount
      B = Break-even yield (3-month U.S. yield)
   Tsm = Time in days from settlement to maturity
      P = Price of Canadian Treasury Bill
    Ep = Exchange rate at purchase

Equation 7.1b tells us that an exchange rate of better than 1.1604 (e.g., 1.1600) would have to prevail at the Canadian Treasury Bill's maturity to outperform a U.S. Treasury Bill of comparable maturity.

Now then, what if an investor does not want the exchange rate risk associated with a Canadian Treasury Bill? Then eliminate it. How? With a forward contract.

In Part One, we talked about forward rates as these apply to fixed-income securities. We stated that a forward rate is the market's implicit forecast of where future yields will trade. Similarly, among exchange rates, a forward rate is the market's implicit forecast where an exchange rate will trade at some future date. Table 7.1 shows forward "points" for a variety of currencies across varying dates.

Forward points are used to calculate forward rates. For example, 3-month points on the Canadian dollar are quoted as 89/91, bid/offer. To use these forward points to calculate a forward rate, we use Equation 7.2.

$$Z = Ep + V / 10,000 \qquad\qquad (7.2)$$

$$1.1603 = 1.1512 + 91 / 10,000$$

where: Z = Forward rate
V = Forward points, offer-side (Ep is offer-side as well)

Equation 7.2 tells us that the 3-month forward rate is 1.1603. A forward rate of 1.1603 implies that the Canadian dollar will depreciate against the U.S. dollar. The forward rate implies that in three months' time a stronger U.S. dollar will buy $1.1603 Canadian as opposed to the $1.1512 Canadian today.

Observe that our forward rate of $1.1603 Canadian is very close to our break-even exchange rate of $1.1604 Canadian. If we were to make adjustments for respective maturity dates, the differential would widen between the forward rate and break-even rate. The Treasury Bill is valued with 87 days from settlement to maturity, and the forward rate is valued to 90 days. Intuitively, we would expect the break-even rate to be comparable to the forward rate since it ought not to be possible to significantly outperform one security with a comparable security. Forward rates serve to impose a level playing field across nondollar securities when these securities are hedged into U.S. dollars. However, owing to market imperfections, nondollar products may sometimes be used to create a U.S. dollar-denominated asset that yields more than true U.S. securities.

FORWARD POINTS

Table 7.3 provides a sampling of bid/offer forward point values. Forward points are determined by respective Eurorate differentials. A Eurorate is the rate of interest on a security that is backed by deposits outside the Eurorate's home market. A Eurodollar rate, for example, is the yield an

Table 7.3 Forward Points across Markets
May 3, 1991

Country	3-Month	6-Month	12-Month
Canada	89/91	168/172	286/294
United Kindgom	231/229	417/413	703/697

investor might earn on a Eurodollar CD, and the Eurodollar CD might be backed by dollar deposits in London. If we were to take the difference between any two Eurorates, this difference should match the difference between the exchange rate and forward rate if interest rates and currency rates are expressed in basis points.

Table 7.4 shows Eurorates for a variety of countries. Note that the differential in Eurorates between the United States and Canada is 312.5 basis points.

The following equation allows us to convert U.S./Canadian exchange rates and forward rates into basis points to confirm that Eurorate differentials drive forward rates:

$$316 \text{ basis points} = \left(\frac{Z - Ep}{Ep}\right)\left(\frac{360}{Tsm}\right)$$

$$= \left(\frac{1.1600 - 1.1512}{1.1512}\right)\left(\frac{360}{87}\right)$$

We use a forward rate of 1.1600 instead of 1.1603 in this equation because the latter rate was calculated assuming a 90-day investment horizon. The Canadian Treasury Bill matures in 87 days, serving to lower the forward rate by roughly three "pips."

Table 7.4 Eurorates across Markets
Offer-Side Quotes on May 3, 1991

Country	3-Month (%)	6-Month (%)	12-Month (%)
United States	6.0625	6.1875	6.2650
Canada	9.1875	9.2500	9.3750
United Kindgom	11.5625	11.3750	11.2500

Although 316 basis points is not equal to 312.5 basis points, consideration of bid/offer spreads and other transactions costs would make it difficult to structure a worthwhile arbitrage around this 3.5 basis point differential.

If the Eurorate differential between a given Eurodollar rate and any other Eurorate is positive, then the nondollar currency is said to be a *premium* currency. If the Eurorate differential between a given Eurodollar rate and any other Eurorate is negative, then the nondollar currency is said to be a *discount* currency. Table 7.4 shows that both the Pound sterling and Canadian dollar are discount currencies to the U.S. dollar. Subtracting Canadian and Sterling Eurorates from respective Eurodollar rates gives negative values.

There is an active forward market in foreign exchange, and it is commonly used for hedging purposes. When an investor engages in a forward transaction, he or she generally buys or sells a given exchange rate forward. In the preceding example, the investor sells forward Canadian dollars for U.S. dollars. A forward contract commits an investor to buy or sell a predetermined amount of one currency for another currency at a predetermined exchange rate. As such, a forward is really nothing more than a mutual agreement to exchange one commodity for another at a predetermined date and price.

Getting back to our investor who wants to own Canadian Treasury Bills, can he or she use the forward market to hedge the currency risk? Absolutely!

The Canadian Treasury Bills will mature at par, so if our investor wants to buy $1 million Canadian face value of Treasury Bills, he or she ought to sell forward $1 million Canadian. Since the investment will be fully hedged, it is possible to state with certainty that the 3-month Canadian Treasury Bill will earn

$$5.670\% = \left(\frac{(100 / 1.1600) - (97.90 / 1.1512)}{(97.90 / 1.1512)} \right) \left(\frac{360}{87} \right)$$

Note that a return of 5.670% is 15 basis points *above* the return that could be earned on the 3-month U.S Treasury Bill. Therefore, given a choice between a 3-month Canadian Treasury Bill fully hedged into U.S. dollars earning 5.670% and a 3-month U.S. Treasury Bill earning

5.520%, the fully hedged Canadian Treasury Bill appears to be the better investment.

Rather than compare returns of the above strategy with U.S. Treasury Bills, many investors will only do the trade if returns exceed the relevant Eurodollar rate. In this instance, the fully-hedged return would have had to exceed the 3-month Eurodollar rate. Why? If an investor purchases a Canadian Treasury Bill, he or she accepts a sovereign credit risk. That is, the risk that the government of Canada may default on its debt. However, when the 3-month Canadian Treasury Bill is combined with a forward contract, another credit risk appears. In particular, if an investor learns in three months' time that the counterparty to the forward contract will not honor the forward contract, the investor may or may not be concerned. If the Canadian dollar appreciated over three months, then the investor would probably *welcome* the fact that he or she was not locked-in at the forward rate. However, if the Canadian dollar depreciated over the three months, then the investor could well suffer a dramatic loss. The counter-party risk of a forward contract is not a sovereign credit risk. The conventional way to perceive forward contract risk is to view it as bank risk. We can accept this view since banks are the most active players in the currency forwards marketplace. Accordingly, many investors will compare the yield of a fully hedged nondollar Treasury Bill with the relevant *Eurorate,* not with a comparable U.S. Treasury Bill yield.

It often comes as a surprise to investors that it may be possible to create synthetic U.S. securities with nondollar assets that outperform true U.S. money market securities. This surprise may stem from the theory of covered interest rate arbitrage.

COVERED INTEREST RATE ARBITRAGE

Covered interest arbitrage theory states that a fully hedged nondollar security ought to provide a return that is equal to the return of a comparable U.S. security. Covered interest arbitrage generally holds among comparable Eurorates. When it does not, there is an arbitrage opportunity. The problem with applying covered interest arbitrage to nonEurorate securities is twofold. First, as we've discussed, forward rates are driven by Eurorate differentials, not Treasury Bill rate or other yield differentials.

Second, all Treasury Bills are not created equal. Across international markets Treasury Bills may be subject to disparate issue sizes, varying auction cycles and fiscal dynamics, and unique sources of demand.

Finally, an investor should know that there are more choices available than simply buying a nondollar money market security that is either unhedged or fully hedged. For example, an investor may decide to sell forward only half of a nondollar security's full face value. With this approach, an investor is partially covered should the currency move against him or her and is partially exposed should the currency move in his or her favor.

Eurodollar Futures and International Money Markets Summary

- It is possible to create synthetic U.S. dollar products with nondollar securities and forward exchange rate contracts, and sometimes with a significant pick-up in yield.

8

Floating Rate Notes

A floating rate note (FRN) is a coupon-paying fixed-income product whose coupon is linked to a variable-rate index (hence the name). Although Libor (the London interbank offer rate) is the most common index among FRNs, other indices have grown in popularity including U.S. Treasury Bill rates.

An FRN's coupon is determined at "reset" dates. For example, an FRN linked to 3-month Libor may reset its coupon at 3-month intervals, an FRN linked to 6-month Libor may reset at 6-month intervals, and so forth. Once a coupon's value has been determined, it is generally paid at the next reset period. Figure 8.1 helps to demonstrate the coupon reset/coupon payment cycle.

At time t, an investor purchases a newly issued FRN linked to 3-month Libor at a price of par. The amount of the first coupon payment is also determined at time t. At time t plus three months, the first coupon is paid at the rate determined at time t, and a new coupon is set relative to the prevailing rate for 3-month Libor. At time t plus six months, the second coupon is paid at the rate determined at time t plus three months, and a new coupon is reset relative to the prevailing rate for 3-month Libor. This process continues until the FRN matures.

Generally, an FRN's coupon will be something other than an unadjusted index rate. For example, in April 1991, both American Express and Chrysler Financial had Libor-linked FRNs trading in the marketplace, yet the former had a credit rating from Moody's of A2 while the latter had

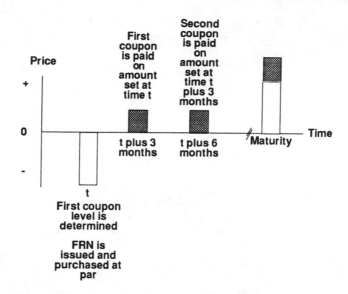

FIGURE 8.1 Coupon reset/coupon payment cycles for FRNs.

a credit rating from Moody's of Ba3. Rating agencies exist that evaluate the credit risks of a variety of borrowers including corporations, governments, and supranational organizations. In Appendix B we provide an overview of the various ratings used to distinguish among credits.

Clearly, we would expect Chrysler Financial's FRNs to pay a coupon higher than American Express's FRNs to compensate, in part, for Chrysler Financial's greater credit risk. This was indeed the case. Chrysler Financial's coupon paid 3-month Libor plus 100 basis points while American Express's coupon paid 3-month Libor plus 12.5 basis points.

In instances where a borrower has particularly strong credit, the coupon is commonly set at the appropriate index rate *minus* a given number of basis points. For example, sovereigns including Germany and Ireland have borrowed at rates below respective Libor rates. When an FRN pays a predetermined number of basis points above or below an index rate, this value is called a quoted margin.

Thus far, we've only talked about FRNs whose coupons are reset and paid at common intervals. There are FRNs whose coupons are reset on one cycle (say, weekly), while coupons are paid on another cycle (say, quarterly). An FRN with this type of coupon reset/coupon payment cycle is said to be a mismatch FRN.

Why is there a market for both "regular" and mismatch FRNs? Because there is demand for both regular and mismatch FRNs. Yes, you may quote me on that.

With a regular FRN, the coupon payment is determined by the prevailing level of a given index *on the day* a reset is made. Further, the coupon is generally paid in arrears. That is, for a 3-month Libor-based FRN, the coupon is generally set at time t and paid three months later at time t plus three months. With a mismatch FRN, the coupon payment is determined by an *average* of levels relative to a given index over reset periods. Accordingly, the coupon is paid in *average arrears* where the coupon payment in three months' time is determined over the preceding three months.

For an FRN linked to a 3-month Treasury Bill that resets weekly and pays quarterly, the quarterly coupon payment is determined by the average of weekly 3-month Treasury Bill yields. Thus, for an investor who believes that 3-month Treasury Bill yields will rise, a mismatch FRN may be just the ticket. First, the coupon of the mismatch FRN will appreciate in value as yields rise while an investor's return is "locked-in" with a Treasury Bill held to maturity. Second, if Treasury Bill yields rise, a mismatch FRN's coupon payment may exceed a regular FRN's coupon payment for the same investment horizon. In a market environment of rising yields, a mismatch FRN's *average* index rate *across* reset dates should exceed a regular FRN's *single* index rate prevailing at *one prior* reset date. Figure 8.2 helps to demonstrate this.

Figure 8.2 shows that if yields rise between time t and time t plus three months, the coupon payment on a regular FRN may be less than the coupon payment on a mismatch FRN.

In Table 8.1 we show weekly reset values for a Treasury Bill-linked FRN issued by SLMA. While the average weekly reset value was 7.77% over three months' time, the single yield value at the beginning of the 3-month investment horizon was 8.09%. The *average* interest rate over time can be very different from a *single* interest rate at any one point in time.

If yields were to decline between reset periods, a mismatch FRN's coupon payment would probably be less than a regular FRN's coupon payment.

To summarize, in a market of rising yields we would expect mismatch FRNs to outperform regular FRNs, and in a market of declining yields we would expect regular FRNs to outperform mismatch FRNs. Further, in a market of rising yields we would expect mismatch FRNs to outperform regular Treasury Bills, and in a market of declining yields we might

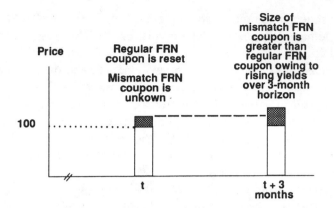

At time t, the coupon for a regular FRN is reset and is represented by the shaded rectangle. It is this amount that will be paid at time t plus three months. At time t the future coupon payment for the mismatch FRN is unknown. However, if yields rise, the mismatch FRN coupon payment at time t plus three months will be greater than the regular FRN's coupon payment for the same investment horizon.

FIGURE 8.2   Regular versus mismatch coupon levels with rising yields.

see regular Treasury Bills outperform mismatch FRNs. We assume that the Treasury Bills would be held to maturity.

In Part One, we demonstrated that a security's price trades at par when its bond-equivalent yield is equal to its coupon. Similarly, among regular highly-rated FRNs, the price of the FRN tends to move close to par when a coupon is paid. The explanation for this is that the coupon is reset *to the market*. That is, the coupon is reset to the market level of its respective index adjusted for the quoted margin. "Highly-rated" FRNs refers to securities with an Aaa rating from Moody's or an AAA rating from Standard and Poor's.

And just as regular higher-rated FRNs tend to reset closer to par relative to lower-rated FRNs, regular shorter-dated FRNs tend to reset closer to par relative to longer-dated FRNs, and regular FRNs that pay coupons on a frequent basis tend to trade closer to par relative to FRNs that pay coupons on a less frequent basis.

In sum, for purposes of evaluating an FRN as a substitute for a money market security, the comparison is likely to be most easily accomplished if it is a regular FRN, if it has a high credit rating, if it has a relatively short time to maturity, and if it has frequent reset periods.

Table 8.1 Average versus Single Value Yield Levels over a Given Reset Period

Date	Rate (%)
10/25/90	8.09
10/30/90	8.00
11/06/90	7.95
11/14/90	7.93
11/20/90	7.96
11/27/90	7.89
12/04/90	7.94
12/11/90	7.73
12/18/90	7.64
12/26/90	7.37
01/02/91	7.37
01/08/91	7.37
Average rate: 7.77%	

Note: For a regular FRN linked to 3-month Treasury Bill rates, the coupon probably would have been set in mid-October at something above 8.0%. The coupon would be paid in mid-January. For a mismatched FRN linked to 3-month Treasury Bill rates and reset on a weekly basis, we see that the January coupon payment would pobably have been *below* 8.0%. As shown above, the average weekly Treasury Bill rate from 12/25/90 to 1/8/91 is 7.77%

But what about FRNs with less-than-stellar credit ratings; don't they tend to reset close to par along with highly-rated FRNs? Generally, no. Since an FRN's coupon is typically "fixed" (over the life of the FRN, the coupon paid is always equal to the appropriate index rate adjusted for the quoted margin), price is the only variable to adjust to such phenomena as real or perceived risks of holding a less-than AAA/Aaa-rated security. Thus, while a less-than AAA/Aaa-rated security may well reset close to par in the various stages of its life, it is less likely to consistently reset close to par relative to highly rated FRNs. The term "credit spread" is often used among fixed-income investors to describe the dynamic price/yield behavior among securities with different credit ratings and varying real or perceived credit risks.

And what about highly-rated mismatch FRNs; do they tend to reset close to par along with regular FRNs? Generally, yes. When the last reset is made on a mismatch FRN and the coupon is paid, then a highly-rated issue may well be priced close to par. The FRN begins a new coupon cycle with a "clean slate" in the same way as a regular FRN.

In short, prices of highly-rated FRNs tend to trade close to par. However, supply and demand fundamentals may push an FRN's price appreciably above par, and an interest rate cap may push an FRN's price below par. An interest rate cap limits how high an FRN's coupon may go. Thus, if yields rise above the cap rate, price tends to fall. Other bells and whistles such as callable or puttable features may also affect price in a significant way.

FRNS: MONEY MARKET SECURITIES OR NOTES AND BONDS?

At this point, the reader may be asking if an FRN is more like a money market security or more like a note or bond. Table 8.2 lists an FRN's characteristics in respective categories.

Duration may provide some insight as to whether an FRN is better valued as a money market security or note/bond. To put this differently, when the price of an FRN changes, is the change consistent with what would be implied by the duration of a money market security, or with what would be implied by the duration of a note or bond? Taking Equation 3.7 from Chapter 3 and solving for modified duration, we have

$$\text{Dmod} = \frac{P^e - Pd}{Pd \cdot \Delta Y}$$

where: Dmod = Modified duration
  Pe = Estimated price
  Pd = Dirty price
  ΔY = Change in bond-equivalent yield

By calculating implied modified durations over a range of observed prices, an investor may discern if the FRN behaves more like a note or bond as opposed to a money market security.

To be more precise, a "two-tiered" duration analysis is sometimes used with FRNs. The first-tier duration, sometimes referred to as a "Libor duration," measures an FRN's price sensitivity from one coupon payment to the

Table 8.2   FRNs: Money Market Securities or Notes and Bonds

Money Market Characteristics	Note/Bond Characteristics
Generally linked to money market indices such as Treasury Bills or Libor	May have a fixed maturity of up to or more than 10 years
Highly-rated traditional FRNS tend to trade to par when coupons are paid	Are coupon-bearing securities

next. It is this duration that best characterizes a high-quality, shorter-dated, frequent-pay FRN. The second-tier duration, sometimes referred to as a "spread duration," measures an FRN's price sensitivity from settlement date to maturity date. Spread duration becomes longer as an FRN's price falls significantly below par. It is this duration that best characterizes a lower-quality, longer-dated, semipay FRN. Thus, for FRNs best characterized by first-tier durations, these assets may be considered to be money market substitutes.

DETERMINING VALUE

If an investor is interested only in holding an FRN until the next coupon is paid, it is an easy matter to calculate an expected return. Solving for a simple interest money market yield, we have

$$\left(\frac{(\text{Pds} + \text{F} \cdot \text{C} / \text{N}) - \text{Pdp}}{\text{Pdp}}\right)\left(\frac{360}{\text{Tsm}}\right) \tag{8.1}$$

where: F = Face value of security
C = Coupon
N = Number of coupon payments per year
Pdp = Dirty price at purchase of security
Pds = Dirty price at sale of security
Tsm = Time from settlement to maturity

Unless the next coupon to be paid is the final coupon payment (that is, the issue matures with the next coupon payment), an estimate is required for Pds. If the FRN being valued happens to be a highly rated FRN that is expected to reset close to par, then an investor may be comfortable with plugging in an estimated price of something close to par.

It is more of a challenge to value an FRN beyond one coupon cycle; an FRN's stream of coupon payments has to be discounted to a present value. In Part One, we stated that the present value calculation for coupon-bearing securities assumes that all coupons are discounted at the same rate; that is, the bond-equivalent yield. Similarly, among FRNs, it is assumed that all future cashflows are discounted at a constant rate. However, generally two conventions are used to determine an FRN's yield: simple margin and discounted margin.

Simple margin is a measure of return in basis points that is either added to or subtracted from an index rate to derive an FRN's yield. If 3-month Libor is 8.0% and a regular FRN linked to 3-month Libor has a simple margin of 0.25%, then the FRN's return implied by the simple margin value is 8.25% (8.0% + 0.25% = 8.25%).

The formula for simple margin is

$$Sm = \frac{F - Pc}{Tsm} + Q \qquad\qquad (8.2)$$

where: Sm = Simple margin
        F = Face value
        Pc = Clean price (excludes accrued interest)
     Tsm = Time from settlement to maturity
        Q = Quoted Margin: The fixed spread in basis points relative to
           the index rate; may be positive or negative

If Pc should happen to be par, then the first term on the right side of Equation 8.2 becomes undefined, and Sm = Q. In words, a simple margin equation posits that an FRN's return is equal to its index rate plus or minus its quoted margin whenever price is par. Since there is an inverse relationship between price and yield, we would expect the value of Sm to rise with a fall in Pc, and we would expect the value of Sm to fall with a rise in Pc. This is indeed the case.

Simple margin is not unlike a current yield calculation among traditional coupon-bearing securities. Current yield, Yc, is defined as

$$Yc = \frac{F \cdot C}{Pc} \qquad (8.3)$$

When Pc is equal to par, current yield is equal to yield-to-maturity. By yield-to-maturity we mean a yield calculated with the assumption that all cashflows are discounted at the same rate. A bond-equivalent yield is also a yield-to-maturity, but a yield-to-maturity may not be a bond-equivalent yield. That is, a bond-equivalent yield assumes semiannual cashflows. A yield-to-maturity may be calculated for a security with just about any cashflow cycle.

In Part One, we showed that a coupon-bearing security priced at par will have a yield-to-maturity equal to the security's coupon. Thus, a similarity between simple margin and current yield is that they may be used to provide a quick, easy, and reasonable estimate of a security's return *if* the security is priced at par *and* if future cashflows are paid and invested at the same rate to maturity. Simple margin and current yield calculations are also similar in that they fail to consider accrued interest.

A difference between simple margin and current yield equations is the way that they treat prices deviating from par. The simple margin equation takes the difference between face and current price values and amortizes this price difference over the life of the FRN. The amortization is a straight-line amortization and is calculated in the first term of Equation 8.2. A current yield equation does not amortize differences from par. A security priced at 110 or 90 is assumed to mature at a price of 110 or 90. In actuality, the security is going to mature at a price of 100. Therefore, for a security held to maturity, a current yield *overstates* a security's potential total return when a security is priced above par, and a current yield *understates* total return when a security is priced below par.

Finally, a weakness of both simple margin and current yield calculations is that they fail to consider coupon income. Coupon income is defined as any coupons paid plus any earnings from investing those coupons over time. If respective securities are priced at par, then this is not an issue. However, at any other price level, these equations will not provide an accurate value for prospective total returns.

Just as yield-to-maturity overcomes many of the problems inherent with using current yield on traditional coupon-bearing securities, discounted margin overcomes many of the problems inherent with using simple margin on FRNs.

When discounted margin is added to or subtracted from the relevant index rate, this value equates an FRN's future cashflows to its present value. If 3-month Libor is 8.0% and a regular FRN linked to 3-month Libor has a discounted margin of 0.33%, then the return implied by the discounted margin value is 8.33%. The formula to calculate discounted margin is

$$Pd (1 + (I + D) \, T_1 \, / \, 360) - C_1 = \frac{(Ia + Q) \, T_2 \, / \, 360}{(1 + (Ia + D) \, T_2 \, / \, 360}$$

$$+ \frac{(Ia + Q) \, T_3 \, / \, 360}{(1 + (Ia + D) \, T_3 \, / \, 360) \, (1 + (Ia + D) \, T_2 \, / \, 360)}$$

$$+ \ldots \frac{(Ia + Q) \, (T_N \, / \, 360) = F}{(1 + (Ia + D) \, T_N \, / \, 360) \, \ldots \, (1 + (Ia + D) \, T_2 \, / \, 360)} \quad (8.4)$$

where: Pd = Dirty price
          I = Index rate for the time from settlement to next coupon
          D = Discounted margin
          C_1 = Next coupon
          Ia = Assumed index rate over the life of the FRN
          Q = Quoted margin
          T_1 = Time in days from settlement to next coupon
   $T_2 \ldots T_N$ = Time in days from one coupon period to the next

The careful reader will observe similarities between Equation 8.4 and the formula for present value provided in Part One. Each cashflow in Equation 8.4 is discounted at a rate assumed to be constant over the life of the FRN, which is analogous to our constant yield-to-maturity assumption for traditional coupon-bearing securities. And since Equation 8.4 requires an assumption as to the level of future coupon payments, the convention is to assume that all future coupons will be the same as the coupon at the time the FRN is purchased. When evaluating various types of FRNs, it is important to bear in mind that discounted margins are directly comparable only if they share common indices and reset periods.

As to the *common index* requirement, a Treasury Bill index clearly is not equivalent to a Eurodollar index. For this reason, it is not possible to make a direct comparison between a Treasury Bill-linked FRN and a Eurodollar-linked FRN. Indeed, a popular spread trade among investors is the TED spread. The TED spread, or Treasury Bill versus Eurodollar spread (usually of 3-month maturities), is a commonly used barometer of perceived market risk, or equivalently, market volatility.

A common way of trading the TED spread is with futures contracts. For example, to buy the TED spread, the investor buys 3-month Treasury Bill futures and sells 3-month Eurodollar futures. He or she would purchase the TED spread if it is believed that perceptions of market risk or volatility will increase. In short, buying the TED spread is a bet that the spread will widen. If perceptions of increased market risk become manifest in moves out of risky assets (namely, Eurodollar denominated securities that are dominated by bank issues) and into safe assets (namely, U.S. Treasury securities), Treasury Bill yields would be expected to edge lower relative to Eurodollar yields and the TED spread would widen. Examples of events that might contribute to perceptions of market uncertainty would include a weak stock market, banking sector weakness as reflected in savings and loan or bank failures, a national or international calamity, and so forth.

Thus, different indices reflect different sensitivities to the marketplace, and it may not be appropriate to compare the yield of one with the yield of another using the assumption that they are equivalent measures of return. Further, it may not even be appropriate to compare directly two measures of return of two securities from the same market sector. For example, one FRN may be indexed to 3-month Treasury Bills while another FRN may be indexed to 6-month Treasury Bills. Although both FRNs are linked to Treasury securities, they are at different points on the yield curve. If the yield curve is flat among Treasury Bills, then there may not be much of a distinction to be made between respective indices. However, if an appreciable yield spread exists between these indices, and/or if the yield spread is expected to change in any way, then the differences in maturity become quite important.

Regarding *common reset* periods, two issues are not directly comparable if one FRN resets quarterly whereas another resets on a semiannual basis. In the case of a quarterly-pay security, an investor has the opportunity to reinvest proceeds four times a year, not just twice as with a semiannual pay FRN. The opportunity to reinvest funds with a greater frequency argues that the quarterly-pay security ought to trade at a higher yield if that yield is expressed on a true semipay basis. That is, the yield on the quarterly-pay security ought to reflect a greater return potential. To compare these two securities on an apples-to-apples basis, it is necessary to quantify the quarterly-pay security in semiannual terms or state the semiannual pay security in quarterly terms. This conversion is easily accomplished by modifying a third, and the most appropriate, measure of an FRN's yield. This yield measure is very much like a yield-to-maturity and is probably the most accurate and consistent measure of an FRN's value. The formula is as follows:

$$Pd = \frac{F \cdot C_1 / f}{(1 + Y / f)^{Tsc/Tln}} + \cdots + \frac{F \cdot C_{N/f}}{(1 + Y / f)^{N + Tsc/Tln}}$$

$$+ \frac{F / f}{(1 + Y / f)^{N + Tsc / Tln}} \tag{8.5}$$

where: Pd = Dirty price
C_1 = Next coupon
$C_2 \ldots C_N$ = Estimates of future coupons (index plus quoted margin)
Y = Yield-to-maturity
f = Frequency of coupons (2 for semi-annual pay FRNs)
Tsc = Time in days from settlement to next coupon
Tln = Time in days from last coupon to next coupon
N = Respective number of whole coupon payments
F = Face value of FRN

As written, Equation 8.5 may be used to calculate the yield-to-maturity for an FRN. To use Equation 8.5 to compare an FRN with one coupon frequency with an FRN of another coupon frequency, a few modifications are required. These modifications are presented in Equation 8.6:

$$Pd = \frac{F \cdot C_1 / F}{(1 + Y / f^*)^{(1/(f/f^*))}} + \cdots + \frac{F \cdot C_{N/f}}{(1 + Y / f^*)^{1 + 1/(f/f^*)}}$$

$$+ \frac{F / f}{(1 + Y / f)^{N + 1/(f/f^*)}} \tag{8.6}$$

where: f = Frequency of base security's coupon payments

          f* = Frequency of converted coupon payments. For example, to convert the yield of a security with monthly coupon payments into a bond-equivalent yield, f would be equal to 12 and f* would be equal to 2.

Equation 8.6 may be used to compare FRNs with different reset periods assuming the securities share the same index. To make the comparison, it is necessary to convert respective frequency bases. For example, assume an investor wants to compare a semipay FRN with a monthly-pay FRN on a semiannual basis. The semipay FRN can be calculated using Equation 8.5 with the frequency (f) equal to two. To calculate yield on the monthly-pay FRN on a semiannual basis using Equation 8.6, the frequency (f) is set equal to 12 and the conversion frequency (f*) is set equal to 2. In this way, an apples-to-apples comparison may be made.

Table 8.3 provides semiannual yield equivalents across various frequencies. Semiannual equivalent values are calculated using Equation 8.6. For example, a monthly-pay FRN with a yield-to-maturity of 12% would have a semiannual yield of 12.30%. All else being equal, a security that pays a coupon every month has more value relative to a security that pays a coupon every six months. The former is worth more because the investor gets cash sooner that may be invested in other interest-bearing assets. Accordingly, converting a monthly-pay yield into a semipay yield generates a higher yield. The higher yield reflects the greater value of owning a monthly-pay asset relative to a true semipay asset. However, that is not the end of the story. When an investor evaluates monthly pay versus semipay

Table 8.3   Comparing Semipay Yields with Various Frequencies*

Semipay	Monthly-pay	Quarterly-pay	Semipay	Annual-pay
8.00	8.13	8.08	8.00	7.85
10.00	10.21	10.13	10.00	9.76
12.00	12.30	12.18	12.00	11.66
14.00	14.41	14.25	14.00	13.54
16.00	16.54	16.32	16.00	15.41

* If an investor holds a monthly-pay security and wants to know the semipay equivalent of a 12% yield, it is 12.30%.

securities, he or she will also want to consider if the securities are based on the same index. If the monthly-pay FRN is indexed to 1-month Libor while the semipay FRN is indexed to 6-month Libor, then the outlook for 1- versus 6-month Libor rates is an important consideration. For example, if the yield curve is expected to steepen in a significant way with a sharp drop in 1-month rates relative to 6-month rates, the semipay FRN may be the better investment even after compounding effects are considered.

Equation 8.5 is intended to calculate the yield for a regular FRN. In contrast to a regular FRN where at least the value of the next coupon payment is known with certainty, the coupon of a mismatched FRN is only known when it comes time for the coupon to be paid. Thus, to calculate a yield for a mismatched FRN, it is necessary to have an assumption about the value of the next coupon to be paid. These assumptions may span the gamut from simply plugging in the current value of an index to incorporating a near-term yield forecast. As there are various conventions used to calculate yields for mismatch FRNs, we simply urge the reader to be cognizant of the assumptions employed.

For an investor who seeks out opportunities to enhance yield among money market securities, an appropriate strategy would be to round-up a basket of FRNs to evaluate from one coupon payment period to the next. As a *rolling* money market security, an FRN may generate returns that exceed the return on traditional money securities by several basis points.

BEAR AND BULL FLOATERS

The coupon of an FRN is linked to an index of some kind like a 3-month Treasury Bill rate. Thus, as the 3-month Treasury Bill rate increases, so too does the coupon.

An innovative type of FRN is the so-called bull floater, also called an inverse floater. With an inverse floater, the coupon rises as yields decline.

A bull floater is generally more price sensitive than a traditional fixed-rate asset. This is because a higher (lower) yield both decreases (increases) future coupon cashflows and raises (lowers) the yield at which those cashflows are valued. A higher (lower) yield increases (decreases) the value of future coupon cashflows by more than the change in the discounted value of those cashflows at the new yield. In Figure 8.3 we show price/yield profiles for a variety of fixed-income securities.

Price

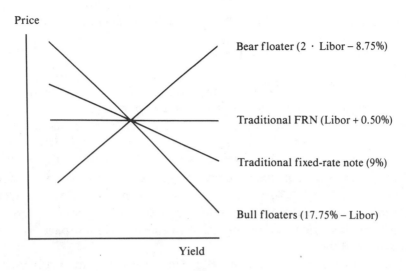

Bear floater (2 · Libor – 8.75%)

Traditional FRN (Libor + 0.50%)

Traditional fixed-rate note (9%)

Bull floaters (17.75% – Libor)

Yield

FIGURE 8.3   Price/yield profiles for a variety of fixed-income securities.

The traditional note and bull floater securities intersect at par. However, the bull floater outperforms the traditional note as yields fall, and underperforms the traditional note as yields rise.

Bull floaters tend to be most popular when investors expect a decline in interest rates at the short-end of the yield curve. An incentive to issue a bull floater may be that an issuer can achieve a lower net cost of funds relative to more traditional means of raising capital.

Just for the sake of setting up this example, let's assume that an issuer is contemplating a bull floater with the option of borrowing at either a fixed rate of 9% or 6-month Libor plus 50 basis points. Further, assume that the issuer wants the bull floater to mature in three years, and wants coupons paid on a semi-annual basis.

The structure of most bull floaters is that they pay a reference rate less Libor. The reference rate is generally unchanged over the life of the bull floater. For example, if the reference rate is determined to be say, 17.75%, then the value of 17.75% minus Libor will increase as Libor falls. That is, the bull floater will pay a higher coupon as interest rates edge lower. If our issuer can enter into a 3-year swap to either pay or receive a fixed rate of 8.75% against 6-month Libor, when would the issuer be indifferent between issuing fixed- or floating rate debt?

If our reference rate were 17.75%, the indifference rate would be

17.75% − Libor − (8.75% − Libor) = 9%.

Note that 9% is equal to our issuer's fixed rate cost of borrowing. The above formula assumes that the issuer agrees to receive 8.75% fixed and pay Libor on an interest rate swap with a notional principal equal to the par value of the FRN. Thus, our issuer has an incentive to issue a bull floater instead of fixed-rate debt for a reference rate of anything below 17.75%. However, to protect the issuer against the possibility that Libor could rise above 17.75%, a cap would have to be purchased. To compensate for the cost of the cap, the reference rate could be reduced. When evaluating this strategy, it is important to consider counterparty risks of the swap and the cap.

The methodology to evaluate a bear floater is not dramatically different from a bull floater. A typical structure of a bear floater would be to take twice the level of Libor and subtract a reference rate from that product. For example, $2 \cdot \text{Libor} - 8.50\%$ might be the relevant valuation for a bear floater. An incentive for a borrower to issue this type of debt may exist when a reference rate is high enough to make the effective borrowing rate less than the relevant fixed cost of funds.

In sum, borrowers may have an incentive to issue bull or bear floaters if it is possible to secure a cost of funds which is less than the relevant fixed cost to borrow. Investors may desire the unique price/yield characteristics of bull or bear floaters for a given market expectation.

Floating Rate Notes Summary

- An FRN is a coupon-paying fixed-income product whose coupon is linked to a variable-rate index.
- Although many FRN coupons are reset when coupons are paid, some FRN coupons are reset more often and these are called mismatch FRNs.
- Coupon payments on a mismatch FRN will exceed coupon payments on a regular FRN if the index rate rises over the life of the mismatch FRN. Conversely, coupon payments on a mismatch FRN should fall below coupon payments on a regular FRN if the index rate falls over the life of respective FRNs. We assume, of course,

that respective FRNs are linked to the same index, pay coupons on the same cycle, and are of comparable credit quality.

- The price/yield behavior of an FRN over intracoupon payment cycles suggests that highly-rated FRNs behave more like money market securities than notes or bonds.

- A regular highly rated FRN may be considered a substitute for a money market security since it generally resets close to par when coupons are paid.

- Any FRN in its last coupon period may be evaluated as a substitute for a money market security.

- The convention for calculating a yield on an FRN is to solve for its discounted margin, which is added to its index. This value also serves as an estimate for the return on the security.

- Although it is not appropriate to compare an FRN linked to one index with an FRN linked to another index, with an adjustment it is possible to compare an FRN on one coupon cycle with an FRN on another coupon cycle.

- For any FRN held beyond one coupon payment, an assumption is required as to what future coupon payments will be. The convention is to assume that future coupon payments will be equal to the coupon level prevailing at the time of investment.

- Bear and bull floaters are nontraditional FRNs, and may be desirable owing to their unique price/yield dynamics.

PART THREE

SYNTHETIC NOTES, BONDS, AND OPTIONS

In Part Two, we generally limited our investment criteria to two things: maturity dates and credit quality. When we considered various strategies, we did not delve into the minutiae of respective durations, convexities, and so forth. Why not? One reason is we generally assumed these investments would be held to maturity. If two securities are of comparable credit risk and will be held to maturity, the relevant investment criterion may simply be which security yields more. Since money market securities tend to be held to maturity, there is little value in knowing one's interest rate exposure between settlement and maturity dates as characterized by such measures as duration and convexity. Finally, differences in duration or convexity often aren't very significant among money market securities that have common maturity dates.

But as we move further along the yield curve to consider synthetic notes and bonds, we need to revisit the assumption that a given security will be held to maturity. It's one thing to assume that a 3-month Treasury Bill will be held to maturity, yet quite another to assume that a 30-year Treasury Bond will be held to maturity. Thus, in this part, we first consider short-term synthetic strategies for notes and bonds, making extensive use of duration, convexity, and total returns. Then, in Chapters 12 through 16, we consider long-term synthetic strategies for notes and bonds.

9
Creating Duration

CREATING DURATION WITH CASH SECURITIES

As duration and convexity are important measures of a fixed-income asset's price sensitivity to changes in yield, it is useful to have an appreciation for how duration and convexity behave across securities and maturities.

Table 9.1 shows modified duration values for a STRIPS, a 4% coupon issue, and a 12% coupon security. Although all securities start out with the same modified duration at six months to maturity, modified durations evolve quite differently as maturity dates lengthen. The modified duration of the STRIPS appears to grow in a straight-line fashion. The modified durations of the 4% and 12% coupon securities grow as maturities lengthen, but in a less dramatic way. At a term-to-maturity of 30

Table 9.1 Modified Durations as Maturity Dates Lengthen across Securities (All securities assumed to be priced at an 8.0% yield-to-maturity)

Term-to-Maturity	STRIPS	4% Coupon Bond	12% Coupon Bond
6 months	0.481	0.481	0.481
1 year	0.962	0.952	0.935
2 years	1.923	1.865	1.772
5 years	4.808	4.359	3.837
10 years	9.615	7.679	6.289
20 years	19.231	11.505	9.200
30 years	28.846	12.834	10.738

years, the difference between the modified duration of the STRIPS and the modified durations on the 4% and 12% coupon securities is more than 10 years. The greatest differential between the modified duration of the 4% coupon and 12% coupon is only about two years.

In sum, modified durations may be comparable or markedly different across securities with common maturity dates. And what may at first appear to be an appreciable difference in modified durations might reduce to something rather insignificant as maturities shorten.

Table 9.2 shows annualized returns for three fixed-income securities with comparable modified durations. Annualized returns are calculated across various changes in yield level and across two investment horizons.

Table 9.2 Total Returns for 3- and 6-Month Investment Horizons across Securities (%)

Yield Change in Basis Points	3-Month Horizon		
	STRIPS of 2/15/94 MD 2.643*	7%/5-15-94 MD 2.646*	12.625%/8-15-94 MD 2.624*
+100	−2.38	−2.57	−2.19
+75	−0.05	−0.19	0.12
+50	2.32	2.21	2.47
+25	4.72	4.66	4.85
0	7.15	7.13	7.26
−25	9.61	9.64	9.70
−50	12.11	12.18	12.18
−75	14.63	14.76	14.69
−100	17.19	17.37	17.24

Yield Change in Basis Points	6-Month Horizon		
	STRIPS of 2/15/94	7%/5-15-94	12.625%/8-15-94
+100	2.77	2.71	2.93
+75	3.86	3.80	4.00
+50	4.95	4.91	5.07
+25	6.05	6.01	6.16
0	7.15	7.13	7.26
−25	8.26	8.25	8.36
−50	9.38	9.38	9.47
−75	10.51	10.52	10.59
−100	11.64	11.67	11.72

* MD = Modified duration.

Several pieces of information can be extracted from Table 9.2, though two in particular need to be highlighted here. First, securities that have comparable modified durations may exhibit very different return profiles. Second, the length of an investment horizon can have a significant effect on a security's total return.

The top half of Table 9.2 shows annualized returns for a 3-month horizon. The STRIPS underperforms the 12.625% coupon bond when yields rise or fall. By contrast, the STRIPS underperforms the 7% coupon bond when yields fall but outperforms the 7% coupon bond when yields rise. The 12% coupon bond outperforms the 7% coupon bond except when yields fall by a significant amount. These scenarios assume that yield spreads remain constant among these securities across changes in yield.

The bottom half of Table 9.2 shows annualized returns for a 6-month horizon. The 12.625% coupon bond outperforms the 7% coupon bond across all changes in yield, and the STRIPS outperforms or runs about even with the 7% coupon bond across a broader range of changes in yield.

Aside from considerations related to relative performance, there are differences in the magnitude of returns over investment horizons. For example, with a 3-month horizon, the difference between high and low return values is 18 basis points at a change in yield of −100 basis points across our three securities. With a 6-month horizon, the difference between high and low return values is only 8 basis points at a change in yield of −100 basis points.

With a 3-month horizon the difference between high and low return values is 38 basis points at a change in yield of +100 basis points across our three securities. With a 6-month horizon, the difference between high and low return values is 22 basis points at a change in yield of +100 basis points. Further, while 3-month returns are in the high teens at −100 basis points, 6-month returns are not substantially above 10% at −100 basis points.

In sum, for securities with comparable modified durations, respective return profiles can differ in a rather significant way over relatively short investment horizons. As investment horizons lengthen, respective differences in return profiles can be expected to become less pronounced.

Herein is an important consideration when creating synthetic notes or bonds: An outlook on the timing and direction of changes in the yield curve can be critical. And yet such a consideration is implicit with any investment. When an investor does something as simple as buy a 6-month Treasury Bill to be held to maturity, he or she is implicitly betting that 3-month Treasury Bill rates will be lower in three months' time. And when an investor buys a 2-year Treasury Note, he or she is implicitly betting that the return profile of that issue will be superior to any other asset with a comparable modified duration.

So how is it that securities with comparable modified durations may have very different return profiles? Different convexities and security characteristics. Convexity was 0.083 for the STRIPS, 0.086 for the 7% coupon bond, and 0.090 for the 12.525% coupon bond. Further, the higher yield of the 12.625% coupon bond (7.26%) helped to boost its holding period return relative to the STRIPS (7.15%).

The main point about Tables 9.1 and 9.2 is that it's not enough for a fixed-income investor to have a duration target. There are, however, a number of fixed-income investors whose only objective is to maintain a fixed-income portfolio's modified duration near some predetermined level. What this mandate fails to consider is that a duration target can be met in any number of ways with any number of securities. Thus, it is imperative that a fixed-income investor not only appreciate his or her assets' sensitivity to changes in yield as implied by modified duration but consider other factors as well. By other factors, I mean convexity, length of investment horizon, and yield curve outlook, to name just a few.

Table 9.2 shows how return profiles can differ across securities with comparable modified durations. Table 9.3 shows how return profiles can differ across *pairs* of securities that have comparable *average* modified durations. Again, the objective here is to demonstrate that securities with comparable modified durations may have very different return profiles. Thus, when duration is created, an investor will want to evaluate the respective securities used under a variety of scenarios.

In column A of Table 9.3, a 6-month Treasury Bill and 10-year Treasury Note are combined in a ratio of 1:1.321 to produce an average modified duration of 4.091. The objective is to match the modified duration of the on-the-run 5-year Treasury Note, which is 4.091. As we move from column A to column C, we are presented with two other combinations of securities that match the modified duration target. This strategy of combining two securities is known as barbelling.

Since the securities in Table 9.3 span the yield curve from 6-month Treasury Bills to a 10-year Treasury Note, we generate total returns using a variety of yield curve scenarios. This contrasts with Table 9.2, where we assumed parallel shifts in the yield curve. This parallel shift assumption was not entirely inappropriate considering that the difference between

Table 9.3   Total Returns for 3-Month Investment
Horizons across Pairs of Securities (%)

Yield Change in Basis Points	3-Month Horizon Target Modified Duration: 4.091 Benchmark Security: 7.625%/5-31-96		
	(A) (1) 6-Month T-Bill (2) 8%/5-15-01 T-Note Ratio: 1:1.321*	(B) (1) 7%/5-15-94 T-Note (2) 7.875%/4-15-98 T-Note Ratio: 1:1.326*	(C) (1) 5-15-94 STRIPS (2) 5-15-97 STRIPS Ratio: 1:0.953*
+100	−7.62	−7.61	−8.32
+50	−0.54	−0.21	−0.54
+25	3.21	3.63	3.50
0	7.12	7.56	7.63
−25	11.11	11.59	11.85
−50	15.29	15.71	16.19
−100	24.14	24.27	25.22
Steepening**	4.74	6.18	5.73
Inversion**	9.55	9.07	9.65

* Ratio of security (1) to security (2). Ratios are determined by market value-weighted durations that match the duration of the target security.

** By steepening or inversion, we mean a widening or narrowing in spread between bond-equivalent yields of the overnight Fed funds rate and 30-year Treasury Bond. We assume that the steepening or inversion occurs with a 50 basis point change at either end of the yield curve. For example, an inversion assumes that the 30-year yield falls by 50 basis points while the overnight Fed funds rate rises by 50 basis points. For a steepening, the opposite changes in yield are assumed.

the shortest and longest maturity dates across securities was but six months.

The yield curve scenarios in Table 9.3 include parallel shifts up and down, an inversion, and a steepening. And just as in Table 9.2, there are dynamic interrelationships among these return profiles. With a 3-month investment horizon, the 3-year/7-year Treasury Notes combination outperforms the other two security combinations when the yield curve makes a parallel shift to higher yield levels. The STRIPS combination outperforms the other two security combinations when the yield curve is unchanged or makes a parallel shift to lower yield levels. The 3-year/7-year Treasury Notes combination dominates when the yield curve steepens, and the STRIPS combination dominates when the yield curve inverts.

Although modified durations are equivalent across our pairs of securities, there are differences in convexities and yields-to-maturity. The 6-month Treasury Bill/10-year Treasury Note combination had the highest convexity followed by the 3-year/7-year Treasury Notes combination and STRIPS combination. The convexities of these last two combinations were quite similar. The STRIPS combination had the highest combined yield-to-maturity followed by the 3-year/7-year Treasury Notes and 6-month Treasury Bill/10-year Treasury Note combinations.

With a 6-month horizon, the 3-year/7-year Treasury Notes combination again dominates the other two security combinations when the yield curve makes a parallel shift to higher yield levels. The STRIPS combination again outperforms the other two security combinations when the yield curve is unchanged or makes a parallel shift to higher yield levels. And consistent with results generated under the 3-month horizon, the 3-year/7-year Treasury Notes combination dominates when the yield curve steepens while the STRIPS combination dominates when the yield curve inverts.

There are two important points regarding Table 9.3. First, the exhibit reinforces the notion that there are a variety of ways to meet a target duration, and with unique return profiles for each strategy. Second, there is much less of a spread between high and low returns in Table 9.3 relative to Table 9.2. This suggests that the investor may benefit from spreading assets across the yield curve when creating duration if variability of total returns is of concern.

Cash Duration Summary

- Duration can be created in a variety of ways with cash securities.
- Securities with comparable modified durations may exhibit very different return profiles over time.
- Creating duration with pairs of securities instead of with single securities can moderate the extremes of return profiles over time.
- To identify the optimal duration–creation strategy for a fixed-income investor at a given point in time, it is useful to have an outlook on the yield curve, the relevant investment horizon, and the investment philosophy of the investor. By investment philosophy, we mean how aggressive or conservative the investor would like to be over time.

CREATING DURATION WITH TREASURY NOTE AND BOND FUTURES CONTRACTS

The price behavior of a Treasury futures contract is really quite simple. Treasury futures prices move inversely to the direction of yields. Just as the price of a Treasury Note or Bond will decline (rise) as yields rise (fall), so too will the price of a Treasury future. However, the nature of a given price response can be very different across these securities. One reason for this is that a Treasury Note or Bond is a cash security while a Treasury future is more like a forward contract.

When a Treasury Note or Bond is bought or sold, the full value of the security is exchanged. When a Treasury future is bought or sold, margin and transactions costs are the only up-front "costs" for an investor. Margin is a deposit in the form of cash or interest-bearing securities to back an investor's good faith to honor a trade. Since margin can be posted in the form of interest-earning assets, an investor may not view this as a cost if the futures strategy is successful and the investor is able to take back his or her margin plus interest at the end of the trade.

The initial margin requirement for a Treasury Bond future is determined by the International Monetary Market (IMM) division of the Chicago Mercantile Exchange and is currently $2,700 per contract for speculative accounts and $2,000 per contract for hedging accounts. The initial margin requirement for a Treasury Note future is currently $1,350 per contract for speculative accounts and $1,000 per contract for hedging accounts.* Individual firms may require their customers to post margin above these minimum levels, and the IMM may choose to raise margin requirements when there is a dramatic increase in market volatility.

A futures contract is marked-to-market on a daily basis. That is, when an investor is long a futures contract and the market rallies, the investor's margin account is credited by the amount of the futures' appreciation on that day. And when the market falls, the investor's margin account is debited by the amount of the futures' decline on that day.

The discussion of Treasury Bill futures in Part Two introduced the notion of a "cash-and-carry." A cash-and-carry trade is executed when

---

* Treasury Note futures include 2-, 5-, and 10-year contracts. Since the 10-year note future is about the most actively traded among these three, the present discussion is limited to this contract. Appendix C provides a sketch of existing contracts.

the investor purchases a deliverable Treasury issue and simultaneously goes short Treasury futures.

Equation 9.1 provides the formula for calculating the holding period return on a cash-and-carry trade using Treasury Bonds and Treasury Bond futures. In the marketplace, this holding period return is more commonly known as an implied repo rate.

Assume that the holding period for this trade is the time between the settlement date and the last possible delivery date of the relevant futures contract. If the trade is held to the last delivery date, the investor will earn an implied repo rate equal to

$$\left(\frac{Q \cdot P_f - Pdp + Ad + F \cdot C/N \cdot (1 + R \cdot Tcd/360)}{Pdp}\right)\left(\frac{360}{Tsd}\right) \quad (9.1)$$

where: Q = Factor
P_f = Futures price
Pdp = Dirty price of cash security at purchase date
Ad = Accrued interest at delivery date
    The delivery date is the day when the cash position is delivered against the futures position
F = Face amount of cash security
C = Coupon payments if any over holding period
N = Number of coupon payments per year
R = Term repo rate
Tcd = Time in days from coupon payment to delivery date
Tsd = Time in days from settlement date to delivery date

If no coupon is paid over the holding period, then C is equal to zero in Equation 9.1 and the formula is reduced.

Equation 6.1a provided the implied repo rate for Treasury Bill securities:

$$Ri = ((Pf/Pb) - 1) \cdot 360/Tsd$$

where: Ri = Implied repo rate
Pf = Futures price
Pb = Treasury Bill price
Tsd = Time in days from settlement to delivery

There are two important differences between implied repo rate calculations for a Treasury Bill and a Treasury Note or Bond. First, additional terms are required in Equation 9.1 because of the coupons paid by Treasury Notes and Bonds. Second, Equation 9.1 has a term called a "factor." Unlike a Treasury Bill future, which generally has but one deliverable cash Bill, there is a basket of cash Treasury Notes and Bonds deliverable against any given Treasury Note or Bond futures contract. The factor thus serves to impose a common denominator across all deliverable issues to allow for direct comparisons across otherwise dissimilar securities. A factor is defined as the price (in decimal) that generates an 8.0% bond-equivalent yield on a security from the first delivery date to the security's maturity date rounded to the nearest quarter. If the security is callable, the factor is calculated from the first delivery date to the security's call date rounded to the nearest quarter.

Of all the cash Treasury issues in a given basket at any one point in time, there is generally only one that is the most desirable as a deliverable issue in a cash-and-carry trade. This issue is defined as that Treasury Note or Bond generating the highest holding period return when combined with a futures contract. The deliverable issue that generates the highest holding period return is called the cheapest-to-deliver (CTD).

Table 9.4 presents the basket of deliverable Treasury Bonds for the September 1991 Treasury Bond futures contract on May 24. The 7.5%/11-15-16 was CTD with the highest holding period return of 4.32%.

Just as was the case in Part Two when we discussed Treasury Bill futures, it is perhaps more instructive to view an implied repo rate as a *break-even* repo rate.

For example, if the true term repo rate were ever less than the break-even repo rate, it would be desirable for an investor to execute an arbitrage strategy. If the true term repo rate were less than the break-even repo rate, an investor would (a) buy the deliverable Treasury Note or Bond, (b) go short an equal factor-weighted face amount of Treasury Note or Bond futures, and (c) finance the deliverable Treasury Note or Bond position in the repo market. Since the deliverable Treasury Note or Bond can be financed at the true repo rate for less than the implied repo rate, the return earned on this cash-and-carry trade is a leveraged, arbitraged profit. Steps (a) and (b) constitute a cash-and-carry trade, while steps (a), (b), and (c) constitute a leveraged cash-and-carry trade.

Table 9.4   Cheapest-to-Deliver Securities, 5/27/91

September 1991 Treasury Bond Future*	
Issue	Implied Repo Rate (%)
7.500%/11-15-16	4.32
9.250%/02-15-16	4.31
10.625%/08-15-16	4.19
8.875%/08-15-17	4.17
9.875%/11-15-15	4.11
7.250%/05-15-16	4.06
8.750%/05-15-17	4.01
11.250%/02-15-15	3.95
12.000%/08-15-13	3.83
10.375%/11-15-12	3.81
12.500%/08-15-14	3.76
9.125%/05-15-18	3.67
13.250%/05-15-14	3.59
8.875%/02-15-19	3.58
8.125%/08-15-19	3.55
9.000%/11-15-18	3.53
11.750%/11-15-14	3.35
8.500%/ 02-15-20	3.09
8.750%/08-15-20	2.45
8.750%/05-15-20	2.38
7.875%/02-15-21	2.21
14.000%/11-15-11	2.07

* Includes every deliverable security and its implied repo rate for the September 1991 Treasury Bond future on 5/27/91. The 7.5%/11-15-16 is the CTD because it has the highest implied repo rate of 4.32%. The 9.25%/2-15-16 follows at a close second.

The arbitraged profit from the financed cash-and-carry is equal to the spread between the true term repo rate and the implied term repo rate. The term "arbitrage" means a riskless position.

If an implied term repo rate is greater than the true term repo rate, then the futures' price may be said to be overvalued. It is overvalued because it is trading at a price higher than suggested by the repo market. To put this differently, the Treasury Note or Bond future is pricing the forward value of the deliverable Treasury Note or Bond "richer" than the repo market. When the implied repo rate is greater than the true repo rate, an investor is better off buying the deliverable Treasury Note or Bond (also called the deliverable cash Note or Bond, or cash) instead of going long Treasury Note or Bond futures and investing in term repo. When the implied term repo rate is greater than the true repo rate, then we may say that futures are trading rich to cash.

Conversely, when the implied repo rate is less than the true term repo rate, an investor is better off going long Treasury Note or Bond futures and investing in term repo instead of buying Treasury Notes or Bonds. In this instance, futures are trading cheap to cash.

As a general rule, Treasury Note and Bond futures tend to trade cheap to cash. The explanation for this is that Treasury Note and Bond futures have embedded options that accrue to the investor who is short the futures contracts. Because these embedded options have value, holding period returns on cash-and-carry trades tend to consistently trade below true term repo rates. As there is a vast literature on the topic of options embedded in Treasury futures contracts, this discussion is limited to a few brief comments.

Of all the options said to be embedded in Treasury futures, the three most commonly cited are the Quality option, the Wildcard option, and the Timing or Cost-of-carry option.

Quality Option

For the Treasury Bond futures contract, any Treasury Bond with at least 15 years remaining to maturity or to call as of the first delivery date may be delivered into a long Treasury Bond futures contract. For the Treasury Note futures contract, any Treasury Note maturing in not less than $6^{1}/_{2}$ years or more than 10 years from the date of delivery may be delivered into a long Treasury Note futures contract. Although only one deliverable bond is generally CTD at any one point in time, the CTD may change several times between a given valuation date and the delivery date. There are unique profit opportunities associated with each change in CTD, and an investor is free to switch into more attractive cash/futures combinations over time. The transitory behavior of the CTD has value to the holder of a short futures position, and the Quality option quantifies this value.

Since there are more securities in the Treasury Bond futures' deliverable basket relative to the Treasury Note futures' deliverable basket, the Quality option tends to have a greater quantitative significance for the Treasury

Bond future. Further, the securities in the Treasury Bond futures' deliverable basket are less homogeneous, and this also gives rise to a higher value for the Quality option. This heterogeneity stems largely from the fact that the Treasury Bond futures' deliverable basket includes callable bonds. However, these callable bonds will disappear altogether from the deliverable basket over the next few years. The Treasury Bond futures' deliverable basket will become more homogeneous, and the Quality option will lose some of its value.

Wildcard Option

On each day between the first business day of the delivery month and the seventh business day before the end of the delivery month, the holder of a short futures position has until 9 P.M. Eastern Standard Time to notify the exchange of his or her intention to deliver. Delivery means that deliverable securities are provided in exchange for a cash payment. The investor who is short the futures contract sells the deliverable securities, and the investor who is long the futures contract buys those securities. To determine how much ought to be paid for the delivered securities, an invoice price is set at 3 P.M. The invoice price is calculated from the future's settlement price at 3 P.M. EST on the day that a delivery notice is given. The cash market does not close until 5 P.M. EST, so there is a two-hour window of opportunity when an investor holding a short future may profit from a decline in the cash market.* The Wildcard option thus values the opportunity to profit from different trading hours for cash and futures.

Timing or Cost-of-Carry Option

The timing or cost-of-carry option attempts to quantify the optimal time to make delivery. If there is a positive cost-of-carry, then there is an incentive to put off delivery until the last possible delivery date. By cost-of-carry we mean the difference between the return earned on a cash

---

* In actuality, the market often does not "close" at 5 P.M., but remains open for as long as there is a trader willing to make a market. Indeed, even if one is hard pressed to find a market-maker in the United States after 5 P.M., it may not be difficult to find a market-maker in Tokyo where the trading day is just getting underway.

security and the cost to finance that cash security in the repo market. If that difference is positive, then there is a positive cost-of-carry. Cost-of-carry is usually positive when the yield curve has a normal or positive shape. Conversely, if there is a negative cost-of-carry, then there is an incentive to make delivery on the first possible delivery date. Negative cost of carry exists if there is a negative difference between the return earned on a cash security and the cost to finance that cash security in the repo market. Cost-of-carry is usually negative when the yield curve has a negative or inverted shape. In sum, the cost-of-carry option may be viewed as an option on the slope of the yield curve. And since the slope of the yield curve is such an important factor when evaluating cash-and-carry trades, Equation 9.1 ought to be calculated to the latest (earliest) possible delivery date when the yield curve has a normal (inverted) shape.

Now that we've reviewed Treasury future characteristics, let's delve into the details of defining a Treasury future's duration.

Calculating a Future's Duration

In Part One, we stated that calculating duration typically requires consideration of a security's cashflows. Since a Treasury Bond future does not require an initial payment, generate coupons, or pay principal at maturity, it does not generate the cashflows generally associated with fixed-income securities. However, a Treasury future is deliverable into Treasury issues that do experience cashflows, and this link allows us to calculate a Treasury future's duration.

Many investors use the duration of the CTD as a proxy for the duration of the respective futures contract. This is not correct because a futures contract does not trade to the cash price of the underlying security. A futures contract trades to the *forward* price of the underlying security. Thus, to build our methodology to calculate a futures' duration, let's start with a formula that quantifies a futures price as a forward price. Equation 9.2 identifies the value of a future by incorporating the forward value of the CTD and the CTD's factor. Specifically, the forward value of the CTD is in the numerator of Equation 9.2, and the CTD's factor is in the denominator:

$$Z = \frac{Pdp \cdot (1 + Ri \cdot Tsd / 360) - Ad + (F \cdot C / N) \cdot (1 + Ri \cdot Tcd / 360)}{Q}$$

$$(9.2)$$

where: Z = Theoretical futures price
         Pdp = Dirty price of CTD at purchase date
         Ri = Implied term repo rate
         Tsd = Time in days from settlement date to delivery date
         Ad = Accrued interest on CTD at delivery date
         F = Face amount of CTD
         C = Coupon payments over holding period (if any)
         N = Number of coupon payments per year
         Tcd = Time in days from coupon payment to delivery date
         Q = CTD Factor

We use an implied repo rate in Equation 9.2 instead of the market repo rate, because the implied repo rate best quantifies the convergence between the futures' invoice price and the CTD's price at delivery.

To be even more precise when calculating a future's duration, we ought to allow for the fact that Treasury Note and Bond futures have embedded delivery options. Since the delivery options accrue to one who is short the futures contract, we need to adjust Equation 9.2 by *subtracting* the embedded delivery option values. If we let E represent the embedded delivery option values, we may rewrite Equation 9.2 as

$$Z = \frac{Pdp \cdot (1 + Ri \cdot Tsd / 360) - Ad + (F \cdot C / N) \cdot (1 + Ri \cdot Tcd / 360)}{Q} - E$$

$$(9.2a)$$

where: E = Embedded delivery option values; the compound option values of the Wildcard, Quality, and Cost-of-carry options

We conveniently sidestepped the issue of valuing E, the embedded delivery options. Several papers have been written on this topic, and a review on valuing embedded delivery options goes beyond the scope of this text.* We didn't mention it in Chapter 6, but Treasury Bill futures have embedded Wildcard and Cost-of-carry options as well.

---

* Papers that may be of interest include "Valuation and Optimal Exercise of the Wild Card Option in the Treasury Bond Futures Market," by Alex Kane and Alan J. Marcus, *The Journal of Finance,* March 1986; "The Quality Option Implicit in Futures Contracts," by Gerald D. Gay and Steven Manaster, *Journal of Financial Economics,* September 1984; and "Treasury Bond Futures: Valuing the Delivery Options," by Marcelle Arak and Laurie S. Goodman, *The Journal of Futures Markets,* 1987.

If there is no coupon payment from the settlement date to the delivery date, then C is equal to zero in Equation 9.2a and the formula is reduced. However, if a coupon is paid over the holding period, then Equation 9.2a is not entirely correct. Multiplying Pdp by $(1 + Ri \cdot Tsd / 360)$ implies that no coupon is paid over the holding period. To be more precise, Pdp must be financed up to the time the coupon is paid (Tsc), and only Pcp (clean price of CTD at purchase date) has to be financed from the time the coupon is paid until the delivery date (Tcd). To calculate this more accurate theoretical futures price, we solve for

$$Z = [(Pdp \cdot (1 + Ri \cdot Tsd / 360) \cdot Tsc / Tsd) \qquad (9.2b)$$
$$+(Pcp \cdot (1 + Ri \cdot Tsd / 360) \cdot Tcd / Tsd)$$
$$-Ad + (F \cdot C / N) \cdot (1 + Ri \cdot Tcd / 360)] / Q - E$$

In our discussion of the Quality option, we stated that this option will lose some of its value as the Treasury Bond futures' deliverable basket becomes more homogeneous. The basket will become more homogeneous as callable bonds become ineligible to deliver. We can readily see from Equation 9.2b that an implication of this is that the value of E will decline. Concomitantly, the value of Z will rise. Thus, as callable bonds disappear as eligible deliverable securities, Treasury bond futures contracts can be expected to trade more expensive to cash.

The formula for a theoretical Treasury Bill futures price appeared in Chapter 6 as Equation 6.1:

$$Pf = Pb (1 + R \cdot Tsd / 360)$$

where: Pf = Futures price
      Pb = Treasury Bill price
       R = Term repo rate
    Tsd = Time in days from settlement date to delivery date

The reader will note the similarities between this formula and Equation 9.2a, particularly if no coupon is paid. Rewriting Equation 9.2a if no coupon is paid over the investment horizon, we have

$$Z = \frac{Pdp \cdot (1 + Ri \cdot Tsd / 360) - Ad}{Q} - E$$

The intuition behind Equation 9.2a is that a Treasury future's price is generally determined by the price of the CTD (Pdp) and the implied repo rate (Ri). The price of a Treasury issue is generally calculated with just one yield; that is, the bond-equivalent yield. However, Equation 9.2a tells us that a Treasury future's price is calculated using *two* yields. First, there is the bond-equivalent yield (à la Pdp), and second, the implied repo rate (Ri).When there is a delayed sale or purchase of a cash security, the alternative investment vehicle is generally considered to be the repo market. Thus, with the importance of both the repo market and cash securities when identifying a Treasury Note or Bond futures' fair market value, we find ourselves with two yields in a theoretical futures price formula. This was also the case when we calculated theoretical Treasury Bill futures prices in Chapter 6 using Equation 6.1. Equation 6.1 considers both the repo rate and an implied rate of discount. The implied rate of discount comes from Pb, the price of the deliverable Treasury Bill.

Now that we have a working definition for a futures price as defined by Equation 9.2b, we may derive a modified duration for a futures contract. The duration may be calculated in much the same way as a duration would be obtained for the CTD, but with an important difference. Instead of using the standard next-day settlement price of the CTD, the forward price is used as defined by the numerator of Equation 9.2b. This forward price is in turn used to calculate a forward modified duration. When this forward modified duration is obtained, we calculate the future's DV01 as

$$DV01^f = D^f mod \cdot P^f d / 10,000 \cdot Q \qquad (9.3)$$

where: $DV01^f$ = Forward DV01; that is, the DV01 for the futures contract
$D^f mod$ = Forward modified duration of the CTD
$P^f d$ = Forward dirty price of the CTD which incorporates the value of the future's embedded options
Q = Factor of the CTD

In sum, although a Treasury issue and a Treasury future are very different securities—the former as a cash instrument and the latter as a forward contract—they can nonetheless be linked by duration.

Figure 9.1 shows modified duration values for the 8.75% Treasury Bond of 2-15-2020 across a range of yields. It is readily seen that modified

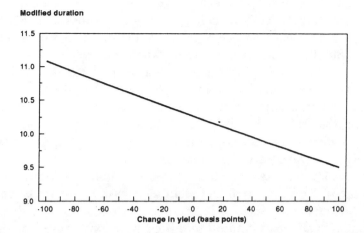

FIGURE 9.1   Modified duration: 8.75% 5-15-2020.

duration changes by less than one year as the yield level rises or falls by 100 basis points. To be precise, modified duration falls from 10.258 to 9.502 when the yield level rises by 100 basis points. Modified duration rises from 10.258 to 11.079 when the yield level falls by 100 basis points.

Figure 9.2 shows modified duration values for the September 1990 Treasury Bond futures contract across a range of yields. In contrast to Figure 9.1, modified duration values may change dramatically across yields. Modified duration ranges from a low of 8.095 to a high of 10.698.

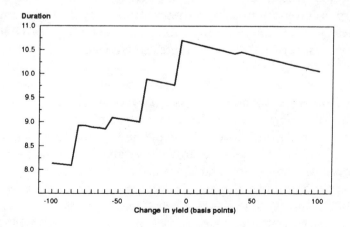

FIGURE 9.2   Duration of bond future: September 1990 contract.

The difference between high and low duration values is 2.603. This exceeds the difference between high and low duration values on the Treasury Bond by more than one year. Moreover, in contrast to Figure 9.1, duration evolves in a steplike pattern as we go from low-yield levels to high-yield levels. Moving from left to right along the x axis, each "step" represents a shift to a new CTD. Moving from right to left along the x axis, the CTD evolves from lower-coupon/higher-duration securities into higher-coupon/lower-duration securities. We see that duration and yield level have an inverse relationship among individual CTDs. However, since each step puts the futures' duration at a higher level, it may be argued that duration and yield level have a direct relationship across wide ranges of yields.

To understand why a futures' modified duration behaves the way it does, it is necessary to revisit the concept of CTD. A CTD, the reader will recall, is determined by implied repo rates. Whichever deliverable security has the highest implied repo rate is the CTD. When yields rise, low-coupon/high-duration securities tend to outperform high-coupon/low-duration securities. Prices of low-coupon/high-duration securities generally *fall* by *less* in relation to high-coupon/low-duration securities. Thus, in an environment of rising yields, low-coupon/high-duration securities tend to carry the higher implied repo rates. Conversely, when yields fall, high-coupon/low-duration securities tend to outperform low-coupon/high-duration securities. Prices of high-coupon/low-duration securities generally *rise* by *more* in relation to low-coupon/high-duration securities. Thus, in an environment of falling yields, high-coupon/lower-duration securities tend to carry the higher implied repo rates. In sum, the relative performance of deliverable securities determines respective implied repo rates and, concomitantly, the modified duration of a futures contract.

Figure 9.3 shows modified duration values for the December 1990 Treasury Note futures contract across a range of yields.

In contrast to Figure 9.2, transitions from one CTD to another are much smoother. Again, this can be explained by the fewer number of securities in the Treasury Note future's deliverable basket and the greater homogeneity among the deliverable Treasury Note securities. For example, unlike the basket of deliverable Treasury Bond securities, none of the deliverable Treasury Note issues are callable. Callable issues tend to be characterized by high-coupon/low-duration securities. Modified

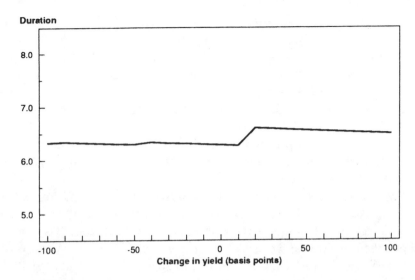

FIGURE 9.3 Duration of note future: September 1990 contract.

duration ranges from a low of 6.300 to a high of 6.600. The difference between high- and low-duration values is 0.30, or a little over three months.

If a note or bond is callable, this means that the issuer (in this instance, the Treasury) has the right to redeem an outstanding issue prior to its maturity date. This early redemption occurs at a predetermined date (the call date) and at a predetermined price (the call price). Since all outstanding callable Treasury Bonds are callable at a price of par, a callable Treasury Bond trading above (below) par is said to be trading in-(out)-of-the-money and is (is not) likely to be called. As of May 1991, most callable Treasury Bonds were trading in-the-money.

The significance of having both callable and noncallable Treasury Bonds in a basket of deliverable securities is that there can be a wide range of modified duration values across yields (as per Figure 9.2). Lower-coupon noncall Treasury Bonds have modified durations significantly above higher-coupon callable Treasury Bonds. In a market environment of declining yield levels, the CTD will typically evolve into higher-coupon callable Treasury Bonds as dictated by respective implied repo rates across deliverable issues. Hence, significant changes occur in the Treasury Bond futures' modified duration across yields.

Now that we have an appreciation for a Treasury future's duration dynamics, let's consider a trade where Treasury futures are used to create duration.

In January 1990, the Resolution Trust Corporation (RTC) decided to issue a 40-year bond as part of its capital markets program. The RTC was created by Congress to administer to the plight of failing savings and loan institutions.

Although RTC had previously issued 30-year bonds, the January 1990 40-year issue was unique. At the time there were no existing Agency securities with 40 years to maturity.

When it was first announced that a 40-year bond would be issued, many investors speculated about how this new arrival would trade in the marketplace. What would be its bond-equivalent yield? Since there were no outstanding 40-year Treasury or Agency issues, it was not possible to extrapolate a hypothetical price relative to an existing 40-year security.

To generate a ballpark estimate of the 40-year bond's value, some investors simply assumed that the RTC yield curve would be relatively flat between 30- and 40-year maturities. The RTC had issued a 30-year bond three months earlier. At the time, the Treasury yield curve was relatively flat across 10-, 20-, and 30-year securities, so a flat RTC curve between 30-and 40-year maturities was not unreasonable. It was further assumed that the 40-year RTC would trade at about the same spread to Treasury issues as the 30-year RTC. At the time, the 30-year RTC was trading at about 30 basis points over the 30-year on-the-run Treasury, so that would put the 40-year RTC yield near 8.6%.

Investors who bothered to take the exercise a step further would have discovered that the difference in modified durations between the existing 30-year RTC and a hypothetical 40-year RTC was little more than half of one year. Thus, for holding a security with an extra 10 years of life, the pickup in modified duration was but a proverbial drop in the bucket. What would be the incentive to take on an additional 10 years of investment risk with such a marginal "bang-for-the-buck" if the yield curve were to flatten?

It seems as though there would have been little incentive to own 40-year RTC bonds instead of 30-year RTC bonds. However, while there was a modest difference in modified durations between the 30- and 40-year RTC bonds in *coupon* form, there was a substantial difference in respective modified durations in *stripped* form. Indeed, the modified duration of the stripped 40-year RTC bond was about *10 years* more than the modified duration of the stripped 30-year RTC bond. Stripping the 40-year RTC bonds would extend the maturities of previously existing STRIPS by nearly 10 years with one auction.

Aside from its value in stripped form, the 40-year RTC bond made for an ideal candidate to use as a hedge against existing nongovernment 40-year issues. For example, there was an outstanding 9.625% coupon 40-year bond issued by GTE Florida, Incorporated.

In light of the preceding points, we now have a story for how the 40-year RTC bond might actually trade through (trade at a yield below) the 30-year RTC bond. Namely, the 40-year RTC bond's unique contribution to the STRIPS universe could make it a relatively more desirable security. In actuality, that's exactly what happened. Several days after the 40-year RTC bond was auctioned, its yield spread to the 30-year RTC bond went from positive to negative.

For the investor who believed that the 40-year RTC bond would trade at a narrowing spread to the 30-year RTC bond, one investment strategy could have been to buy the true 40-year RTC while going short a synthetic 40-year RTC. The synthetic 40-year RTC could have been created with a combination of 30-year RTC bonds and Treasury Bond futures. The combination of the 30-year RTC bonds and Treasury Bond futures would be structured such that the initial DV01 of the synthetic would match the DV01 of the true. With any narrowing in spread between the synthetic 40-year RTC and the true 40-year RTC, our investor would win. The narrowing in spread would occur as the bond-equivalent yield of the true 40-year RTC bond edged lower, and/or as the bond-equivalent yield of the synthetic 40-year RTC bond moved higher. Table 9.5 provides a step-by-step overview of the trade.

Table 9.5 shows that while a loss would have been suffered on the true 40-year RTC, a sizable gain on the synthetic 40-year RTC would have more than made up the difference. The objective of the trade was to get a narrowing in spread between the true 40-year RTC bond and the synthetic 40-year RTC bond created with a 30-year RTC bond and futures contracts. Over the investment horizon, the spread between the 40- and 30-year RTC issues went from plus 2 basis points to minus 12 basis points. The net gain on the trade was $137,710 per $10.0 million.

In this section, we have pretty much limited our scope to Treasury Note and Bond futures duration. What happened to convexity? While Treasury

Table 9.5   Step-by-Step Overview of RTC Strategy

January 17, 1990

Step 1: Buy 40-year RTC bond at a bond-equivalent yield* of 8.59%

Step 2: Sell 30-year RTC bond at a bond-equivalent yield of 8.57%

Step 3: Sell 12 March 1990 Treasury Bond futures contracts at 96-10 for every $10 million face value of 30-year RTC bonds

Net effect: The DVO1 of the true 40-year RTC bond is matched against the DV01 of the synthetic 40-year RTC bond created with the 30-year RTC bond and March 1990 futures contracts.

February 2, 1990

Step 1: Sell the 40-year RTC bond at a bond-equivalent yield of 8.71%

Step 2: Buy the 30-year RTC bond at a bond-equivalent yield of 8.83%

Step 3: Buy 12 March 1990 Treasury Bond futures contracts at 93-27 for every $10 million face value of 30-year RTC bonds

	Value on 1/17	Value on 2/2	Gain/(Loss)**	Cumulative
40-year RTC	100.4400	99.4772	(0.9628)	(0.9628)
30-year RTC	97.1073	95.0637	2.0436	1.0808
March future	96-10	93-27	0.2963†	1.3771

Net gain per $10 million face value invested: $137,710

* As an agency security, RTC issues are quoted on a 30/360 basis.

** Includes change in price plus accrued interst.

† Adjusted for $10 million face value position in the 30-year RTC bond.

Notes and Bond futures certainly do have convexity, these assets are generally not thought of as convexity management tools. One reason is that Treasury futures exhibit what is sometimes called "negative convexity."

Negative convexity means that a security's price/yield relationship becomes *less* convex as yields fall. In Part One, we showed that a security's convexity generally increases as yields move away from current levels. If convexity edges lower with declining yield levels, a Treasury futures' price becomes less sensitive to changes in yield. Hence, we have negative convexity, also known as price compression.

What causes the negative convexity? Earlier in this chapter, we stated that high-coupon/low-duration securities outperform low-coupon/high-duration securities as yield levels fall. This is equivalent to saying that high-coupon/low-duration securities become CTD as yield levels fall. Thus, futures contracts exhibit negative convexity because securities with lower durations and lower convexities become CTD at lower yields.

If we arbitrarily chose 9% as the demarcation between low- and high-coupon bonds eligible for delivery against the December 1991 futures contract, half of the high coupon issues were also callable. Generally speaking, callable Treasury issues tend to carry high coupons.

From an investor's perspective, a callable bond can be thought of as a combination of a bond and a short call option. It is a *short* call option because the *issuer* owns the call. It is the issuer who has the right to exercise the call. Under what circumstances would it be prudent for the issuer to exercise the call? When the call is in-the-money. And when would the call be in-the-money? When yields have fallen such that the callable issue is trading above its strike price. The majority of callable bonds are callable at a strike price of par. The issuer would call for early redemption of an outstanding high-coupon security and replace it with a lower-coupon security to enjoy a lower net cost of funds. Thus, the call option takes on value when yields decline. And it is precisely because the call option takes on a value when yields decline that a callable bond experiences negative convexity.

Figure 9.4 shows the price/yield profile for a callable bond. As yield levels decline, the price/yield profile bends back. That's negative convexity.

Figure 9.5 presents two theoretical price/yield relationships for the September 1990 Treasury Bond future. The solid line traces out theoretical futures prices across bond-equivalent yields. The solid line is generated with the assumption that the futures contract tracks whatever Treasury Bond is CTD. The dashed line also traces out theoretical futures prices across bond-equivalent yields but assumes that the futures contract always tracks the 7¼% Treasury Bond of 5-15-2016 as CTD. The 7¼%/5-15-2016 is a noncallable Treasury Bond.

As bond-equivalent yields decline in Figure 9.5, a wedge begins to emerge between the two price/yield profiles. The wedge contrasts the positive (normal) convexity of the 7¼%/5-15-2016 as CTD with the negative convexity of the high factor/callable Treasury Bonds that become CTD as yields decline.

The point to be made about the wedge in Figure 9.5 is that the price/yield profile of a Treasury bond futures contract is unlike the profile of a typical noncall cash security. Accordingly, the fixed-income investor ought to be aware of this and related implications for investment strategies.

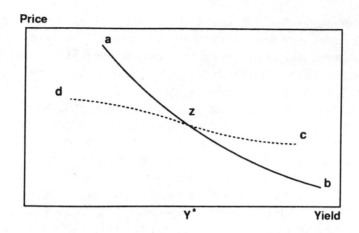

The price/yield profile traced out by azb defines the price/yield relationship for a traditional coupon-bearing fixed-income security. The price/yield profile traced out by dzb defines the price/yield relationship for a callable bond. The fact that dz lies below az highlights the negative convexity of a callable issue. Finally, a putable bond would have the price/yield profile of azc.

FIGURE 9.4 Price/yield profiles for bonds with embedded options.

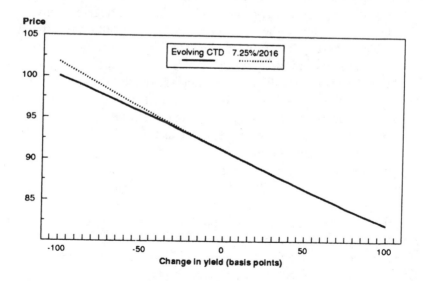

FIGURE 9.5 Theoretical futures prices: Evolving CTD versus 7.25%/2016. September 1990 contract.

To offer a contrast to Figure 9.5, Figure 9.6 shows a theoretical price/ yield relationship between whatever Treasury Bond is CTD and the 10³/8%/11-15-2012 as CTD. The 10³/8%/11-15-2012 is a callable Treasury Bond. As bond yields rise, a wedge begins to emerge between the two price/yield profiles. The wedge contrasts the negative convexity of the 10³/8%/11-15-2012 as CTD with the positive convexity of low-coupon Treasury Bonds that become CTD as yields rise.

The point to be made about the wedge in Figure 9.6 is that the price/ yield profile of a Treasury bond futures contract is unlike the profile of a typical callable cash security. Again, the fixed-income investor ought to be aware of this and related implications for investment risks and opportunities.

Finally, *negative* convexity may have some *positive* attributes. For example, if an investor wants to maximize current income and believes that yields will be relatively stable over the near term, owning some negatively convex securities may be just the ticket. The current income objective can be met with the high coupon cashflows that are often associated with callable cash securities.

So where can we go if we want to buy or sell some convexity? The options market. We explore these opportunities in the following chapter.

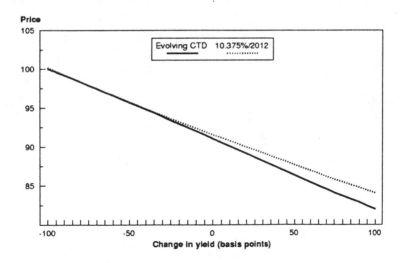

FIGURE 9.6   Theoretical futures prices: Evolving CTD versus 10.375%/2012.
September 1990 contract.

Futures Duration Summary

- Although Treasury Notes and Bonds and Treasury futures respond similarly to changes in yield, they are nonetheless different securities. Treasury Notes and Bonds are cash securities, and Treasury Note and Bond futures are more like forward contracts.
- Despite their differences, the price sensitivity of Treasury issues and Treasury futures can be quantified with duration via DV01s. This measure of price sensitivity is useful when creating duration with futures contracts.
- Duration and yield exhibit an inverse relationship among traditional fixed-income securities, yet duration and yield exhibit a direct relationship among Treasury Note and Bond futures. This direct relationship is explained by the fact that high-coupon/low-duration securities outperform low-coupon/high-duration securities when yields fall, and low-coupon/high duration securities outperform high-coupon/low-duration securities when yields rise. This phenomenon also gives rise to negative convexity among Treasury futures contracts.

10
Creating Convexity

FUTURES OPTIONS

A Treasury Note or Bond option can be thought of as an alternative means to buy or to sell a Treasury issue or Treasury future. For example, with a call option on a Treasury issue or Treasury future, the option's value increases (decreases) as yields fall (rise). This is entirely consistent with the price behavior of a long position in a Treasury issue or Treasury future. Conversely, with a put option on a Treasury issue or Treasury future, the option's value increases (decreases) as yields rise (fall). This is entirely consistent with the price behavior of a short position in a Treasury issue or Treasury future. However, an option differs from Treasury issues and Treasury futures in some rather significant ways.

First, an option is sometimes said to be a wasting asset. That is, an option may well expire worthless. For example, if a call option is purchased in hopes that yields will fall but yields actually rise, the call option may expire with no value. Second, when an option is purchased, it is possible to know one's down-side risk with certainty. The maximum down-side risk is the cost of the option itself. To continue with our previous example, let's say the call option will expire worthless if yields rise 50 basis points. Whether yields actually rise 50 basis points or 100 basis points, the loss on the call option would be the same. That loss would simply be the original cost of the call. Third, unlike a Treasury issue, an option does not pay coupons, and unlike a Treasury future, an option is not marked-to-market. To put it bluntly, an option either gains or loses value over time, and an investor is free to buy or sell the option at his or her discretion.

Figure 10.1 shows a price profile for a September 1991 futures option call. The price profile was created when the option had 66 days to expiration. Not surprisingly, the option value increases when the price of the underlying asset rises, and the option value decreases when the price of the underlying asset falls. However, in contrast to price/yield profiles we saw in Chapter 3, the price profile becomes "flat" in Figure 10.1 as the price of the underlying asset falls by a significant amount. The price profile becomes flat because the maximum loss to an investor who is long a call is the cost of the call.

Figure 10.1 highlights the convexity of the futures option call. The convexity of the futures option call will dissipate over time. As the expiration date draws near, the only convexity of import will be that consistent with the forward value of the underlying security.

Entire books have been written on the subject of options theory, and we do not intend to delve into this realm of financial theory casually. However, we do believe it is important that the reader have an appreciation for how option values are determined, and a brief survey should suffice.

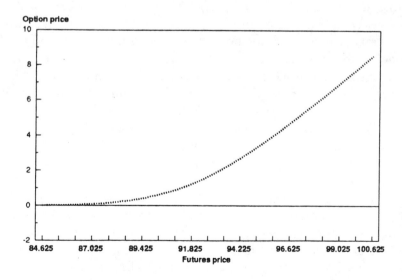

FIGURE 10.1   Price profile of a futures option call.

Five variables determine an option's value. These variables include risk-free rate, price of underlying asset, time to expiration, strike price, and volatility:

Risk-Free Rate. The risk-free rate is exactly what it implies. It is the rate that may be earned on a risk-free asset over the life of the option. While some investors will use a Treasury Bill rate, others will use a repo rate (see Figure 10.2).

Price of Underlying Asset. As stated. When the underlying asset is a cash security, the price ought to be the dirty price. Further, for a call (put) option, the price of the underlying ought to be the offer (bid) price (see Figure 10.3).

Expiration Date. As stated (see Figure 10.4).

Strike Price. Options trade with a variety of strike prices. A strike price is that price which determines whether an option is trading in-, at-, or out-of-the-money. If a call (put) option is purchased with a strike price of 100 and the underlying security is at 100, then the option is at-the-money. If a call (put) option is purchased with a strike price of 100 and the underlying security is at 102, then the option is in-(out-of)-the-money. And if a put (call) option is purchased with a strike price of 100 and the underlying security is at 98, then the option is in-(out-of)-the-money (see Figure 10.5).

Volatility. Of the five variables used to value an option, volatility is perhaps the most elusive. Indeed, volatility is the only variable that cannot be obtained from the business section of most newspapers. Simply put, volatility is a measure of the expected price distribution on the underlying security. For example, if the price of the underlying security is expected to trade over a fairly wide range, then volatility will be large. There is a direct relationship between volatility and an option's value (see Figures 10.6 and 10.7).

Options Convexity Summary

- The unique price/yield behavior of options make these attractive securities to use when creating convexity. Of course, options are popular investment vehicles in their own right.

CALL

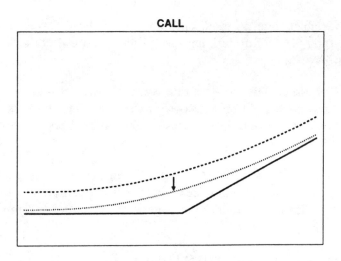

PUT

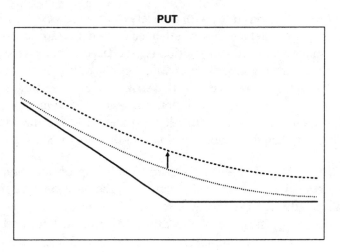

For an increase in the risk-free rate, the value of a call option will decrease and the value of a put option will increase. An increase in the risk-free rate will shift a call option's theoretical value curve lower and will shift a put option's theoretical value curve higher.

FIGURE 10.2   Risk-free rate.

CALL

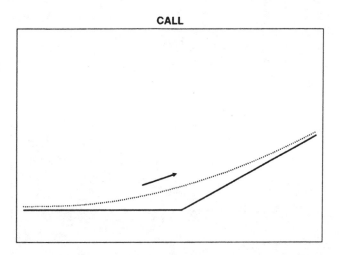

PUT

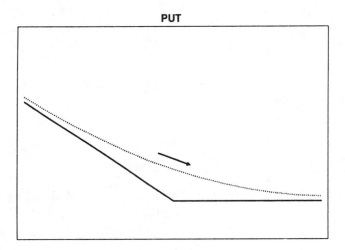

If the value of the underlying security increases prior to maturity, then the value of a call option will increase and the value of a put option will decrease. An increase in the value of the underlying security will result in a movement from left to right along the theoretical value curves shown above.

FIGURE 10.3 Underlying price.

CALL

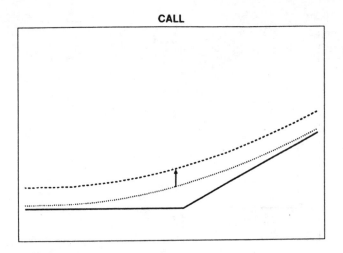

PUT

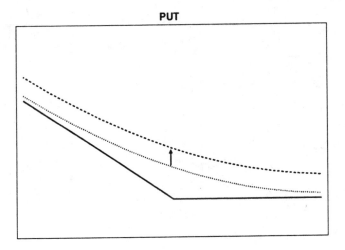

For an increase in an option's time to expiration, the value of both a call option and a put option will increase. An increase in an option's time to expiration will shift an option's theoretical value curve higher.

FIGURE 10.4   Time to expiration.

CALL

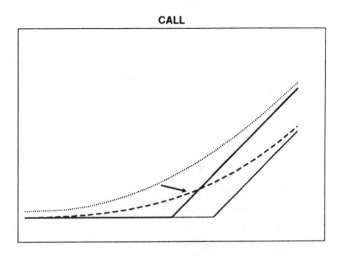

PUT

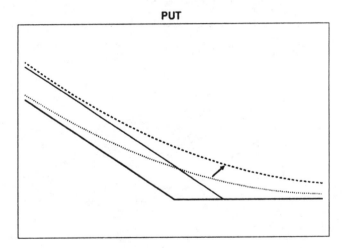

For a higher strike price, the value of a call option will decrease and the value of a put option will increase. A higher strike price will shift a call option's theoretical value curve down, and it will shift a put option's theoretical value curve up.

FIGURE 10.5 Strike price.

CALL

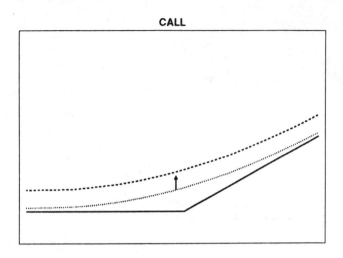

PUT

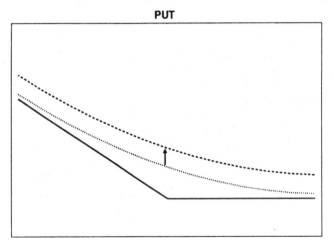

For an increase in volatility, the value of an option will increase. An increase in volatility will shift both a call and put option's theoretical value curve higher.

FIGURE 10.6   Volatility.

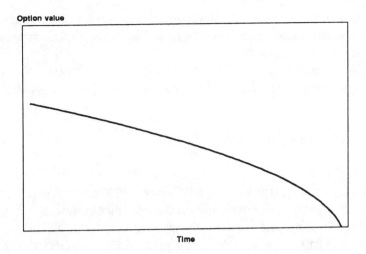

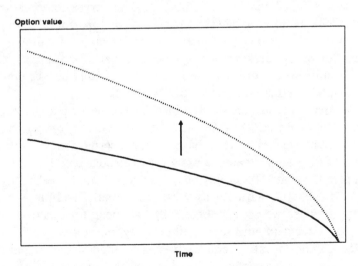

An option is a wasting asset. The top figure shows how an option's value deteriorates over time. As suggested by the figure, an option's time decay is most rapid just prior to its expiration. In fact, 50% of an option's time value decays in the last 25% of its life. The bottom figure shows how an increase in volatility can shift the time decay pattern higher.

FIGURE 10.7 Time decay.

- Given the unique price characteristics of options, it is imperative to consider a variety of investment scenarios for a given strategy and investment horizon.
- When used creatively, options can allow for the creation of products which may outperform traditional cash fixed-income securities.

MORTGAGE-BACKED SECURITIES

Now that we see how futures options may be used to create convexity, when might an investor want to buy convexity? Perhaps when he or she would like to reduce or eliminate a security's price compression. By neutralizing the effects of a security's negative convexity, an investor may create an asset with more traditional price/yield characteristics. For example, we've stated that callable bonds exhibit price compression, and that a callable bond may be thought of as a combination of a long bond and a short call option. To neutralize the effects of a callable bond's negative convexity, an investor might purchase a call option. Purchasing the call option would offset the effect of the callable bond's embedded option. We will return to this idea in Chapter 12.

In Chapter 5 we touched on Mortgage-Backed Securities (MBSs) in the section "Dollar Rolls." An MBS is a fixed-income security comprising one or more mortgages. In this chapter, we concern ourselves with MBSs comprising several mortgages, and we only consider pass-through securities. A pass-through MBS is one that pays out principal over the life of the security, not at its maturity as with traditional fixed-income assets. Henceforth, when we use the term MBS, we mean for this to apply to a pass-through security with several underlying mortgages.

MBSs exhibit negative convexity (also called price compression), which occurs because of the nature of mortgage prepayments across various yields. Mortgage payers have the right to pay-off or refinance their mortgage when mortgage rates fall, and this right may be viewed as being long a call option. For someone who owns a MBS, this early prepayment option may be characterized as a short call. Thus, an investor who owns a MBS is long a bond and short a call option.

To neutralize the effects of the short call embedded in a MBS, an investor might consider purchasing a call option. Why? It might well be possible to create an asset with more traditional price/yield characteristics (i.e., no price compression) that outperforms a security with no embedded options. To see how this would work, we first need to review some fundamental differences between MBSs and traditional coupon-bearing fixed-income securities.

For an investor who owns an MBS, the early pay-down of a mortgage means that a certain percentage of the MBS's principal value is received *prior* to the maturity of the MBS. Since mortgage prepayments tend to accelerate when yield levels decline, this causes a MBS to experience negative convexity. To put this differently, the embedded short calls appreciate in value as yield levels decline. This limits the price appreciation of an MBS.

Since prepayments are an essential part of how an MBS is valued, models have been developed to project prepayment speeds. Prepayment speed means the rate at which a given pool of mortgages is expected to be paid down prior to original maturity. Most mortgages tend to have original terms-to-maturity of 30 years.

Prepayment speed projections are generally made on the basis of prepayment histories, coupon levels, and the ages of respective mortgages within a given pool of securities. A pool is a collection of mortgages that has been bundled together to form one MBS. Thus, one MBS can be thought of as a *portfolio* of individual mortgages, and rarely do all mortgages prepay all at once. While mortgages within a pool generally have the same coupon (or mortgage rate), they may originate from different regions of the country.

There are three components of an MBS's cashflows. These cashflows include (a) coupon payments, (b) scheduled principal amortization, and (c) prepayments. Let's consider the first two cashflows in some detail.

Figure 10.8 shows an interest and principal profile for a level-payment 10.5% 30-year GNMA MBS. GNMA is a corporation of the U.S. government. GNMA stands for Government National Mortgage Association. GNMA MBSs are backed by the full faith and credit of the U.S. Treasury, and GNMAs make up the largest portion of outstanding MBSs. Other MBS facilities of the U.S. government include FNMA (Federal National Mortgage Association) and FHLMC (Federal Home Loan Mortgage Corporation). FNMA (sometimes called "Fannie Mae") and FHLMC (sometimes called "Freddie Mae") are federally chartered, privately owned corporations.

As mortgages are amortized, the holder of an MBS receives less interest income since there are fewer mortgages underlying the MBS.

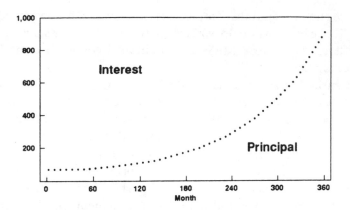

FIGURE 10.8   Level-payment fixed-rate mortgage:
Monthly payments,
10.5%, 30-year term, $100,000 original balance

Thus, principal and interest payments decline over time as shown in
Figure 10.8.

Given the importance of prepayment rates when valuing an MBS,
several models have been developed to forecast prepayment patterns.
Clearly, an investor with a superior prepayment model is better equipped
to identify fair market value.

In an attempt to impose a homogeneity across prepayment assumptions, certain market conventions have been adopted. These conventions facilitate trades in MBSs since respective buyers and sellers know
exactly what assumptions are being used to value various securities.

One commonly used method to proxy prepayment speeds is the Constant Prepayment Rate (CPR). A CPR is the ratio of the amount of
mortgages prepaid in a given period to the total amount of mortgages in
the pool at the beginning of the period. That is, the CPR is the percentage
of the principal outstanding at the beginning of a period that will prepay
over the following period. For example, if the CPR for a given security in
a particular month is 10.5, then the annualized percentage of principal
outstanding at the beginning of the month that will prepay during the
month is 10.5%. As the name implies, CPR assumes that prepayment
rates are constant over the life of the MBS.

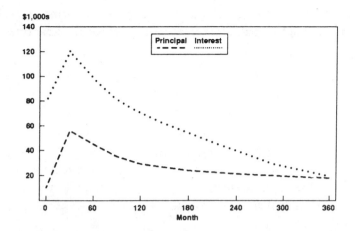

FIGURE 10.9   GNMA 9%: Cashflows, 100% PSA.

In an attempt to move beyond the rather limiting assumption imposed by a CPR—namely, that prepayments are made at a constant rate over the life of an MBS—an alternative measure was proposed. The alternative measure is the Public Securities Association (PSA) model.

The PSA model simply posits that any given MBS will prepay at an annualized rate of 0.2% in the first month that an MBS is outstanding, and prepayments will increase by 0.2% per month until month 30. After month 30, it is assumed that prepayments occur at a rate of 6% per year for all succeeding months.

Generally speaking, the PSA Model provides a good description of prepayment patterns for the first several years in the life of an MBS and has proved to be a standard for comparing various MBSs. Figure 10.9 shows theoretical principal and coupon cashflows for a 9% GNMA MBS at 100% PSA. When an MBS is quoted at 100% PSA, this means that prepayment assumptions are right in line with the PSA model described above. An MBS quoted at 200% PSA assumes prepayment speeds that are twice the PSA model, and an MBS quoted at 50% PSA assumes a slower prepayment pattern.

Since prepayments play such a dominant role when valuing MBSs, we consider two features of a fixed-income security that are greatly influenced by the nature of prepayments: average life and total duration. First, average life.

Average life quantifies the average time to receipt of principal weighted by the amount of principal. Mathematically, average life is expressed as

$$\text{Average life} = \sum_{n=1}^{M} \frac{n \cdot L_n}{\sum_{n=1}^{M} L_n} \tag{10.1}$$

where: M = Maturity of MBS
           n = Period when principal payment is received
              For example, if principal payments are made on a monthly basis, then n is equal to 1 for the first month, 2 for the second month, and so forth
        L_n = Principal amount paid at period n

For a standard coupon-bearing fixed-income security with five years to maturity, its average life would be five years. The numerator of Equation 10.1 would be equal to 1,000 and the denominator of Equation 10.1 would be equal to 100. Since 1,000/100 is 10, the average life in half years is 10. The average life in whole years is 5. The average life of a MBS is generally used as the measure of maturity for comparing mortgage securities with other more traditional fixed-income products.

In Figure 10.10, we show average life values across prepayment speeds. It is readily seen that there is an inverse relationship between average life

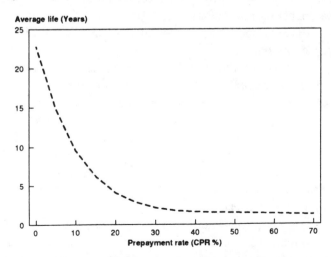

FIGURE 10.10   Average life/prepayment rate profile, 10% GNMA.

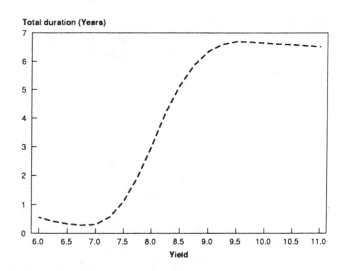

FIGURE 10.11   Total duration/yield profile for GNMA 9%.

and prepayment speeds. As prepayment speeds increase, average life declines. At a prepayment speed of zero we would expect a MBS to appear
much like an ordinary fixed-income coupon-bearing security. Indeed, as
shown in Figure 10.10, a prepayment speed of zero corresponds to an
average life of about 20 years.

Then there is total duration. Total duration is a function of two components: sensitivity of price to changes in yield, and sensitivity of price to
changes in prepayment rates as caused by changes in yield. The former is
calculated by holding prepayment rates constant and is most comparable
to modified duration.

In Figure 10.11, we show total duration values across yield levels for an
MBS. In contrast with what we would expect for a traditional fixed-
income security, Figure 10.11 shows that there is generally a direct relationship between total duration and yield. As yields decline, so too does
total duration. The coupon of the MBS in Figure 10.11 is 9%, and we see
that at yields above this level there is an indirect relationship between
total duration and yield. At yields above 9%, it is unlikely that mortgage
payers will have an incentive to prepay. Accordingly, the inverse relationship between yield and duration at these yield levels is consistent with
what we would expect for traditional fixed-income securities. However,
as yields and prepayments increase, total duration declines.

To calculate the yield on any fixed-income security, it is important to get a handle on the cashflows. Since cashflows on an MBS are uncertain, various assumptions are required. Not surprisingly, a key assumption is the prepayment speed. Any MBS yield calculated on the basis of various assumptions is called a cashflow yield. This is in contrast to a mortgage yield which makes the unrealistic assumption that the MBS is fully amortizing up to the twelfth year at which time it prepays entirely. According

Table 10.1 Differences Between MBSs and Coupon-Bearing Treasuries

	MBSs	Treasuries
Coupons	Paid monthly	Paid semiannually
	Size of payments vary depending on remaining face value	Fixed payments based on par value
	Payment at regular intervals, but with a delay from date coupon is set	Payment at regular intervals
Principal	Paid over life of security*	Paid at maturity of security
	Uncertain principal cashflows give rise to an embedded short call option	
Other	Although GNMA securities are backed by the full faith and credit of the U.S. Treasury with guaranties for the timely payment of principal and interest, FNMA and FHLMC securities are not explicitly backed by the U.S. Treasury. Further, the FHLMC guarantees the timely payment of interest and ultimate payment of principal. These differences in what is guaranteed and by whom help to explain varying yields among these securities.	Backed by the full faith and credit of the U.S. government

* There is a delay from when a homeowner makes a payment and when the servicing institution pays MBS investors. This payment delay differs for each type of pass-through security, and may range from 45 to 75 days. To be precise, these delays are actually 30 days shorter than stated because of the way the payment periods are defined. Prices are discounted to reflect any payment delays.

to this calculation, the assumed number of years until prepayment is independent of the yield level and the age of the MBS. An investor should know that the MBS yield typically quoted in newspapers and other sources is the mortgage yield.

As we discovered in Part One, as much as 70% of a traditional coupon security's total return may be earned from invested coupon income. With an MBS, invested cashflows are all the more important because principal is prepaid along with coupons over the life of the asset. MBS pricing models often assume a variety of prepayment patterns and potential investment rates when valuing a given security.

To summarize this section, Table 10.1 provides an overview of MBS characteristics relative to traditional coupon-bearing securities. In particular, MBSs pay coupons on a monthly basis, principal may be prepaid over the life of the security, and total returns are particularly sensitive to investment rates.

Figure 10.12 presents a theoretical price/yield relationship for an MBS. The flattening of the price/yield relationship at lower yields is attributable to the short calls embedded in an MBS. We add a solid line to Figure 10.12 to show how we might want to alter the price/yield relationship to approximate a traditional coupon-bearing fixed-income security.

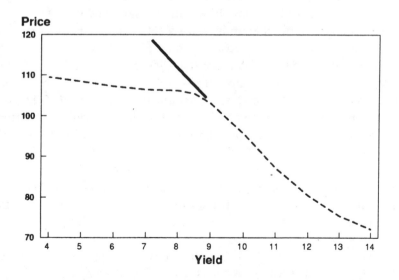

FIGURE 10.12   Price/yield profile for 9% GNMA.

To bend the price/yield relationship in Figure 10.12, we need to buy some convexity. The convexity we want can be created with options. If we are able to create a price/yield profile that outperforms a traditional coupon-bearing fixed-income security—namely, a Treasury issue—an incentive may exist to create synthetic securities out of MBSs and options.

But what kind of options do we want to buy? We can buy over-the-counter (OTC) options on MBSs, OTC options on Treasuries, futures options on MBSs, and/or futures options on Treasuries. There are pros and cons with each of these products. Generally speaking, an advantage to using OTC options is that they can be tailor-made to suit the exacting needs of an investor. The strike price and expiration date can be chosen by whoever purchases or sells the option. A disadvantage to using OTC options is that they may not be as liquid as exchange-traded futures options. Thus, an advantage to using exchange-traded futures options is that they tend to be more liquid than OTC options, and a disadvantage is that strike prices and expiration dates are determined by respective exchanges.

Aside from considerations related to product specifications and liquidity, options products differ by the way in which they respond to the market. For example, futures options respond to the price behavior of futures contracts, and OTC options respond to the price behavior of respective underlying cash securities. The significance of this observation is that different option products should respond differently to market dynamics.

For example, assume that an investor wants to own an option product that trades to the 7¼% Treasury Bond of 5-15-2016. If the CTD (cheapest-to-deliver) happens to be the 7¼%/5-15-2016, then a futures option will provide a decent investment vehicle. However, to be precise, the futures option will expire to a *forward* value of the 7¼/5-15-2016. Futures options expire weeks before the last delivery date of a futures contract, so futures options will expire to a forward value of the underlying security. But even if the CTD is the 7¼%/5-15-2016 at the time of the initial investment, that doesn't mean it will be the CTD over the entire investment horizon. Indeed, as we discovered in the previous section, if yields decline, the CTD will evolve into higher-coupon/lower-duration Treasury Bonds. The futures option will have a weaker link to the price behavior of the 7¼%/5-15-2016.

On the other hand, if an investor buys an OTC option on the 7¼%/5-15-2016, then the investor is assured of a strong correlation between the option and the underlying security over the entire investment horizon. A further distinction is that an OTC option will expire at the *spot* value of the underlying, not at a forward value as with the futures option.

As a parting comment on OTC options, we note that all else equal, we would expect to pay more for an OTC MBS option than an OTC Treasury option. We would expect to pay more for the former owing to its greater credit risk (real or perceived) and uncertain cashflows.

If we consider combining Treasury option products with MBSs, we introduce another dimension of product correlations. Although MBSs are considered to be of the highest credit quality, they nonetheless tend to trade at a positive yield spread to comparable duration Treasury issues. That is, for an MBS and a Treasury issue with the same duration, the MBS will tend to trade at a higher yield. That higher yield reflects perceptions of greater risk for holding a non-Treasury security, and it rewards the risk of taking on the uncertain pattern of cashflows associated with an MBS. If Treasury option products are used in combination with MBSs, there is the risk that yield spreads will change (widen or narrow) between Treasuries and MBSs over the course of the investment horizon. There is also the risk that an MBS will behave less like a traditional coupon-bearing security. That is, there is the risk that an MBS will prepay over the investment horizon.

All else being equal, as an investor insists on using that option product which has the strongest correlation with the underlying security of interest, the more he or she would probably be required to pay up for that option. For example, to approximate the price/yield profile of a traditional coupon-bearing fixed-income security using MBSs and options, it would probably be less expensive to use Treasury futures options instead of OTC MBS options.

In Table 10.2, we combine an MBS with an at-the-money Treasury futures option. We use Treasury futures options because of liquidity, price considerations, and ease of use. In many instances, firms that deal in OTC derivative products require extensive counterparty credit reviews before any trading is permitted. While it is true that counterparty credit checks are required before a firm will allow a customer to trade futures and/or futures options, the review process is usually not as rigorous. This is partly because the respective exchange (the International Monetary Market division of the Chicago Mercantile Exchange, for example) ultimately bears the risk of whether or not an investor makes good on his or her promise to stand by a trade.

Table 10.2   Creating a Traditional Fixed-Income Security with a
Pass-Through MBS and Futures Option Calls

Step 1: Taking the pass-through MBS of interest, we use its effective duration to calculate a DV01. An unseasoned pass-through MBS may greatly simplify matters. An unseasoned pass-through MBS is one that has not yet made any prepayments and is generally a newly issued security.

Step 2: Find a Treasury security with a DV01 that approximates the DV01 of the pass-through MBS. Since this Treasury will serve as our benchmark security, it is important that it be a noncall issue. This Treasury will be the security we attempt to outperform with our pass-through MBS and futures options.

When calculating respective DV01s, it is important to bear in mind that pass-through MBSs settle once a month while Treasuries generally settle the next day. This is relevant because a settlement date affects a DV01. All else being equal, the longer the time to settlement, the lower the DV01. Accordingly, when calculating respective DV01s, an investor will want to ensure that common settlement dates are used.

Step 3: To determine the appropriate strike price of the futures option calls, it is necessary to have an idea of just how much convexity needs to be enhanced. As with Step 1, an unseasoned security may greatly simplify matters since no prepayments have been made. Further, if the pass-through MBS is priced close to par, at-the-money calls might be just the ticket. Out-of-the-money calls might be appropriate for a pass-through MBS trading at a discount, while in-the-money calls might be appropriate for a pass-through MBS trading at a premium.

Assuming that we have an unseasoned MBS priced near par and that at-the-money futures option calls may be used, how many should we buy? A lot depends on our outlook on volatility (both for our Treasury futures options and options embedded in the pass-through MBS), the nature of future yield changes (both on the cheapest-to-deliver securities of the Treasury futures options and the pass-through MBS), and the investment horizon. In short, a variety of what-if scenarios ought to be evaluated in light of how our benchmark Treasury performs.

Step 4: If combining pass-through MBSs with futures options calls proves to generate superior returns relative to a traditional Treasury for expected market dynamics, then the synthetic Treasury ought to be purchased instead of the true.

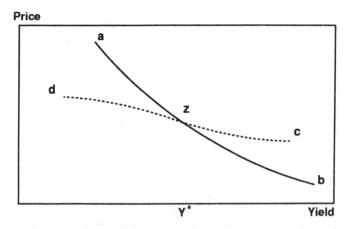

The price/yield profile traced out by azb defines the price/yield relationship for a traditional coupon-bearing fixed-income security. The price/yield profile traced out by dzb defines the price/yield relationship for a pass-through MBS. The fact that dz lies below az highlights the negative convexity of a pass-through MBS.

FIGURE 10.13   Price/yield profiles for bonds with embedded options.

To neutralize the negative convexity of our MBS, at-the-money futures options calls may be used to *bend* the MBS's price/yield profile at lower yields. To determine the number of futures option calls to purchase, we need to know DV01 values for the MBS and the futures option.

If we assume that the yield on our MBS is at Y* in Figure 10.13, then we will want to know the duration of the MBS at that yield level. To be precise, we want to know the total duration and related DV01 of the MBS at that yield. Next, we want to know the DV01 of the futures option. The DV01 of the futures option is simply the DV01 of the underlying futures contract adjusted by the delta of the futures option.

Delta is a measure of an option's price sensitivity to a given change in the underlying security. Delta may range in value between zero and positive one for a call, and between zero and negative one for a put. Figure 10.14 shows how the value of delta changes for a call option as the price of the underlying asset moves in-or out-of-the-money.

Perhaps a more intuitive way to think of delta is that an option's price behavior more closely approximates the price behavior of the underlying

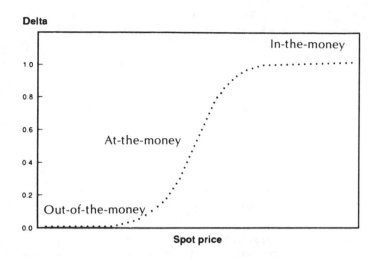

FIGURE 10.14   Delta.

asset as delta approaches an absolute value of one. That is, when delta is equal to 0.9 for a call option, the option is exposed to 90% of the underlying security. To be precise, delta is the change in an option's price divided by the change in the price of the underlying security. As shown in Figure 10.14, the delta for a call option struck at-the-money is about 0.5. As the option becomes more in-the-money, delta moves closer to a value of one. The option trades more and more like the underlying security. And as the option becomes more out-of-the-money, delta moves closer to a value of zero. The option's value is less exposed to changes in price of the underlying security.

In the strategy presented in Table 10.2, we use futures option calls struck at-the-money. We use at-the-money calls because the yield of the MBS is close to its coupon. That is, the prepayment option embedded in the MBS is at-the-money. Since the delta of an option struck at-the-money is about 0.5, the option is exposed to half of the underlying security. However, as yields fall, the delta of the call option will increase. Accordingly, the greater value of the call option will serve to offset the price compression of the MBS. The step-by-step procedure provided in Table 10.2 helps to describe the trade in more detail.

Since purchasing calls requires an up-front payment, this serves to lower the standstill yield of the MBS. Indeed, the standstill yield of the

MBS may fall several basis points below the standstill yield of a comparable duration Treasury issue. However, as yields fall, the MBS/option combination may be expected to outperform a Treasury security with a comparable modified duration. Since the synthetic Treasury may outperform the true Treasury security only when yield levels change, we might conclude that this strategy is appropriate when an investor believes that yield levels are poised to drop.

In sum, an MBS/option combination may significantly outperform a Treasury with the same initial duration as the MBS. However, recognizing the unique price characteristics associated with options (sensitivities to market volatility and time decay, for example), a variety of investment scenarios ought to be considered. Such scenarios would include different assumptions about volatility, length of investment horizon, shape of the yield curve, and so forth.

Options may be combined with any number of fixed-income securities to structure a variety of price/yield profiles. If a particular option strategy allows an investor to outperform a benchmark cash issue, then the strategy ought to be considered as a synthetic alternative to the true security.

11
Creating Notes and Bonds

THE STRIPS MARKET

A Treasury STRIPS (Separate Trading of Registered Interest and Principal Securities) is created by separating (stripping) a Treasury security's coupons from its principal. The principal component of a STRIPS is also referred to as the corpus.

The incentive for stripping a security exists when the sum of its parts is greater than its value as a whole. Respective coupon maturities extend from when the next coupon is to be paid until the final maturity of the corpus when the last coupon is paid.

When a STRIPS is created, a primary dealer simply wires the Federal Reserve to indicate the amount of a given security to be stripped, and the Federal Reserve wires back the information necessary to trade the security in its various pieces. That is, the Federal Reserve assigns a CUSIP to each coupon cashflow and to the corpus. CUSIP stands for Committee on Uniform Securities Identification Procedures, and every Treasury security has one.

To determine if a Treasury security ought to be stripped, each cashflow of a Treasury security is valued at a bond-equivalent yield consistent with the maturity of the cashflow. For a coupon security with 10 years to maturity, this could mean using up to 21 different bond-equivalent yields; one bond-equivalent yield for each coupon payment plus the corpus. If valuing a Treasury coupon security's cashflows at these various bond-equivalent yields suggests that the security is worth more stripped than as a coupon security, then there is an incentive to strip the security.

And just as it is possible to create a Treasury STRIPS from a coupon bond, it is possible to create a coupon bond from Treasury STRIPS. This process of *reconstituting* a security is done when the value of the security as a whole is found to be of greater value than trading the various pieces of the stripped security.

In Table 11.1 we take the 7.875% Treasury Note of 8-15-2001 and value it as a regular coupon security and as a stripped security. Any Treasury security issued after October 1984 and having an original term-to-maturity of ten years or longer is eligible to be stripped.

Column C of Table 11.1 shows that the present value sum of cashflows at a constant bond-equivalent yield of 7.723% is $101.6090. Column E of Table 11.1 shows that the present value sum of cashflows using respective spot rates is $100.5490. The spot rates shown in column D are the bid-side bond-equivalent yield values for outstanding Treasury STRIPS as reported in the *Wall Street Journal.* Recall from Part One that a spot rate is simply the yield on a single cashflow security.

To properly evaluate the stripped value of a given security, it is best to price the coupon security (column C) on the offer-side and to price the stripped pieces (column E) on the bid-side. The rationale for this methodology is that the coupon security is purchased (offer-side), stripped, then sold (bid-side) in stripped form.

Since subtracting the sum of column E from the sum of column C generates a positive value of $10,600 per $1 million face value, this suggests that the Treasury Note is best left as a regular coupon security. Indeed, the positive difference in price suggests that an incentive may exist to reconstitute this security. If the price difference between columns E and C were negative, an incentive would exist to strip this security.

It should be noted that when a security is reconstituted, coupon and principal cashflows may be mixed and/or matched. That is, the corpus of one security may be combined with the coupon cashflows of another security(s). For example, the corpus of the 7.875% Treasury Note of 8-15-2001 may be combined with coupon cashflows stripped from the 7.875% Treasury Bond of 2-15-2021. The reason for this is that all coupon cashflows of a given semipay cycle are melted into one CUSIP. Since both the 7.875%

Table 11.1   Valuing the 7.875% Treasury Note of 8-15-2001 as a
Regular Coupon Security and as a STRIPS

(A) Date	(B) Cashflows	(C) Present Value at Constant Yield of 7.723%	(D) Spot Rates	(E) Present Value at Spot Rates
15-Feb-92	3.9375	3.8122	5.510	3.8472
15-Aug-92	3.9375	3.6705	5.700	3.7377
15-Feb-93	3.9375	3.5340	6.030	3.6175
15-Aug-93	3.9375	3.4026	6.290	3.4946
15-Feb-94	3.9375	3.2761	6.520	3.3698
15-Aug-94	3.9375	3.1543	6.670	3.2496
15-Feb-95	3.9375	3.0371	6.950	3.1157
15-Aug-95	3.9375	2.9241	7.120	2.9917
15-Feb-96	3.9375	2.8154	7.260	2.8716
15-Aug-96	3.9375	2.7107	7.340	2.7605
15-Feb-97	3.9375	2.6100	7.520	2.6378
15-Aug-97	3.9375	2.5129	7.620	2.5277
15-Feb-98	3.9375	2.4195	7.710	2.4214
15-Aug-98	3.9375	2.3295	7.750	2.3254
15-Feb-99	3.9375	2.2429	7.860	2.2211
15-Aug-99	3.9375	2.1595	7.880	2.1338
15-Feb-2000	3.9375	2.0793	7.940	2.0430
15-Aug-2000	3.9375	2.0019	7.970	1.9599
15-Feb-2001	3.9375	1.9275	8.050	1.8712
15-Aug-2001	3.9375	1.8559	8.050	1.7988
15-Aug-2001	100.0000	47.1327	8.080	45.5530
		Sum: 101.6090		**Sum: 100.5490**

The value of the 7.875%/8-15-2001 in coupon form exceeds its value in stripped form.
Its value in coupon form is 101.6090, and its value in stripped form is 100.5490. The
dollar value of the difference is $10,600 per $1 million face value. Thus, there may be an
incentive to reconstitute this issue rather than strip it. However, since this issue was just
recently auctioned at the time of our analysis, it is doubtful that this security existed in
stripped form to make a reconstitution possible.

Treasury Note and 7.875% Treasury Bond pay coupons on a February/
August cycle, we may use the Treasury Bond's coupon cashflows in combi-
nation with the Treasury Note's corpus. It is not possible to combine the
corpus of the Treasury Bond with the coupon cashflows of the Treasury
Note because the Treasury Note's last coupon is paid on August 15, 2001.
The Treasury Bond matures several years later on February 15, 2021.

Finally, although we chose to use actual market spot rates to evaluate the merits of stripping, investors may choose to use other spot rate values such as those generated by various models as discussed in Part One. An advantage to having access to a spot rate model is the opportunity to generate theoretical spot rate values when outstanding STRIPS are not actively traded. When outstanding STRIPS are not actively traded, it may be difficult to identify the fair market value of a STRIPS.

One desirable property of owning a Treasury STRIPS is that its return will equal its yield if the security is held to maturity. With a Treasury coupon security, the return earned on coupon payments over the life of the note or bond can have a significant impact on the security's total value. Invested coupon income can account for nearly two thirds of a Treasury coupon security's total returns over time. There is no reinvestment risk associated with a Treasury STRIPS because the only cashflow is the payoff at maturity.

Since a Treasury STRIPS has a single cashflow, its duration (or price sensitivity to a change in yield) is easily calculated. It is equal to the security's term-to-maturity in years. Modified duration for a STRIPS is equal to the security's term-to-maturity in years divided by $(1 + Y/2)$, where Y is the bond-equivalent yield.

In Figure 11.1 shows Treasury coupon and STRIPS yield curves for March 26, 1991.

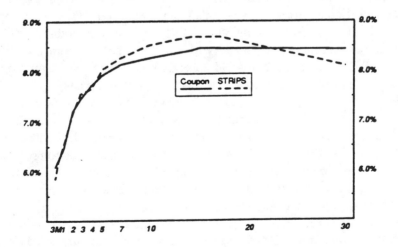

FIGURE 11.1   Treasury coupon curve versus Treasury STRIPS curve.

Figure 11.1 shows that in some maturity sectors, STRIPS yields may trade above coupon yields, and in other maturity sectors the opposite may be true. The economics of the spot and coupon curves is explored in Part One. When STRIPS yields trade above (below) coupon yields, STRIPS are said to trade cheap (rich) to coupon securities.

All else being equal, a coupon cashflow STRIPS will tend to trade cheap to a principal cashflow STRIPS. The rationale is that a coupon cashflow STRIPS is less liquid and thus carries a greater liquidity premium. For example, if $10 million of an 8% Treasury Note is stripped, the corpus cashflow STRIPS will trade to a face value of $10 million. However, any given coupon cashflow STRIPS from that 8% Treasury Note will trade to a face value of only $0.4 million ($10 million · 8%/2).

The careful reader will observe that the corpus cashflow spot rate in Table 11.1 is above the last coupon cashflow spot rate. This is in contradiction to the above paragraph. The anomaly is explained by the fact that the 7.875%/8-15-2001 was just auctioned. It is doubtful that any piece of that issue was yet stripped.

When the STRIPS curve trades cheap to the coupon curve, it may be possible to create duration-weighted trades with a pickup in yield. For example, assume that an investor desires an exposure to the marketplace consistent with the duration of the on-the-run 10-year Treasury Note. On March 21, 1991, the modified duration of the 7.75% 2-15-01 was 6.997, and its yield was 8.14%. On the same day, the Treasury STRIPS of 2-15-98 had a modified duration of 6.90 with a yield of 8.20%. This simple example shows that it was possible to buy the STRIPS with a comparable modified duration of the coupon security yet with a pickup of 6 basis points. We note that STRIPS versus coupon yield spreads tend to be less volatile on a duration-matched basis relative to a maturity-matched basis.

For investors who invest in shorter-dated securities, barbell swaps can be structured with STRIPS. A barbell swap is created by combining two assets to compare against a third. Two Treasury STRIPS might be combined to create a modified duration that matches the duration of a coupon security, yet with a more attractive return profile. The first section of Chapter 9, "Creating Duration with Cash Securities," describes a variety of duration-matching strategies including STRIPS combinations.

Finally, it is important to point out that many investors may not be enthusiastic about STRIPS owing to the unique way they are taxed by the Internal Revenue Service. STRIPS are taxed on the amount of principal that accretes to par even *before* the STRIPS is sold. Normally, any capital gain on a security is recognized when that security is sold. Not so with STRIPS. For an investor who finds himself or herself paying taxes for the capital appreciation of a STRIPS that has not yet been sold, this represents a negative cashflow; taxes are being paid out before any capital gains are taken in.

OTHER STRIPS PRODUCTS

Aside from Treasuries, Refcorp securities and MBSs are other products that may be stripped.

We discussed Refcorp securities in Chapter 9 in the section "Creating Duration with Treasury Note and Bond Futures Contracts." Refcorp STRIPS are generally valued with the same methodology used for evaluating Treasury STRIPS. That is, a Refcorp bond is valued in both coupon-bearing and stripped forms. The issue is stripped if the sum of its pieces is worth more than the issue as a coupon-bearing security. However, since a Refcorp bond is not of the same credit quality as a Treasury security, Refcorp spot rates would be expected to trade above Treasury spot rates. Refcorp is an agency of the U.S. government and is perceived to embody a credit status subordinate to Treasury issues. Accordingly, Refcorp spot rates would be expected to reflect the greater risk associated with holding these securities.

MBSs may be stripped as well, and once stripped the pieces are classified as either IO (interest only) or PO (principal only) securities. A PO is analogous to the corpus of a Treasury or Refcorp STRIPS, and an IO is analogous to the coupon cashflows of Treasury or Refcorp STRIPS. However, owing to the prepayment characteristics of MBSs, POs and IOs behave quite differently over time and across yield levels.

There are three important differences between Treasury STRIPS and STRIPS created with pass-through MBSs. First, Treasury STRIPS do not prepay. Just because a MBS has been stripped does not mean that prepayments are no longer of importance. Prepayment speeds ought to be considered when investing in IOs and POs just as they ought to be considered when investing in any other pass-though MBS. Second, when a pass-through MBS is stripped, all of the coupon cashflows are generally bundled together. This is in contrast to when a Treasury issue is stripped and coupon cashflows are simply melted into respective coupon cycle CUSIPS. Third, IOs do not respond to changes in yield in the same way as POs and Treasury STRIPS. When yields rise, the present value of POs and Treasury STRIPS declines. Recall the inverse relationship between price and yield. However, an IO actually benefits from higher yield levels. An IO benefits from higher yield levels because higher yields mean slower prepayments. Coupon payments on a pass-through MBS are based on the outstanding principal, not the face value of the security as with traditional fixed-income securities. Thus, with slower (faster) prepayments, more (less) of the principal is outstanding, and higher (lower) coupon payments are received.

To be precise, Federal agency STRIPS require that an IO carry a minimum of 1% of the principal of the underlying loans. This minimum principal is required for the security to be accepted by the book-entry system of the Federal Reserve Bank of New York. Privately placed STRIPS may consist of 100% interest and thus constitute a true interest *only* security.

Aside from IOs and POs, there is one other MBS product with STRIPS-like properties. It is the Z-tranche of a collateralized mortgage obligation (CMO).

A CMO is a pass-through MBS that has generally been separated into four tranches. The tranches are A, B, C, and Z. For example, assume that a $400 million pool has been separated into four tranches of $100 million each. The first tranche, A, would receive all of the principal prepayments up to the first $100 million. Tranche A is often called the first-pay tranche. Once the first $100 million in principal prepayments have been made, the second tranche kicks in. The second tranche, B, receives the second $100 million in principal prepayments. Tranche B is usually called the medium-pay tranche. The third tranche, C, receives the third $100 million in principal prepayments, and it is commonly called the slow-pay tranche.

The fourth tranche, the Z-tranche, combines features of STRIPS and MBS pass-throughs. The Z-tranche receives no coupon payments until all previous classes have been paid off. The cashflow from the remaining principal is then paid to investors who own the Z-tranche. While tranches A, B, and C are being paid down, the interest earned on the Z-tranche is instead used to speed the pay-down of the shorter-maturity tranches. Figure 11.2 shows CMO cashflows at 100% PSA.

Millions of dollars

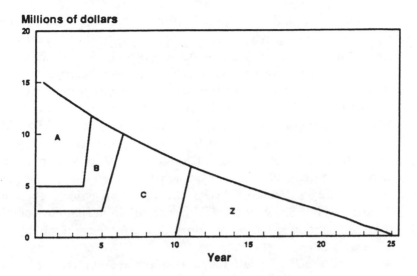

FIGURE 11.2 CMO cashflows at 100% PSA.

In sum, although the Z-tranche of a CMO certainly has some unique characteristics that distinguish it from a typical STRIPS, it does exhibit STRIPS-like properties. The Z-tranche tends to enjoy the highest credit ratings, as do the other tranches; the Z-tranche may not generate cashflows for a number of years, which serves to eliminate investment risk; and Z-tranche yields tend to trade above Treasury STRIPS yields.

Finally, a variety of "feline" zero-coupon securities have been issued. Such products include LYONs, CATs, and TIGRs. These securities are distinguished from STRIPS in that they are issued by non-government sources, and may carry bells and whistles. For example, LYONs are zero coupon convertible securities combining features of convertible and puttable issues.

STRIPS Summary

- STRIPS, or "Separate Trading of Registered Interest and Principal Securities," are issues with a single cashflow that is paid when the asset matures.
- A STRIPS is either the coupon or corpus component of a note or bond that has been stripped. Coupon cashflow STRIPS are

generally less liquid than corpus cashflow STRIPS and will thus tend to trade at higher yields.
- An incentive exists to strip an issue when its present value in stripped form exceeds its present value in coupon-bearing form.
- An incentive exists to reconstitute an issue when its present value in coupon-bearing form exceeds its present value in stripped form.
- While coupon issues are valued at a constant bond-equivalent yield, STRIPS are valued at spot rates that may vary for each cashflow. A spot rate model may be helpful to identify theoretical spot rate values when stripped issues are not actively traded.
- When valuing a Refcorp STRIPS, the methodology for evaluating Treasury STRIPS may be used. However, different spot rates ought to be used since a Refcorp bond does not enjoy the credit quality of a Treasury issue.
- MBSs may be stripped, and the coupon component is referred to as an IO, or interest only. The corpus component is referred to as a PO, or principal only.
- The Z-tranche of a CMO may also be considered to be like a stripped security.
- So-called "feline" zero-coupon securities may prove to be attractive alternatives to Treasury or Agency STRIPS.

SYNTHETIC TREASURY NOTES AND BONDS

Treasury Bills can be combined with Treasury Note or Treasury Bond futures contracts to create synthetic Treasury Notes or Treasury Bonds. In Chapter 9, the section "Creating Duration with Treasury Note and Bond Futures Contracts," stated that Treasury futures tend to trade "cheap" to cash and that this cheapness is explained by delivery options embedded in Treasury futures contracts. The embedded delivery options accrue to the investor who is short Treasury futures contracts. The embedded options tend to have greater value with Treasury Bond futures relative to Treasury Note futures, and this is evidenced by the fact that Treasury Note futures' implied repo rates tend to be well above implied repo rates on Treasury Bond futures.

Since there is a systematic bias in the way Treasury futures are valued relative to cash Treasury securities, it is possible to turn this bias to advantage. To capture the cheapness of Treasury futures with a synthetic strategy, the investor may simply combine Treasury futures with Treasury Bills.

For example, assume that on May 28, 1991, an investor wanted to create synthetically the on-the-run 30-year Treasury Bond with Treasury Bills and Treasury Bond futures contracts. Table 11.2 provides a step-by-step procedure for how this trade could have been executed.

Table 11.2 Synthetically Creating $100 Million Face Amount of a Treasury Bond with Treasury Bills and Treasury Bond Futures

Bond: 8.125%/5-15-2021
Bond's forward dirty price/forward DV01: 99.1634/0.1029
Future's price/DV01: 94-26/0.0999
3-month Treasury Bill: 10-3-91
Treasury Bill's price/Rate of discount: 98.0633/5.49%

Step 1: Go long 1,030 September 1991 Treasury Bond futures contracts
$1.0300 = 0.1029/0.0999$
$1.030 = 1.0300 \cdot 1,000$

We multiply 1.0300 by 1,000 because Treasury Bond futures contracts trade in units of $100,000 and $1,000 \cdot \$100,000$ gives us our $100 million face value.

Step 2: Buy $99,163,400 face value of 3-month Treasury Bills
$\$99,163,400 = 0.991634 \cdot \$100,000,000$
Market value of Treasury Bills is $97,242,853

Evaluation of the trade: On September 19, 1991,* the September Treasury Bond future closed at a price of 99–23. On the same day, the 8.125% Treasury Bond closed at a dirty price of 104.7702. Using the simple interest cash-in/cash-out formula, the synthetic Treasury Bond outperformed the true Treasury Bond by more than 170 basis points. Calculations are as follows:

$$\text{Treasury Bond: } \left(\frac{104.7702 - 98.5960}{98.5960}\right)\left(\frac{365}{113}\right) = 20.23\%$$

$$\text{Synthetic Treasury Bond: } \left(\frac{103.8580 - 97.2429}{97.2429}\right)\left(\frac{365}{113}\right) = 21.97\%$$

* Since the Treasury Bill would not mature until October 3, we assume the discount rate is unchanged on 9-19-91. This is a conservative assumption since short-term rates fell from May to September. A 5.49% rate of discount generates a price of 98.9517, and adding on the appreciation of the futures position gives us a total cash-out value of 103.8580.

Table 11.2 shows that Treasury Bond futures are purchased to match the forward DV01 of the Treasury Bond, and Treasury Bills are purchased to match the forward dirty price of the Treasury Bond. It is important to note that the forward DV01 of the Treasury Bond is not the cash market's forward DV01. The forward DV01 is calculated with the same methodology used to calculate a futures' DV01. The forward DV01 of the Treasury Bond generated with this methodology will tend to be lower than the forward DV01 obtained from the cash market. The lower DV01 is explained by the embedded delivery options that accrue to the holder of a short futures position. Since this synthetic strategy is created with futures contracts, it is imperative that the Treasury Bond's DV01 is that implied by the futures market, not the cash market.

As presented in Table 11.2, the synthetic Treasury Bond outperformed the true Treasury Bond by 174 basis points.

Treasury Notes and Bonds Summary

- Treasury futures tend to trade cheap-to-cash securities, and this is explained by the delivery options embedded in Treasury futures contracts.
- Since delivery options have greater value in Treasury Bond futures relative to Treasury Note futures, the former tend to trade cheaper to cash relative to the latter. The lesser value of delivery options in Treasury Note futures is evidenced by implied repo rates that trade higher relative to Treasury Bond futures.
- The cheapness of Treasury futures can be turned to an investor's advantage by creating synthetic Treasury securities with Treasury Bills and futures contracts.

12
Creating Other Synthetic Assets

CREATING FIXED-RATE ASSETS WITH INTEREST RATE SWAPS

As stated at the beginning of Part Three, note and bond strategies are being presented in two parts. Chapters 9–11 dealt with short-term synthetic strategies. In this chapter, we consider longer-term synthetic strategies.

An interest rate swap involves the exchange of floating interest rate cashflows for fixed interest rate cashflows. Thus, if an investor believes that interest rates will rise over the next several months, he or she may want to enter into an interest rate swap to exchange fixed-rate cashflows for floating-rate cashflows. If interest rates do indeed rise, the investor will gain by paying out the lower fixed-rate cashflows and taking in the higher floating-rate cashflows.

Aside from engaging in an interest rate swap merely to speculate on the direction of interest rates, interest rate swaps may be used to create assets. For example, an investor might create a fixed-rate asset with a floating-rate asset and an interest rate swap. Here's how it would work.

First, an investor would buy the floating-rate asset. For the sake of this example, assume that the floating-rate asset matures in 30 years and pays semiannual coupons linked to 6-month Libor (London interbank offer rate).

Second, an investor would enter into an interest rate swap to pay 6-month Libor and to receive fixed semiannual interest payments. If the investor wants to create a 10-year synthetic fixed-rate asset, then the interest rate swap would have a maturity of 10 years.

Thus, over the next 10 years, our investor would exchange floating-rate payments at 6-month Libor in exchange for fixed-rate payments. In this way, a fixed-rate asset would be created.

In actuality, only the net *difference* in interest payments would be paid. For example, if the payment required from the floating-rate side of the swap exceeded the payment required from the fixed-rate side of the swap, then the floating rate payer would pay the difference between the fixed and floating cashflows.

Why would an investor create a fixed-rate asset instead of buying a traditional ready-made fixed-rate asset? Perhaps because the synthetic offers the potential to earn a substantially higher return. It may also allow an investor to diversify his or her fixed-income portfolio by creating a fixed-rate structure with an asset class that traditionally exists in floating-rate form alone. Finally, it may allow an investor to better match asset and liability streams.

There are securities that lend themselves quite nicely to the creation of synthetic fixed-rate assets, but these are relatively unknown in the United States. These securities are "perpetual" floating rate notes (FRNs). Perpetual refers to the fact that these FRNs have no stated maturity date and could theoretically trade forever. They probably won't. Relatively recent supply and demand phenomena have created a market environment where perpetual FRN prices are attractive.

The perpetual FRN market grew out of the syndicated loan market and started to develop most rapidly in 1982. The late 1980s saw a general decline in the prices of perpetual FRNs as influenced by perceptions of oversupply, foreign regulatory pressures,* and the emergence of other floating rate products including Collateralized Mortgage Obligations (CMOs). Although perpetual FRNs are generally issued by non-U.S. banks, most issues are dollar-denominated.

Given the present status of the FRN market—namely, the relative cheapness of perpetual FRNs on a historical basis—there is a unique

---

*The Japanese Ministry of Finance discouraged the holding of perpetual FRNs, and this put the perpetual FRN market into a tailspin.

investment opportunity to custom-tailor synthetic fixed-rate assets. These synthetic assets may outperform securities with comparable credit risks and maturities. In the investment strategy highlighted in Table 12.1, the synthetic fixed-rate asset earns a return nearly 200 basis points above a 10-year U.S. Treasury Note. Figure 12.1 provides a flowchart of the trade.

When we state that our synthetic fixed-rate asset provides a return of 195 basis points over a 10-year Treasury Note, there is a hitch. The qualification is that the 195 basis points are predicated on the assumption that the price of the perpetual FRN is 91.25 at the end of 10 years. That is, we assume that the price of the perpetual FRN at the end of the investment horizon is the same as it was at the start of the investment horizon. Is this realistic? Probably not. But since the price of the perpetual could be just about anything at the end of 10 years, we need to assume an ending price value. Table 12.2 provides total returns under a variety of end-price scenarios. We show that the price of the perpetual FRN can drop 8 points and still provide a return more than 100 basis points over the 10-year Treasury Note's yield.

Since the price of the perpetual FRN could be substantially lower at the maturity of the interest rate swap, many investors will take out insurance

Table 12.1   Creating a Synthetic Fixed-Rate Asset with a
Floating Rate Note and an Interest Rate Swap

Step 1: Buy the Barclays, AA-Series 1 perpetual FRN at a price of 91.25

Step 2: Enter into a 10-year interest rate swap *to receive* at a semiannual rate of 8.89%

8.89% = 10-year Treasury yield + Swap spread
     =   8.00%   +   0.89%

and *to pay* at a rate of 6-month Libor

Since the FRN pays 6-month Libor plus 3/16% and only Libor is paid on the swap, an additional 3/16% accrues to the investor. Thus,

9.08% = 10-year Treasury yield + Swap spread + Residual gain/loss
     =   8.00%   +   0.89%   +   3/16%

Note: It is important that all yields be expressed on an apples-to-apples basis. Treasury yields are generally stated as Actual/Actual, while swap spreads and Libor are generally stated as 30/360, and Actual/360 respectively.

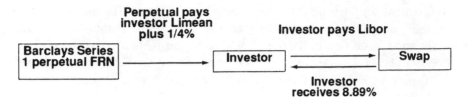

NOTES: Libor, London interbank offer rate, is the offer rate commonly quoted in the swap market. Limean is the mean (or average) of Libid (the bid rate) and Libor. The difference between Libor and Libid is generally 1/8%, and the difference between Libor and Limean is generally 1/16%.

If Limean is equal to Libor less 1/16% over the life of the interest rate swap, the investor gains 3/16% from the net exchange of interest rate cashflows. The investor receives Limean plus 1/4% (equal to Libor plus 3/16%) on the perpetual FRN yet pays out only Libor on the interest rate swap.

A total return of 9.95% is calculated as

$$9.95\% = \text{Swap coupon/FRN price} = 9.08\%/91.25$$

FIGURE 12.1   Creating a fixed-rate asset with an FRN
and an interest rate swap.

against this possibility by purchasing a STRIPS. Refcorp STRIPS are popular insurance vehicles because they carry AAA/Aaa ratings and tend to trade cheaper to Treasury STRIPS. The rationale for purchasing a STRIPS is that the price of the STRIPS will accrete toward par over the investment horizon. Thus, at the maturity of the interest rate swap, the accreted value of the STRIPS can help defray any price loss on the perpetual FRN.

Table 12.2   10-Year Horizon Analysis Given
Various Ending Prices for the Perpetual FRN

FRN Price	Rate of Return (%)	Spread to 10-Year Treasury Note (basis points)
95.25	10.24	224
93.25	10.09	209
91.25	9.95	195
89.25	9.80	180
87.25	9.65	165
85.25	9.50	150
83.25	9.34	134

To use a STRIPS as insurance, an investor could purchase any face amount of a STRIPS up to 100%. Just what percentage of the face amount is purchased depends on how much insurance the investor wants. For example, an investor might purchase $40 face amount of a STRIPS per $100 face amount of the perpetual FRN. To estimate how much of the perpetual's price would be protected, the investor must provide an estimate for the bond-equivalent yield of the STRIPS in 10 years' time. It is then a simple matter to subtract the estimated price of the STRIPS from its price at the time of purchase; the difference is the amount of price insurance that may offset any price loss on the perpetual FRN.

To determine the effect of a STRIPS on total returns, we simply add the price of the STRIPS to the price of the perpetual FRN. Table 12.2 shows total returns for 100% insurance using a 30-year STRIPS with a 7.94% bond-equivalent yield. Even with our worst case scenario of an 8-point drop in the price of the FRN, we still generate a total return of more than 100 basis points over the 10-year Treasury Note's yield if the yield on the STRIPS is unchanged at the end of the investment horizon. Moreover, we show that with an 8-point drop in the price of the perpetual FRN *and* a 200-basis-point rise in yield on the STRIPS, the total return is about 80 basis points over the 10-year Treasury Note's yield.

To better understand just how the purchase of a STRIPS serves to protect the perpetual FRN's principal value, consider the following. First, the base price or purchase price of the perpetual FRN is 91.25. As shown in Table 12.2, a total return of 9.95% is earned if there is no insurance and if the ending price of the perpetual FRN is unchanged. Table 12.3 shows that a total return of 9.74% is earned with insurance if the ending price of the perpetual FRN is unchanged. Thus, since the difference in total returns is 21 basis points (9.95% vs. 9.74%) when the price of the perpetual FRN is unchanged, we might say that the cost of insurance is 21 basis points.

In sum, since the price risk of a perpetual FRN can be substantial, it is imperative that an investor be comfortable with the risk of the perpetual FRN he or she is purchasing. In the jargon of the street, it is important for the investor to like the "name," and to believe that the perpetual FRN has good longer-term prospects.

As to other risks of the trade, an interest rate swap bears counterparty risk. The other side of the interest rate swap may disappear if the counterparty defaults. Since no principal changes hands and interest rate payments are simply net out at regular intervals (every six months in the case of a

Table 12.3   10-year Horizon Analysis with
STRIPS Insurance Given Various Ending
Prices for the Perpetual FRN*

	Rate of Return (%)	
FRN Price	No Change in Yield on STRIPS	200 Basis Point Increase in Yield on STRIPS
95.25	10.01	9.63
93.25	9.88	9.49
91.25	9.74	9.36
89.25	9.61	9.22
87.25	9.47	9.08
85.25	9.34	8.93
83.25	9.20	8.79

*Total returns are based on a $100 face amount of STRIPS purchased for every $100 face amount of perpetual FRNs.

semiannual interest rate swap), this risk may not be substantial. However, there could be a significant cost to replace an interest rate swap that has been broken. This cost could be offset, in part, with the FRN and/or STRIPS. Other risks would include the liquidity of respective markets.

Finally, in Chapter 8, it was noted that FRNs may make for attractive money market substitutes. Just as it is possible to create fixed-rate assets with interest rate swaps and FRNs, it is possible to create floating-rate assets with interest rate swaps and fixed-rate securities. Instead of buying an FRN and entering into an interest rate swap to pay floating-rate payments and receive fixed-rate payments, an investor would buy a traditional coupon security and enter into an interest rate swap to receive floating-rate payments and pay fixed-rate payments. To evaluate the merits of such a trade, an investor will want to weigh the liquidity, returns, and yield outlooks related to respective strategies. A variety of FRNs trade in the marketplace, with perpetuals, fixed maturities, and other structures.

Swaps Summary

- Interest rate swaps may be combined with FRNs to create synthetic fixed-rate assets.

- Perpetual FRNs are attractively priced in the current market environment, and total returns on synthetic fixed-rate assets could be several basis points over Treasury issues.
- Creating fixed-rate assets with FRNs involves the risk that the price of a perpetual FRN could be dramatically lower at the maturity of an interest rate swap. This would serve to lower total returns. STRIPS can be purchased as insurance against a lower price on a perpetual FRN, and the price of that insurance can be estimated in terms of the basis points forfeited on total returns.
- Since the price of a perpetual FRN is an important factor when determining total returns, an investor should be comfortable with a name before the trade is done.

CREATING NONCALL SECURITIES WITH CALLABLE ISSUES AND SWAPTIONS

There are a variety of ways to engineer an interest rate swap. For example, as we saw in the previous section, the most common type of interest rate swap involves the exchange of floating-rate interest payments for fixed-rate interest payments. However, there are many other types of swaps including *basis swaps*. With a basis swap, each counterparty might pay a floating rate where one rate could be a 1-month commercial paper rate while the other may be 3-month Libor. There are also *currency swaps* where counterparties agree to exchange fixed interest payments in one currency for floating interest payments in another currency. And there are option swaps or *swaptions* where a counterparty has the right to enter into an interest rate swap at a future date. Since swaptions are among the more exotic of all swap products, we examine this transaction in some detail.

Return profiles for a bond, a forward, and a generic interest rate swap are presented in Figure 12.2. Notice that the return profiles in Figure 12.2 are quite similar. In Figure 12.2a, an investor's profit increases (decreases) as the difference widens (narrows) between the clean sale price of the bond (Pcs) and its clean purchase price (Pcp). Figure 12.2a considers changes in the price of the bond only. It does not consider coupon income.

In Figure 12.2b, an investor's profit increases (decreases) as the difference widens (narrows) between the sale price of the forward (Ps) and its purchase price (Pp).

(a) Bond

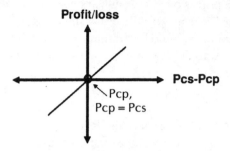

(b) Forward

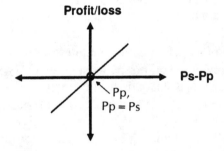

(c) Interest rate swap

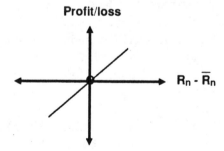

FIGURE 12.2   Profit/loss profiles.

And in Figure 12.2c, where we assume that our swap investor receives floating interest rate payments and pays fixed interest rate payments, his or her profit increases (decreases) as the difference widens (narrows) between the original floating-versus fixed-rate spread $(R_o - \overline{R}_o)$ and subsequent floating-versus fixed-rate spreads $(R_n - \overline{R}_n)$.

Of the three return profiles shown in Figure 12.2, Figures 12.2b, and 12.2c are perhaps the most closely related. Indeed, many investors value Libor-based interest rate swaps relative to a string or strip of Eurodollar futures contracts. A strip of Eurodollar futures is a series of individual contracts across successive maturity dates. The strip is generally bought or sold all at one time.

For example, assume that an investor wants to devise a strategy whereby he or she is rewarded if Libor rates rise relative to a fixed-rate stream of cashflows. One possibility would be to engage in an interest rate swap where he or she would exchange fixed-rate cashflows for floating-rate cashflows. Another possibility would be to sell a strip of Eurodollar futures contracts. If Eurodollar rates were to rise, the forward price of the Eurodollar contracts would decline and the investor would gain. Thus, a strip of Eurodollar futures contracts may be viewed as a *portfolio* equivalent of an interest rate swap.

While we are considering various equivalents to an interest rate swap, there are two other products worth a mention: Forward rate agreements (FRAs), and 3- and 5-year swap futures contracts.

An FRA is a forward agreement to exchange a fixed-rate cashflow for a floating-rate cashflow. For example, in the lingo of the market, an investor may have an interest in buying a 6×9 ("6 by 9" or "six against nine") FRA. That is, an investor wants to benefit from a rise in 3-month Libor (9 minus 6) in six months' time. Thus, in six month's time the difference is calculated between the agreed fixed rate and 3-month Libor, the reference rate. If 3-month Libor is higher than the agreed fixed rate at the forward settlement date, the buyer of the FRA receives a decompounded payment equal to the difference between the two interest rates multiplied by the agreed principal amount and period of the forward rate (three months).

An FRA differs from a Eurodollar futures contract in two respects. First, an FRA is not marked-to-market on a daily basis. The only time money changes hands with an FRA is at the settlement date. Second, an FRA's settlement date may be tailor-made to suit an investor's exact requirements. A given Eurodollar futures contract expires at one fixed date.

If that one expiration date doesn't correspond with an investor's particular needs, then he or she may be out of luck. The settlement date on an FRA can be set to any forward date of interest.

An investor may find that 3- and 5-year swap futures contracts provide a viable alternative to an interest rate swap. These particular products were introduced in June 1991 by the Chicago Board of Trade (CBOT). As with any traditional fixed-income products, the price sensitivity of the swap futures contracts varies inversely with the level of interest rates. However, in contrast to traditional fixed-income products, the swap futures contracts have a fixed value of one basis point. The value of one basis point on the swaps futures is $50.

The swaps underlying the futures contracts can be thought of as fixed-rate notes with maturities of three and five years combined with short positions in floating rate notes. The floating rate notes would pay coupons every six months at 6-month Libor. The 3- and 5-year swap futures tend to exhibit the price behavior of a 3- and 5-year note, respectively. However, one distinction is that the swap futures would not exhibit convexity.

A conventional approach to value a swap yield is to make use of the forward rates in a strip of Eurodollar futures contracts. The conversion of a strip rate to a bond-equivalent rate may be achieved by solving for

$$Yb = (((365 / 360) \cdot Ym + 1)^{1/2} - 1) \cdot 2$$

where: Yb = Bond-equivalent yield
         Ym = Money market yield

By comparing these calculated swap yields against true swap yields, it is easier to determine if swap futures are trading at a fair market value.

The swap futures make for natural hedging instruments against interest rate swaps. For example, assume that an investor wants to hedge a 5-year interest rate swap and must choose between a strip of Eurodollar futures contracts or the 5-year swap futures contract. Advantages of the latter would include the fact that it has a larger basis point value. Thus, fewer swap futures contracts would be used relative to the number of Eurodollar futures contracts that would be required. Further, since the Eurodollar futures contract is tied to 3-month forward rates, the effect of compounding would cause a one basis point move in the strip to produce a greater than one basis point change in a swap yield. For this reason, even more Eurodollar futures contracts would be required to achieve the same net result as provided by swap futures contracts. Finally, when structured properly, Eurodollar futures must be distributed with declining weights across a number of contract months. This distribution offers protection against changes in the yield curve. With a swap future, this distribution is implicitly priced into the contract. And since the longest-dated Eurodollar futures contract matures at the end of four years, the 5-year swap future offers an additional year of potential strategies.

Although this chapter highlights ways in which swap futures contracts may outshine Eurodollar futures contracts, both products ought to be considered to determine if one is somehow mispriced relative to the other. Factors such as supply and demand fundamentals, market volatility, and investor preferences can occasionally skew one market value relative to another.

Corporate treasurers and/or bond issuers may find the swap futures to be attractive hedge vehicles. To the extent that swap yields reflect a credit spread relative to Treasury yields, the swap futures may be a good way to hedge banking or corporate notes or a firm's cost of funds.

As to more speculative strategies, swap futures may be spread against Eurodollar strips or Treasury notes. The former strategy would be an attempt to arbitrage any difference between swap and strip yields. The latter would be a variation of a TED (Treasury Bills vs. Eurodollars) spread trade and would attempt to capture any variation of credit spreads, and/or spreads related to supply/demand between market classes.

Swap futures could also be spread against one another. For example, an investor might go short 3-year swap futures and go long 5-year swap futures to capture a flattening of the yield curve. Since the value of one basis point is $50 for both contracts, they may be bought or sold at a ratio of 1:1 to execute trades on a duration-weighted basis.

If an interest rate swap is equivalent to a strip of Eurodollar futures, swap futures, and an FRA, which strategy carries the least credit risk? The term "credit risk" means an investor's exposure to the fact that the counterparty may not make good on the trade.

Generally speaking, the strip of Eurodollar futures is the least risky of the three strategies from a counterparty perspective. A strip of Eurodollar futures is marked-to-market on a daily basis, so any problem with counterparty risk will tend to surface in short order. Further, trading in futures contracts requires that an investor post a margin deposit. In contrast to a Eurodollar futures contract, an FRA behaves like a true forward contract. That is, no payment is required by respective counterparties until the FRA settles. For this reason, the counterparty risk of an FRA may be said to be greater than a Eurodollar future. With an FRA, an investor has to wait until the forward settlement date to see if the counterparty will make good on the contract. With a Eurodollar future, an investor will know at the end of the day if the counterparty has defaulted on the contract. However, considering that the counterparty on a Eurodollar future is the futures exchange, it is unlikely that the exchange will default on a trade. It is unlikely to default on a trade because to do so would impinge the exchange's credibility overnight. Moreover, the financial futures exchanges have procedures for making good on any contract that would otherwise fail. Finally, an interest rate swap is generally considered to be riskier than either a Eurodollar futures contract or an FRA. An interest rate swap generally has a longer maturity than either a Eurodollar futures contract or an FRA, so a default anytime prior to expiration could have a detrimental impact. A default might be welcome if the trade is going the wrong way for an investor on the other side of a swap, but if all else is equal, an interest rate swap would be the riskier investment relative to the products reviewed above.

Now that we've reviewed some of the ways interest rate swaps may be evaluated, let's go a step further and consider swaptions.

As stated above, a swaption is an option on an interest rate swap. A swaption may be of interest to an investor who wants to create a synthetic noncall bond with a callable bond and a swaption. If a synthetic noncall bond can be created such that it is more desirable than a true noncall bond, then an attractive investment opportunity may exist.

As stated earlier, a callable bond may be thought of as a combination of a bond and a short call option. Figure 12.3 shows a profit/loss profile for this combination prior to the maturity of the callable bond. Figure 12.3 considers changes in the price of the callable bond only. It does not consider coupon income.

In contrast to Figure 12.2a, Figure 12.3 shows that the price of the callable bond exhibits price compression at prices above 100 because of the embedded short call. Without the embedded short call, the profit/loss profile would continue along the straight line.

How can we bend the profit/loss profile in Figure 12.3 to better capture the price dynamics of a noncall bond? Neutralize the effects of the embedded short call! How can we do that? Buy a call swaption.

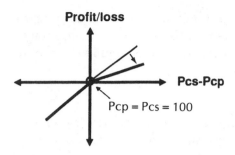

FIGURE 12.3   Profit/loss profile for a callable bond.

With a call swaption, an investor has the right (not the obligation) to receive fixed-rate cashflows in exchange for paying floating-rate cashflows. In the lingo of the swaps market, this may be described as a *receiver* option. Figure 12.2c shows a profit/loss profile for an investor who pays fixed and receives floating. The investor gains when interest rates rise. We want to create the opposite profit/loss profile. Since price compression becomes a problem when yields fall, we want our swaption to take on value when yields decline. When interest rates fall, it is desirable to pay declining floating-rate cashflows and to receive higher fixed-rate cashflows. Hence, under this scenario, a call swaption would appreciate in value. The price appreciation of the call swaption would counter the price compression of the callable bond. Presumably our investor's floating-rate cashflows would be linked to a noncall bond with a maturity equal or comparable to the callable bond.

Purchasing the call swaption provides the convexity required to bend the profit/loss profile in the desired way.

What would be the most an investor would want to pay for the call swaption? All else being equal, an investor would not want to pay more than what it would cost to buy a comparable maturity noncall bond. Callable bonds tend to trade at yields higher than comparable noncall bonds. The higher yield is generated by the embedded short call option, and this serves to compensate an investor for taking on call risk.

Since a call swaption would require an up-front payment, this adds to the effective cost of the callable bond. The higher effective cost of the callable bond means that its yield is reduced. If the yield on the combination of the callable bond and call swaption is less than that of a comparable noncall bond, it may not be advantageous to do the trade. An investor will want to consider the strategy under a variety of scenarios with various yields, volatilities, and investment horizons.

Summary

- There are a variety of interest rate swaps including basis swaps, currency swaps, swaptions, and many others.
- By combining interest rate swaps with fixed-income products, it is possible to create new and innovative securities. Many times it is possible to create synthetic assets with these securities such that the synthetic product is more attractive than the true.
- An interest rate swap can be thought of as a strip of Eurodollar futures contracts, a swap futures contract, and/or an FRA. These products may be used by investors to evaluate the fair market value for an interest rate swap.
- It is possible to create a synthetic noncall bond with a call swaption and a callable bond. When evaluating such a strategy, it is important to consider a variety of scenarios with different assumptions related to yields, volatilities, and investment horizons.

VARIATIONS ON A THEME: SYNTHETIC OPTIONS

When we talk about creating options, what we really want to do is replicate an option's profit/loss profile. This may be achieved in a variety of ways, with pros and cons for each approach. The methodologies considered here make use of options, forwards, futures, cash securities, and interest rate swaps.

Why would an investor choose to create a synthetic option rather than buy or sell the real thing? One reason might be the perception that the option is trading rich to its fair market value. Since volatility is a key factor when determining an option's value, an investor may create a synthetic option when he or she believes that the true option's implied volatility is too high. That is, when an investor believes that the expected price dynamics of the underlying variable are not likely to be as great as that suggested by the true option's implied volatility. If the realized volatility is less than that implied by the true option, then a savings may be realized.

Synthetic Options and Fair Market Value

An advantage of creating an option with forwards and Treasury Bills is that it may result in a lower cost option. A disadvantage of this strategy is that it requires constant monitoring. To see why, we need to revisit the concept of delta.

As we discussed in Part Three, delta is a measure of an option's exposure to the price dynamics of the underlying security. Delta is positive for a long call option and negative for a long put option. Delta is positive for a long call because a call trades to a long position in the underlying security. Delta is negative for a long put because a put trades to a short position in the underlying security. The absolute value of an option's delta becomes closer to one as it moves in-the-money, and becomes closer to zero as it moves out-of-the-money. An option that is at-the-money tends to have a delta with an absolute value close to 0.5.

Let's say that an investor desires an option with an initial delta of 0.5. If a true option is purchased, delta will automatically adjust to price changes in the underlying security. For example, if a call option is purchased on the current 10-year Treasury Note, delta will automatically move closer to one as yields fall. Conversely, delta will move closer to zero as yields rise. With a synthetic option, delta must be monitored constantly because the delta of a synthetic option will not automatically adjust itself to price changes in the underlying security.

If an initial delta of 0.5 is required for a synthetic call option, then an investor will go long a forward to cover half (0.5) of the underlying security's face value, and Treasury Bills will be purchased to cover 100% of the underlying security's forward value. We cover 100% of the security's forward value because this serves to place a "floor" under the strategy's profit/loss profile.

If yields fall and the implied value for delta increases, a larger forward position will be required. If yields rise and the implied value for delta decreases, a smaller forward position will be required. The more volatile the underlying security, the more expensive it will become to manage the synthetic option. This is consistent with the fact that an increase in volatility serves to increase the value of a true option.

The term "implied delta" means the value delta would be for a traditional option when valued using the objective strike price and expected volatility. Just how we draw a synthetic option's profit/loss profile depends on a variety of assumptions. For example, since the synthetic option is created with Treasury Bills and forwards, are the Treasury Bills financed in the repo market? If yes, this would serve to lever the synthetic strategy. It is an explicit assumption of traditional option pricing theory that the risk-free asset (the Treasury Bill) is leveraged. That is, the Treasury Bill is financed in the repo market.

If repo financing on a synthetic option were structured with a string of overnight repos, this would be consistent with creating a synthetic American option. An American option may be exercised at any time. Conversely, if the repo financing were structured with a term repo, this would be consistent with an European option. An European option may be exercised only at the maturity of the option. Since there is no secondary market for repo transactions, and since an investor may not have the interest or ability to execute an off-setting repo trade, a string of overnight repos may be the best strategy with synthetic options.

When a cash position is financed in the repo market, there is either a positive or negative cost-of-carry. The term "cost-of-carry" means the difference between the rate of return earned on the risk-free asset and the cost of borrowing (financing) that risk-free asset. A positive (negative) cost-of-carry exists when the rate of return on the risk-free asset is greater (less) than the cost of financing.

Figure 12.4 shows profit/loss profiles for financed and unfinanced positions in Treasury Bills at maturity. We see that the return for a financed position is always less than the return for an unfinanced position. This is true whether the position is financed at either a positive or negative cost-of-carry. The return for a financed position is lower because of financing costs.

In panels (a), (b), and (c) of Figure 12.4, the profit/loss profiles of the Treasury Bills are independent of the underlying security's price. This is to say that the profit/loss profiles of the Treasury Bills have nothing to do with the underlying security's price. Of course, this assumes that the underlying security is not a Treasury Bill, but presumably a longer-dated asset like a Treasury Note or Bond. There is an independence between the Treasury Bill return and the underlying security's price because *regardless* of what happens to the price of the underlying over time, the Treasury Bill will generate a known return if held to maturity. Since that return will be the same no matter what happens to the price of the underlying, the profit/ loss profile is drawn as a straight line across all potential prices of the underlying asset.

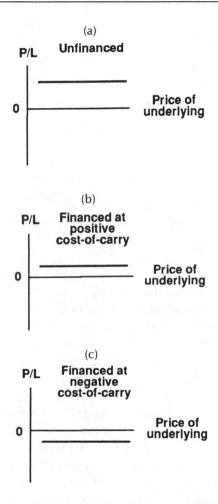

FIGURE 12.4   Profit/loss profiles for Treasury Bills at maturity under various financing assumptions.

A forward is the second leg of a synthetic option strategy. The forward price of a security also depends on the asset's cost-of-carry. If there is a positive (negative) cost-of-carry, then the forward price will tend to be less (greater) than the current price. Figure 12.5 shows forward prices for positive, negative, and zero cost-of-carry. It is readily seen that a forward price lies below (above) the current price with a positive (negative) cost-of-carry and is equal to the current price with a zero cost-of-carry.

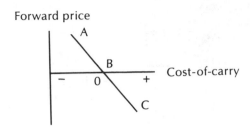

Forward price

A = Forward price with a negative cost-of-carry
B = Forward price with a zero cost-of-carry, equal to current price
C = Forward price with a positive cost-of-carry

FIGURE 12.5   Forward prices for various cost-of-carry assumptions.

By going long a forward, we are entering into an agreement to purchase the underlying security at the forward price. Thus, if the actual market price lies anywhere above (below) the forward price at the expiration of the forward, then there is a profit (loss). There is a profit (loss) because we purchase the underlying security at a price below (above) the prevailing market price, and in turn sell that underlying security at the higher (lower) market price. Of course, once the underlying security is purchased, our investor may decide to hang onto the security rather than sell it immediately and realize any gains (losses). An investor may choose to hold onto the security for awhile in hopes of improving returns.

A long option embodies the *right* to purchase the underlying security. This is in contrast to a long forward (or a long future), which embodies the *obligation* to purchase the underlying security. Thus, an important distinction to be made between a true option and an option created with Treasury Bills and forwards is that the former does not commit an investor to a forward purchase.

Although there is no secondary market for a forward transaction, an offsetting trade may easily be made if an investor wants to reverse the synthetic option strategy prior to expiration. For example, one month after entering into a 3-month forward to purchase a 10-year Treasury Note, an investor may decide to reverse the trade. To do this, our investor would simply enter into a 2-month forward to sell the 10-year Treasury Note. In short, these forward transactions would still *require* an investor to buy and sell the 10-year Treasury Note at some future date. However, these offsetting transactions allow the investor to "close-out" the trade prior to the maturity of the original forward transaction. "Close-out" appears in quotes because the term conveys a sense of finality. Although an offsetting trade is indeed executed for purposes of completing the strategy, the strategy isn't really dead until the forwards mature in two months' time. And when we say that an *offsetting* forward transaction is executed, we mean only that an opposite trade is made on the same underlying security and for the same face value. The forward price of an offsetting trade could be higher, lower, or the same as the forward price of the original forward trade. The factor that determines the price on the offsetting forward is the same factor that determines the price on the original forward contract: cost-of-carry.

If we now assume that we have a positive cost-of-carry for both the Treasury Bill and forward legs of our synthetic option, Figure 12.6 shows how these combined positions would fit together.

If our synthetic call option were originally designed to have a delta of 0.5, then our investor would go long a forward to cover half of the underlying security's face value, and he or she would purchase Treasury Bills equal to 100% of the underlying security's forward value. One half of the underlying security's face value is our benchmark for the forward position because the target delta is 0.5. If the target delta were 0.75, then three quarters of the underlying security's face value would be our benchmark. If the price of the underlying security were to rise (fall), then the forward position would be increased (decreased) to increase (decrease) the implied delta. The term "implied delta" means the value for delta if our synthetic option were a true option.

The preceding example assumes that the synthetic option is intended to underwrite 100% of the underlying asset. For this reason our at-the-

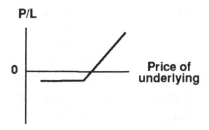

FIGURE 12.6 Combination of financed Treasury Bill and a forward position at the end of investment horizon.

money synthetic option requires holding 50% of the underlying's face value in our forward position. If our synthetic option were to move in-the-money with delta going from 0.5 to close to 1.0, we would progressively hold up to 100% of the underlying's face value in our forward position.

It is a simple matter to determine the appropriate size of the forward position for underwriting anything other than 100% of the underlying asset. For example, let's assume that we want to underwrite 50% of the underlying asset. In this instance, we would want to own 50% of the underlying's face value in Treasury Bills and 25% of the underlying's forward value for an at-the-money option. The delta for an at-the-money option is 0.5, and 50% times 0.5 is equal to 25%. Thus, we want to own 25% of the underlying's forward value in our forward position.

Again, the delta of a synthetic option will not continuously adjust itself to price changes in the underlying security. Forward positions must be actively managed, and the transactions costs implied by bid/offer spreads on successive forward transactions are an important consideration. Thus, how well the synthetic option performs relative to the true option is greatly dependent on market volatility. The more transactions required to manage the synthetic option, the greater its cost. Although the Treasury Bill leg of the synthetic option in Figure 12.6 is financed at a positive cost-of-carry, the horizontal piece of the profit/loss profile is drawn below zero to reflect expected cumulative transactions costs at expiration. Thus, expected volatility may very well be the most important criterion for an investor to consider when evaluating a synthetic versus a true option strategy. That is, if an investor believes that the true option is priced rich on a volatility basis, he or she may wish to create a synthetic option. If the realized volatility happens to be less than that implied by the true option, then the synthetic option may well have been the more appropriate vehicle for executing the option strategy.

Finally, the nature of discrete changes in delta may pose special challenges when an investor wants to achieve a delta of zero. For example, there may be a market level where the investor would like to close out the synthetic option. Since it is unlikely that an investor can monitor the market constantly, he or she would probably leave market orders of where to buy or sell predetermined amounts of forwards or Treasury Bills. However, just leaving a market order to be executed at a given level does not guarantee that the order will be filled at the prices specified. In a fast-moving market, it may well be impossible to fill a large order at the desired price. An implication is that a synthetic option may be closed out, yet at an undesirable forward price. Accordingly, the synthetic option may prove to be a less efficient investment vehicle relative to a true option. It is for this reason that creating synthetic options may only be a worthwhile consideration when replicating option markets which are less efficient. That is, a synthetic strategy may prove to be more successful when structured against a specialized option-type product with a wide bid/ask spread as opposed to replicating an exchange-traded option.

Aside from using Treasury Bills and forwards to create options, Treasury Bills may be combined with Treasury Note or Bond futures, and Treasury Bill futures may be combined with Treasury Note or Bond futures and/or forwards. However, the investor needs to consider the nuances of trading in these other products. For example, a Treasury bill future expires into a 3-month cash bill; it does not expire at par. Further, Treasury Note and Bond futures trade to an underlying CTD, and the CTD may change at any time.

Synthetic Options Created with Options and Cash Securities

Figures 12.7 and 12.8 show how options may be combined with cash securities to create new options. Again, when we talk about creating options, we mean replicating an option's profit/loss profile.

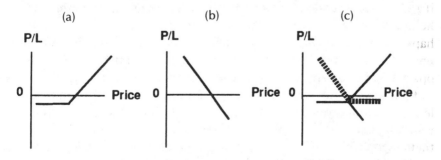

Combining a long call (a) with a short bond (b) creates a synthetic put option (c).

FIGURE 12.7 Combining a long call with a short bond to create a synthetic put option.

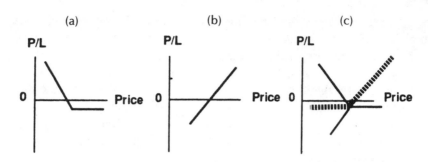

Combining a long put (a) with a long bond (b) creates a synthetic call option (c).

FIGURE 12.8   Combining a long put with a long bond
to create a synthetic call option.

Figure 12.7 demonstrates that combining a long call with a short cash position generates a profit/loss profile consistent with a long put. Figure 12.8 shows that combining a long put with a long cash position generates a profit/loss profile consistent with a long call. To create short option positions, all that is required is to reverse the above transactions. For example, to create a short put, an investor would short a call option and go long a cash position.

We assume that the cash positions in both Figures 12.7 and 12.8 are consistent with respective options. For example, if the cash security is the 10-year Treasury Note, then the option should trade to the 10-year Treasury Note as the underlying security. Further, we assume that the 10-year Treasury Note is financed in the repo market.

When might a synthetic option be created with options and cash? Assume that a manufacturer will receive a payment in yen and wants to protect against an appreciation of the dollar versus yen. The purchase of a yen put would hedge against a strengthening dollar, and the combination of a yen put and yen cash implies a yen call. The profit/loss profile of a yen call is such that the manufacturer is protected with a floor if the dollar appreciates, and enjoys upside potential if the dollar depreciates.

Finally, synthetic options may be created with forwards and/or futures, though special care must be given to monitor changes in the implied delta, particularly as changes occur with the CTD security.

Synthetic Forwards Created with Options

Finally, a long call combined with a short put creates a synthetic long forward. Conversely, a short call combined with a long put creates a synthetic short forward. These positions are shown graphically in Figure 12.8a.

Futures Options as Option Substitutes

Finally, futures options may be considered to be viable substitutes for over-the-counter (OTC) options. As we discussed in Chapter 10, the underlying asset for a futures option is the relevant futures contract which in turn trades to the forward value of the cheapest-to-deliver (CTD) security. For an OTC option, the option generally trades to the forward value of a cash security. Thus, the underlying cash security of a futures option (the CTD) may change many times over the life of the futures option, and the underlying cash security of an OTC option is generally the same over the life of the option.

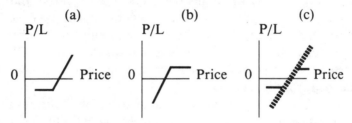

Combining a long call (a) with a short put (b) creates a long forward (c).

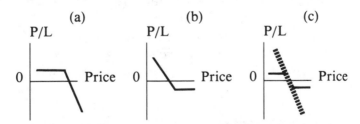

Combining a short call (a) with a long put (b) creates a short forward (c).

FIGURE 12.8a   Combining options to create forwards.

Let's say that an investor desires the profit/loss profile associated with a call option on the 7¼% Treasury Bond of 5-15-16. Further, assume that the CTD for the futures contract is the 7¼%/5-15-16. If our investor believes that the 7¼%/5-15-16 will remain the CTD over the life of the futures option, then he or she may find the futures option to be a viable alternative to an OTC option on the 7¼%/5-15-16. An arbitraguer might even consider selling the OTC option and buying the futures option (or vice-versa) if a significant price difference exists between the two assets. Factors which the investor would want to consider include (a) the probability that the 7¼%/5-15-16 will remain CTD over the life of the futures option, (b) the liquidity and fair market values of respective options, and (c) dynamics of respective underlying securities.

As to point (c), a futures option trades to the forward value of the relevant futures contract which in turn trades to the forward value of the CTD. Futures options tend to expire about one month prior to the expiration of the underlying futures contract. An OTC option may simply trade to the forward value of the underlying cash security. Thus, even if the 7¼%/5-15-16 remains the CTD over the life of the futures option, the profit/loss profile of the futures option will not exactly mirror the profit/loss profile of the OTC option. Aside from different underlying securities, the price dynamics of a futures option will reflect such phenomena as embedded delivery option values associated with the underlying futures contract.

In Figure 12.9 we show a hypothetical distribution of futures prices at option expiration under two scenarios: no change in CTD, and an evolving CTD. These two distributions highlight the dynamics of CTD variability, and help to explain the price action between OTC Treasury options and exchange-traded futures options.

In sum, futures options may be used as alternatives to OTC options, but an investor ought to be aware of the factors which may cause respective options to exhibit different profit/loss profiles over time.

Synthetic Options Created with Interest Rate Swap Products

Another type of synthetic option is an interest rate cap or floor. Caps and floors are interest rate swap products. An interest rate cap is a put option, and an interest rate floor is a call option.

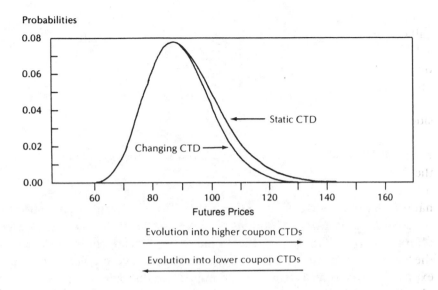

FIGURE 12.9 Distribution of futures prices (at option expiration).

With a traditional interest rate swap, an investor either pays fixed interest rate cashflows and receives floating rate cashflows, or vice versa. With
an interest rate cap/floor, an investor receives/pays cashflows only if interest rates rise/fall. Figures 12.9 and 12.10 provide profit/loss profiles for an
interest rate cap and an interest rate floor. The profit/loss profiles look
very much like the profit/loss profiles of traditional put and call options.

Options pricing methodology may be used to value an interest rate cap
or floor, but there are some unique considerations relative to standard
interest rate options. For example, an interest rate swap is really a strip of

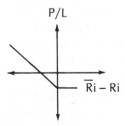

FIGURE 12.10 Creating a put option with an interest rate cap.

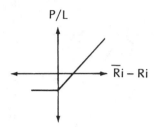

FIGURE 12.11   Creating a call option with an interest rate floor.

options. A cap is a strip of put options, and a floor is a strip of call options. A cap or floor is a strip of options because each reset period in the swap offers an opportunity to profit from the desired change in interest rates. Thus, for a 2-year cap with semiannual resets, an investor who purchases the cap is purchasing a strip of four 6-month put options.

To value a 2-year cap, an investor would want to know the forward structure of interest rates at semiannual dates for two years out, and the term structure of volatility at semiannual dates for two years out. Accordingly, respective options could be valued at appropriate points across the life of the cap. By summing across all values of the put options, we may derive a fair market value for the cap.

Part One introduced the notion of a forward rate, and we have since reviewed this variable in a variety of contexts. In short, a forward rate is the market's implicit forecast for the future level of interest rates. However, this is the first time we've introduced the notion of a term structure of volatility.

A term structure of volatility is created by plotting volatilities against respective expiration dates. At-the-money options are generally used for plotting implied volatility values. If yield volatility is used, the term structure is normally inverted. That is, shorter-dated volatilities tend to be above longer-dated volatilities. The intuition behind this is that a relatively greater change in yield is required among shorter-dated securities to generate a given change in price relative to a longer-dated security. If we were to consider the volatility term structure for prices instead of yields, the term structure would generally have an upward slope.

Another factor contributing to the inverted slope of a yield volatility term structure is that shorter-dated securities tend to be more responsive to the slightest change in monetary policy. Since October 1979, the goal of the Federal Reserve has been to target growth of the money supply. As one result, interest rates are free to respond to such events as open market operations and changes in the Federal Funds and discount rates. As these management tools of the Federal Reserve are at the front-end of the yield curve, shorter-dated yields tend to be among the most volatile.

In sum, when valuing a series of options over any period of time, it may be worthwhile to consider the market's volatility at each node rather than use one average volatility to serve as a proxy for the entire term structure of volatilities.

Finally, what are the pros and cons of caps and floors versus traditional option products? One potential argument in favor of caps and floors instead of traditional option products is that different factors influence these two categories of products. For example, exchange-traded futures options trade to an underlying Treasury security. A cap or floor trades to whatever underlying index is used. Thus, if implied volatilities were perceived to be trading cheaper outside the Treasury market, an investor might prefer to use a cap or floor as his or her option vehicle of choice. An argument against using a cap or floor may be that it is relatively illiquid. For this reason, a cap or floor might be most appropriate for an investor knowing that he or she would like to hold the strategy to expiration.

Synthetic Options Summary

- Synthetic options may be created with combinations of for-wards, Treasury Bills, options, futures, cash, and interest rate swap products.
- One incentive to create synthetic options may be an investor's perception that an option is trading too rich or cheap as implied by the option's volatility. However, this may only prove profitable when attempting to replicate an option with a wide bid/ask spread.
- Market inefficiencies between exchange-traded futures options and OTC options may allow for unique trading strategies.
- Synthetic options may be created with interest rate swap products, and differences across markets may allow an investor to structure an options strategy at less cost with a cap or floor.

PART FOUR
SYNTHETIC FIXED-INCOME PORTFOLIOS

In Part Four we consider synthetic strategies for entire portfolios of fixed-income securities. As we will see, a portfolio of fixed-income securities offers a very different set of challenges and opportunities relative to fixed-income products as individual securities.

13

Creating Portfolio Duration

CREATING PORTFOLIO DURATION WITH TREASURY NOTES AND BONDS

In Chapter 9, in the section "Creating Duration with Treasury Note and Bond Futures Contracts," we demonstrated that pairs of securities with equivalent modified durations may exhibit very different return profiles. One explanation for the different return profiles is that the security pairs have different convexities. Other explanations for different return profiles might include different coupon levels and supply/demand considerations. As to the former, a significant portion of a higher coupon security's total returns may be the coupon income generated and the proceeds earned on investing that coupon income over time. As to the latter, supply/demand fundamentals that drive the STRIPS market may be very different from supply/demand fundamentals which influence Treasury coupon-bearing securities. As mentioned in Chapter 11, "Creating Notes and Bonds" STRIPS are created or reconstituted at the whim of the firms that traffic in these securities. By contrast, the Treasury generally auctions its bills and coupon-bearing securities at regular intervals with pre-announced issue sizes.

In this chapter, we move beyond the two-security examples of Part Three and consider *portfolio* dynamics of duration-matched strategies.

Many portfolio managers are evaluated on the basis of how well their portfolio performs relative to a benchmark (bogey). Often that bogey is the duration of a benchmark security like the on-the-run 2-year Treasury Note.

The rationale for a duration-based bogey may be that a portfolio manager would like his or her risk quantified in terms of an easily understood measure of price/yield sensitivities. Recall that duration is a measure of a fixed-income asset's price sensitivity to a change in yield. Further, many times a bogey is used to determine just how well a portfolio is faring relative to a particular sector of the yield curve.

Clearly, a portfolio manager would like for his or her portfolio to match or outperform the bogey. We know from Part Three that combinations of duration-matched securities may generate very different return profiles, so our portfolio manager will want to identify that portfolio of securities generating the *optimal* return profile for a given duration target.

Most portfolio mangers operate under a variety of guidelines or constraints. Some of those guidelines are formally imposed by a prospectus or board of directors, and others reflect a portfolio manager's individual style. Such guidelines might include limitations on or exclusion of less-than-investment-grade debt (debt with credit ratings of BBB/Baa2 or lower), restrictions on derivative products like futures and options, and/or prohibitions against nondollar securities.

Even among portfolio managers who invest exclusively in Treasuries, certain investment criteria are often imposed. For example, portfolio managers often insist on holding a minimum variety of securities at any one time. Such a requirement could be justified on the grounds that he or she does not want to have all of his or her eggs in one basket. For example, it may not be prudent for a portfolio manager to hold a predominance of high coupon bonds, even though some high coupon bonds might be appropriate for generating current income. The point to be made is that before an optimization model may be used, any constraints must be recognized and incorporated.

Our approach to optimization is rather straightforward. Namely, we generate expected return profiles for all those combinations of fixed-income securities that satisfy our constraints. That one combination of securities generating the best return profile is the optimal portfolio. In Table 13.1, we provide a sample listing of portfolio constraints, and in Table 13.2 we provide a sample methodology to identify an optimal portfolio.

Table 13.1   Constraints for a Treasury Portfolio Designed to Duration-Match the On-the-Run 5-Year Treasury Note

Constraint	Rationale
Total market value of securities must be $200 million	We have $200 million to invest
No short coupons	We want to maintain a relatively liquid portfolio, and one way to achieve this is by excluding less liquid short coupon securities
Minimum amount invested in any one security must be $10 million	Consistent with the point above, we want to maintain a relatively liquid portfolio
No Treasury Bills with three months or less to maturity	We do not want to be active portfolio managers; restricting the minimum maturity of our investments may help to minimize our market activities
No more than 10% of the portfolio's market value may be invested in any one maturity year or security	We want to ensure that our portfolio is diversified along the yield curve and across security types
At least 10% of the portfolio's market value must be allocated to each sector of the yield curve, defined as follows: 3 months to 2 years; 2 years to 5 years; 5 years to 7 years; 7 years to 10 years; and 10 years to 30 years	As with the point above, we want to ensure that our portfolio is diversified along the yield curve
The portfolio is to be duration-matched to the on-the-run 5-year Treasury Note	We do not want an exposure to the market that exceeds the exposure implied by a 5-year Treasury Note's duration

Presumably, an optimal portfolio would be composed of a variety of securities. A variety of securities supports the notion that the portfolio is well diversified and is well positioned for a variety of interest rate scenarios. For example, the presence of STRIPS would be consistent with satisfying a high convexity/aggressive niche, and the presence of high

Table 13.2   A Sample Methodology to Identify an Optimal Portfolio*

Step 1: Generate a log normal yield distribution for every portfolio that is a candidate for the optimal portfolio. Let the mean of the distribution be the standstill yield of the relevant portfolio, and let the standard deviation of the distribution be the bogey security's yield volatility.

Step 2: Use the yields generated by the log normal distributions in Step 1 to calculate expected returns for a given investment horizon. Total returns ought to include capital gains/losses plus coupon income. Note that if the investment horizon is less than one year, then the value for volatility in Step 1 ought to be adjusted accordingly.

Step 3: Total returns calculated in Step 2 are weighted by respective probabilities as implied by the log normal yield distribution.

Step 4: The optimal portfolio is identified by finding that combination of duration-weighted securities generating the greatest expected return subject to the duration target and any other constraints.

* Software is available from the Addison-Wesley and Benjamin-Cummings Publishing Companies for performing monte carlo simulations. The software, @RISK, is an add-on to Lotus 123.

coupon/callable issues is consistent with providing for a current income/defensive niche.

We would expect to find—not surprisingly—that imposing significant constraints results in "optimal" portfolios that are . . . *less* than optimal. This result would not be surprising since the more we limit our portfolio's universe of securities, the more we limit our universe of opportunities.

Table 13.3 provides an example of how probability-weighted expected returns might be generated for a particular duration-weighted portfolio. This type of analysis can be applied to all combinations of securities that satisfy our constraints, and the one portfolio with the best expected return would be our optimal portfolio.

The probabilities in Table 13.3 do not follow a normal distribution. That is, the sum of probabilities above the portfolio's standstill yield is not equal to the sum of probabilities below the portfolio's standstill yield. The term "standstill yield" means the portfolio's bond-equivalent yield at the time probabilities are assigned. The sum of probabilities above the yield is 32.6%, and the sum of probabilities below the yield is 30.6%. If yield levels were best characterized by a normal distribution, then the

Table 13.3   Probability-Weighted Total Returns*

Change in Yield Level (basis points)	Portfolio Return (%)	Probability (%)	Probability-Weighted Portfolio Return (%)
+150	−4.34	0.4	−0.02
+100	−0.76	6.4	−0.05
+50	2.90	25.8	0.75
0	6.64	36.8	2.44
−50	10.47	22.5	2.36
−100	14.39	6.8	0.98
−150	18.40	1.3	0.24
		100.0	**6.70**

* Probability-weighted total return: 6.70%.

sum of probabilities would be equal on either side of the standstill yield. However, yields are often said to exhibit a log normal distribution. Figures 13.1 and 13.2 provide a picture of both normal and log normal distributions. The normal distribution in Figure 13.1 is symmetrical on either side of the standstill yield, and the log normal distribution in Figure 13.2 is asymmetrical on either side of the standstill yield. The reason yields are said to exhibit an asymmetry is that they never take on a negative value. Yields are always positive. Because yields have a natural

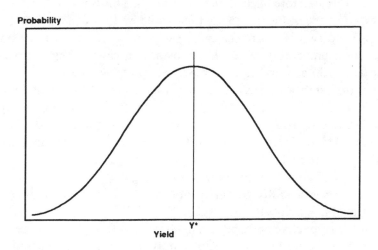

FIGURE 13.1   Normal distribution.

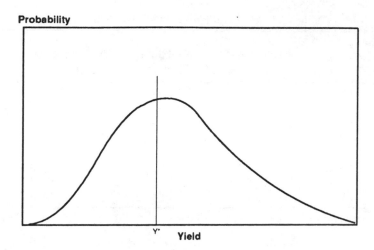

FIGURE 13.2   Log normal distribution.

positive bias, they tend to exhibit an asymmetrical or log normal type of distribution.

Another observation about Table 13.3 is that the highest probabilities are assigned to those yield levels closest to the standstill yield. This is intuitively consistent with the notion that small yield changes around prevailing market levels are more likely than large swings. This is not to say that large swings won't occur. Indeed, to say that would be to assign a probability of zero to yield swings of greater than, say plus or minus 50 basis points. Assigning a probability of any kind to these greater changes in yield is consistent with the view that such moves are possible.

Once probabilities are assigned, how are they used? When total returns are calculated across yield levels, those total return values are multiplied against respective probabilities. Note that the sum of all individual probabilities in Table 13.3 comes to 100%. When probability-weighted total returns are summed, that one number represents 100% of all probable outcomes. In Table 13.3, the probability-weighted total return is 6.70%. Note that the probability-weighted total return exceeds the standstill return by six basis points (6.70% vs. 6.64%).

How are respective probabilities determined? It might be entirely subjective. That is, an investor might simply assign a probability to each yield level. Another more objective method would be to borrow from the market's implied distribution of yield levels. Drawing on information from Part Three, we know that one way to measure the implied distribution of yield levels is to use volatility. Volatility may be thought of as an annualized standard deviation of expected yields.

If we accept that yields exhibit properties consistent with either a normal or log normal distribution, then we can describe a probability distribution with only two variables; a mean and a standard deviation. We let a portfolio's standstill yield proxy as a mean. Thus, with a standstill yield and a yield volatility, we can derive probabilities for a given trading range because there are some universal properties of any normal or log normal distribution. For example, for any normal or log normal distribution, there is a 68.26% likelihood that a variable will take on a value that falls within plus and minus one standard deviation from its mean. Figure 13.3 provides a normal distribution and presents the probability characteristics it implies.

Of course, if an investor has a particular market view that he or she wishes to express with the portfolio, then optimal portfolios may be built

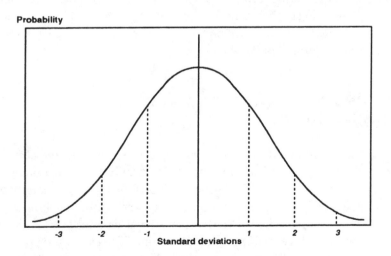

Plus and minus one standard deviation encompasses 68.26% of all expected values. Plus and minus two standard deviations encompasses 95.44% of all expected values. And plus and minus three standard deviations encompasses 99.74% of all expected values.

FIGURE 13.3   Normal distribution with standard deviations.

around such an outlook as well. For example, if our portfolio manager believes that yields will fall in a dramatic way, then probabilities may be skewed toward lower yields to reflect that expectation.

In sum, different combinations of fixed-income securities generate different expected returns, even among duration-matched portfolios. Probability-based optimization models may be of value to identify an optimal duration-weighted portfolio.

Portfolio Duration with Notes and Bonds: Summary

- Different combinations of fixed-income securities generate different expected returns, even among duration-matched portfolios.
- For a portfolio manager whose portfolio is duration-weighted to a particular bogey, it may be desirable to have a model identify the optimal combination of fixed-income assets.
- The more constraints imposed on a given portfolio, the less optimal that portfolio can be expected to perform.
- Probability-based returns may be used to identify the optimal portfolio. Imposing probabilities serves to quantify the likelihood of trading at particular yield levels and may create a meaningful context for creating optimal portfolios.

CREATING PORTFOLIO DURATION WITH TREASURY FUTURES

Just as futures and options may be used to create duration and convexity with individual securities, these products may be used to manage the duration and convexity of fixed-income portfolios. For example, a portfolio manager may believe that a near-term event will cause longer-term yields to rise but that yields will decline soon after. Further, assume that our portfolio manager will have his or her portfolio evaluated within the next few weeks, and his or her bonus will be tied to the portfolio's value. In this instance, the portfolio manager may be interested in reducing his or her portfolio's duration over the near term. It would be a shame to have put in the time and effort to build a solid portfolio with an above-average performance only to be evaluated at a time when yields have risen.

What can our portfolio manager do? Go short some Treasury Bond futures.

When a portfolio manager goes short Treasury bond futures, the duration of a portfolio is shortened. Accordingly, the portfolio's value is less sensitive to parallel shifts in the yield curve. To be more precise, the value of the portfolio is less sensitive to increases in yield at the *long* end of the yield curve. By going short Treasury Bond futures, our portfolio manager is saved from having to sell out a portion of his or her longer-dated cash securities that might later be repurchased.

Conversely, what if our portfolio manager believes longer-term yields will decline yet rise soon after? Go long some Treasury Bond futures. When a portfolio manager goes long Treasury Bond futures, the duration of the portfolio is lengthened. Accordingly, the portfolio's value is more sensitive to parallel shifts in the yield curve. To be more precise, the value of the portfolio is more sensitive to decreases in yield at the long end of the yield curve.

To determine the appropriate number of futures contracts to go long or short to meet a given duration target, we may use Equation 13.1:

$$N = \frac{(Dt \cdot Vt) - (Di \cdot Vi)}{Df \cdot Pf \cdot 1,000} \tag{13.1}$$

where: N = Number of futures contracts to go long (if N is positive) or to go short (if N is negative)

Dt = Target duration of portfolio

Vt = Target market value of portfolio

Di = Initial duration of portfolio

Vi = Initial market value of portfolio

Df = Duration of futures contract

Pf = Price of futures contract

1,000:   Since futures contracts trade at a face value of $100,000 per contract, we multiply the denominator by 1,000 to put the ratio in terms of millions of dollars

For example, assume that a portfolio currently has a market value of $10 million and a duration of 8. Further, assume that the portfolio manager wants to increase the portfolio's duration to 10 while maintaining the portfolio's market value. If the duration of the relevant futures contract is 9.5 and the futures price is 94-13, then the portfolio manager ought to go long 22 futures contracts.

Portfolio managers ought to bear in mind that any calculation involving duration implicitly assumes that the yield curve shifts in a parallel fashion. This is a convenient assumption and rarely characterizes the true behavior of the yield curve on a day-to-day basis. Further, as we have discussed in previous sections, the price sensitivity of a futures contract can change in a dramatic way over time owing to changes in the cheapest-to-deliver security. Thus, a portfolio manager will want to continuously monitor the futures' duration to ensure that the portfolio is neither over- nor underexposed to the market.

Finally, unlike futures contracts, going long an option requires an up-front premium. This is important because anything that changes a portfolio's dollar value (like buying options) will necessarily affect the portfolio's duration. When a long option position is initially added to a portfolio, the duration of the portfolio is changed by both the up-front cost of the option *and* the option's duration. In contrast, when a long futures position is initially added to a portfolio, the duration of the portfolio is changed but at no dollar cost except for posting margin. And as we have said previously, margin may be posted in the form of interest-bearing assets. Since a given portfolio is likely to hold those interest bearing assets required for posting margin, a simple transfer of assets may be made from the portfolio to the margin account. In this instance, a future's contribution to the portfolio's duration is a function of the future's duration alone. For this reason, options contracts generally are not as attractive as futures contracts for duration management. However, options are popular vehicles for managing convexity.

Futures Options and Convexity

To use options to create convexity for a fixed-income portfolio, the principle is the same as discussed in Part Three for individual securities. In short, purchasing options is consistent with going long convexity, and selling options is consistent with going short convexity. Thus, to give a portfolio a little "kick" when a dramatic change is expected in yields, going long calls and/or puts may be appropriate. Namely, a portfolio manager would want to buy calls to enhance convexity when yields are expected to fall, and to buy puts when yields are expected to rise. And as stated in Part Three, a variety of scenarios ought to be considered to evaluate the best possible strategy. These scenarios would include various assumptions on volatility, investment horizons, and yield levels.

Portfolio Duration with Fixed-Income: Summary

- Just as futures and options may be used to manage the duration and convexity of individual securities, these products may be used to manage the duration and convexity of fixed-income portfolios.
- Owing to the unique price behavior of derivative products, portfolio managers ought to continuously monitor respective durations and convexities. Further, a variety of scenarios ought to be evaluated to identify the most appropriate strategy.

CREATING PORTFOLIO DURATION WITH INTEREST RATE SWAPS

The previous section explained how futures contracts may be used to modify a portfolio's duration. This section describes how an interest rate swap may be used to achieve the same objective.

With an interest rate swap, a stream of fixed-rate cashflows is exchanged for a stream of floating-rate cashflows, or vice versa. If a portfolio manager is of the view that the yield curve will steepen, he or she may have an interest in preserving the market value of his or her portfolio. For example, the greater value of the portfolio may lie at the long end of the yield curve. When a yield curve steepens, shorter-term yields generally decline and longer-term yields rise. Thus, securities at the short end of the yield curve appreciate in value, while securities at the long end of the yield curve depreciate in value. Instead of shortening duration by selling Treasury Bond futures contracts, our portfolio manager could buy an interest rate swap. When an investor is long an interest rate swap, he or she receives fixed-rate cashflows and pays floating-rate cashflows.

Figure 13.4 shows how the yield curve might steepen, and Figure 13.5 shows the return profile for our interest rate swap.

We can see from Figure 13.5 that a positive return is earned if the floating rate falls relative to the fixed rate. In Figure 13.4, the steepening of the yield curve appears more or less centered around the 5-year Treasury Note yield. Thus, if the interest rate swap is structured such that

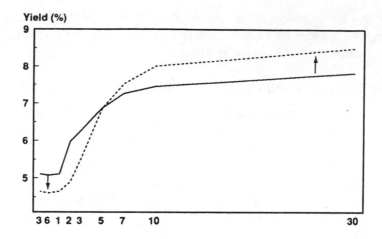

FIGURE 13.4   Yield curve steepens.

fixed-rate cashflows are linked to the 5-year Treasury Note yield and floating-rate cashflows are linked to the 3-month Treasury Bill yield, then a profit is earned as the yield curve steepens. The profit earned on the interest rate swap would serve to offset any loss incurred on the longer-dated securities.

If the interest rate swap is to be the duration-management vehicle of choice, what should be the notional value of the swap? Every basis point

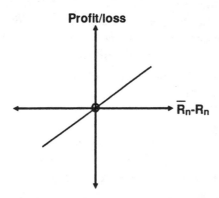

FIGURE 13.5   Profit/loss profile for an interest rate swap. Investor receives fixed ($\overline{R}n$) and pays floating (Rn).

differential on an interest rate swap is equal to a dollar value of 0.01% times the notional value of the swap. Thus, all our investor needs to do is to provide his or her best guess of the market value at risk. For example, let's say our investor determines that $1 million of the portfolio is at risk if the yield curve steepens in the way he or she expects. Accordingly, our investor might want a notional value of a swap that would generate $1 million in revenue as the yield curve steepens.

Assume that the interest rate swap is structured so that our investor receives the 5-year Treasury Note yield fixed and pays the 3-month Treasury Bill yield floating. Further, assume that our investor expects the spread between the 5-year Treasury Note and 3-month Treasury Bill to widen by 20 basis points as the yield curve steepens. Since 0.2% times $500 million is equal to $1 million, our investor would presumably want a notional swap value of about $500 million.

Now that we see how an interest rate swap may be used to manage duration, why would we use this vehicle instead of cash securities or futures contracts? One reason may be that interest rate swaps are off-balance sheet products. That is, banking institutions are not required to report forward products on their balance sheets. "Forward products" refers to futures, options, swaps, forwards, standby commitments, and letters of credit— anything that embodies a forward transaction in an underlying asset(s). As to using an interest rate swap instead of futures contracts, a portfolio manager may be prohibited from using derivative products. Finally, futures contracts are marked-to-market on a daily basis, whereas payments on interest rate swaps are net out at regular, predetermined intervals.

Portfolio Duration with Interest Rate Swaps: Summary

- An interest rate swap may be viable alternative to futures contracts as a duration-management vehicle.
- To determine the appropriate notional value of a swap, it is desirable that the investor have an idea of the portfolio's market value at risk.
- An incentive for using an interest rate swap instead of cash securities to manage duration may be that an interest rate swap is an off-balance sheet transaction. That is, for a banking institution, forward products are not required to be recorded on the balance sheet. Further, a portfolio manager may be prohibited from using derivative products or may not like the mark-to-market requirements of a futures contract.

14
Designing Portfolio Returns

Before delving too deeply into the topic of designing portfolio returns, we ought to acknowledge that there are a variety of opinions about the nature of return distributions. The prevailing school of thought argues that expected returns are best characterized by a normal distribution. (Figure 13.1 shows a normal distribution.)

What is striking about Figure 13.1—also known as a bell curve—is that it is symmetrical. If we were to draw a line down the middle of the distribution at the risk-free rate of return, the right half would be the mirror image of the left half. This property is tantamount to asserting that there is an equal likelihood of generating higher or lower returns relative to the risk-free rate over time. Higher returns would be associated with the right half of the distribution while lower returns would be associated with the left half of the distribution. And since the distribution is symmetrical, the probability of higher returns is 50% and the probability of lower returns is 50%. The notion that a given investment has a 50/50 chance of generating a return superior to the risk-free rate at any given point along the investment horizon has an intuitive appeal.

In Figure 14.1 we show hypothetical normal distributions for 2- and 10-year Treasury note total returns at time of issue for a 1-month horizon. The wider 10-year distribution is explained by its greater modified duration relative to the 2-year.

Probability

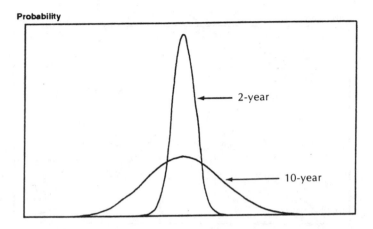

2-year

10-year

FIGURE 14.1 Normal distribution.

If returns are best characterized by a normal distribution, what does this imply for fixed-income prices and yields? Statistical theory suggests that if a variable is best characterized as exhibiting a normal distribution in percentage changes (total returns), then it is probably best characterized as log normal in levels (prices or yields). Figure 14.2 presents a log normal distribution.

What is immediately obvious about Figure 14.2 is that it is not symmetrical. If we were to draw a line through the part of the distribution that splits probabilities into two equal pieces, those two pieces would not be mirror images.

Normal and log normal distributions are statistical benchmarks that are rarely if ever replicated in the real world. If variables like yield, price, or expected returns happen to *approximate* a particular type of distribution, then imposing that distribution may serve to greatly simplify the quantitative tasks of modelling a given process. However, such an imposition is a statistical convenience, and the reader should not think that real-world variables always fit into a given distribution in any complete or consistent way.

Figure 14.3 shows a histogram for a 10-year Treasury Note from January 1990 to October 1991. A histogram provides a picture of how often a variable takes on particular values over time. For example, we see from

Probability

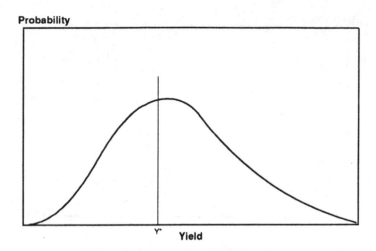

FIGURE 14.2 Log normal distribution.

Figure 14.3 that the 10-year Treasury Note yield traded near 8.2% about 25% of the time.

Figure 14.3 might best be described as being more log normal than normal. Note that we are taking pains not to say that the distribution is definitively log normal, just that it appears to be more log normal than normal. What is the intuition behind this? For one thing, a yield cannot

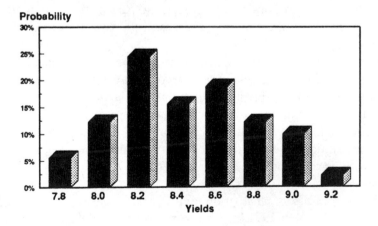

FIGURE 14.3 Histogram for 10-year Treasury Note yields. January 1990–October 1991.

be negative. An expected return may be negative, but a yield cannot be negative.

If we accept the notion that yields are distributed as log normal, what does this imply for price distributions? One response might be that since yields drive prices and vice versa, a log normal distribution for yields must imply a log normal distribution for prices.

But let's not forget about convexity. We know from Part One that convexity enhances a security's price appreciation when yields fall, and cushions a security's price depreciation when yields rise. In the absence of convexity, we would expect a linear relationship between price and yield. Albeit, a linear relationship that changes over time as a security approaches maturity. Specifically, the price/yield relationship will become less elastic as maturity approaches and duration shortens. Thus, in the absence of convexity, we would expect prices to be characterized by a log normal distribution.

In the presence of convexity, we would not expect a linear relationship between price and yield. With convexity, a given change in yield would result in a larger proportional change in price when yields fall relative to when yields rise. Accordingly, we would expect the price/yield dynamics of a high convexity security to exhibit less of a linear relationship relative to a low convexity security. We might even expect the price distribution of a highly convex security to appear more normal than log normal. The limited price appreciation imposed by non-negative yields would be countered in part by the price-enhancing properties of convexity as yields rise. Thus, with convexity, we might expect prices to be characterized by a more normal looking distribution.

In sum, for any discussions involving probability distributions, references to normality or log normality are for purposes of illustration only. It is doubtful that the variable being discussed has a normal or log normal distribution in the truest sense of the terms. However, assuming that a variable may be approximated by one distribution or another may greatly simplify the operations required to generate a solution of some kind. Just don't neglect these assumptions when acting on the solution.

OPTIONS

In Chapter 10, we stated that put options appreciate in value as yields rise. A price/return profile for a put option at expiration is shown in

Figure 14.4. Returns improve as the price of the underlying security declines.

Figure 14.5 shows the price/yield profile for a cash Treasury security combined with an at-the-money put option. The put option serves as a cushion of sorts to protect returns against a dramatic fall in yields. In fact, combining a put with a cash Treasury security generates a profit/loss profile that resembles a long call.

Finally, Figure 14.6 presents probability distributions for expected returns on a Treasury Bond with and without put protection. The term "put protection" refers to an out-of-the-money put to ensure against rising yields.

In Figure 14.6, distribution A is normal and distribution B is skewed. The downside protection in distribution B is created with the put option. Upside potential is preserved while downside risk is limited. The cost of the downside protection is reflected in the relatively lower expected return of Rb relative to Ra.

As we will see in Part Five, a call option may be created with a put option and an underlying cash position. Thus, distribution B is broadly consistent with the return distribution for a call option.

Just as a put option may be combined with an individual security to design a security's expected return distribution, a put option may be combined with a *portfolio* of securities to redesign a portfolio's expected return distribution. Why would a portfolio manager be interested in designing his or her portfolio's expected returns? Perhaps because the peace of mind of limiting losses to some predetermined return is worth its cost. To determine a strike price(s) for the put option(s), our portfolio

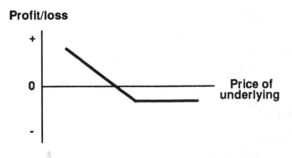

FIGURE 14.4   Profit/loss profile for a put option.

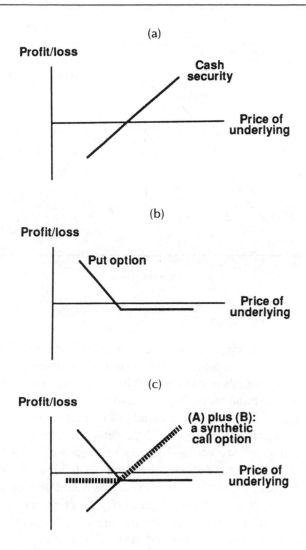

FIGURE 14.5 Creating a synthetic call option with a cash security and a put option.

manager must identify the minimum desirable portfolio return. Since that minimum portfolio return presumably corresponds to a particular market scenario—for example, yields fall by 50 basis points along the yield curve—the strike price(s) would have to be consistent with that market level generating the minimum desired portfolio return.

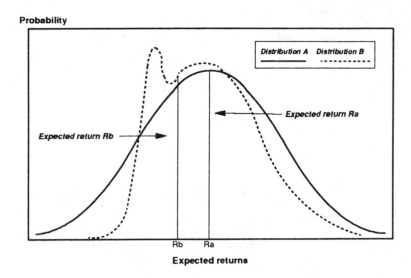

FIGURE 14.6   Distribution of portfolio returns.

The task of identifying a strike price(s) may be considerable. For example, a portfolio manager may wish to make various assumptions as to the nature of the portfolio's dynamics should yields rise. That is, yields may rise more by way of a steepening in the yield curve as opposed to near-parallel shifts. After evaluating a variety of market scenarios, a portfolio manager would perhaps be better able to determine the precise nature of his or her desired put protection. Further, this analysis would presumably address the issue of how to choose the appropriate blend of options so as to afford the best protection. For example, would put options across various segments of the portfolio's maturity range be more meaningful than put options at the long end of the maturity range alone? Concentrating put options among longer-dated securities would perhaps be most appropriate for a steepening yield curve.

In sum, a portfolio manager will want to allow for a margin of error and may want to consider contingency plans for purposes of fine-tuning an initial outlook.

Aside from designing portfolio expected returns with a portfolio of fixed-income assets and put options, an investor may synthetically create a fixed-income portfolio distribution with Treasury Bills and call options.

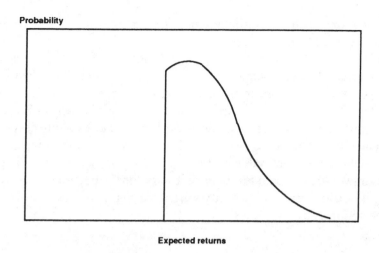

FIGURE 14.7   Distribution of portfolio returns.

Figure 14.7 shows an expected return probability distribution for a portfolio invested 90% in Treasury Bills and 10% in at-the-money call options. Just as we discussed with the put option strategy above, a portfolio manager's choice of options is quite important for our synthetic approach. Namely, the expected nature of a potential change in yields may affect the decision regarding the call options' underlying securities.

FIXED-INCOME PORTFOLIO PLUS PUT OPTIONS

Perhaps the greatest advantage of using put options is that delta will serve as an automatic safety valve. As discussed in Part Three, delta is a measure of an option's exposure to the price of the underlying security. The term "automatic safety valve" means that the delta of a put option increases as rates rise, and decreases as rates fall. Since a put option trades to a *short* position in the underlying security, the floating value of delta acts to *decrease* duration when rates *rise* and *increase* duration when rates *fall*. This is exactly the kind of protection we want. Related to the floating properties of delta, there may be less monitoring and fewer adjustments required over time when working with options instead of synthetic options created with forward/cash combinations. Further, forward/cash combinations require continuous monitoring to ensure an appropriate exposure to the marketplace.

As to the disadvantages of using put options, desired strike prices on exchange-traded options may not be available, or volume (and hence, liquidity) may not be deep in the strike prices of interest. And if over-the-counter (OTC) options are used, liquidity may be of concern. Finally, if put options are used, an investor would have paid more than necessary for the portfolio insurance if the realized volatility were anything less than that implicit in the option's cost. Of course, this may go the other way. An investor would have paid less than necessary for the portfolio insurance if the put option's realized volatility were anything more than that implicit in the option's cost.

TREASURY BILLS PLUS CALL OPTIONS

This strategy would probably have the greatest appeal to a portfolio manager who wants a limited, protected exposure to the fixed-income marketplace. For example, a portfolio manager may be primarily responsible for capturing investment opportunities in the equity market, yet wants a manageable exposure to an expected rally in notes and bonds. Thus, rather than take the time to selectively build a fixed-income portfolio of cash securities, our portfolio manager might simply buy Treasury Bills and a selection of fixed-income call options.

A disadvantage of this strategy may be that the portfolio manager is only as diversified as the relative number and type of call options purchased. If a portfolio manager limits himself/herself to exchange-traded futures options, 10-year Treasury Note and Bond futures options are about the only securities with sufficient liquidity. If the portfolio manager goes the route of over-the-counter options, then liquidity may be a concern.

THEORY VERSUS PRACTICE

This chapter concludes with a comment on designing portfolio returns in the context of financial theory.

Modern Portfolio Theory (MPT) generally asserts that investors choose among efficient portfolios on a mean-variance basis. That is, there is a trade-off between risk and return. Intuitively, this makes perfect sense. The greater our expected risk, the more we would expect to be compensated for taking on that risk. An expected return is generally proxied by the mean of historical returns. Expected risk is generally proxied by the standard deviation of historical returns.

MPT posits that all else being equal, investors will choose among those portfolios generating the greatest expected return for the lowest expected risk.

Figure 14.8 shows what is commonly referred to as the efficient frontier. The efficient frontier traces out optimal portfolios constructed on the basis of a mean-variance methodology.

In Figure 14.8, portfolio D is inefficient because it lies inside the efficient frontier. It is possible to move to a higher expected return for the same level of risk by shifting from portfolio D to portfolio B.

Point A in Figure 14.8 is the so-called minimum variance portfolio (MVP). It is generally reserved for the safe asset. For our purposes, the MVP consists of Treasury Bills. Moving to the northeast, we come to portfolio B, which has a greater expected risk relative to portfolio A but also has a greater expected return. Portfolio B consists of Treasury Bonds. Portfolio C has call options.

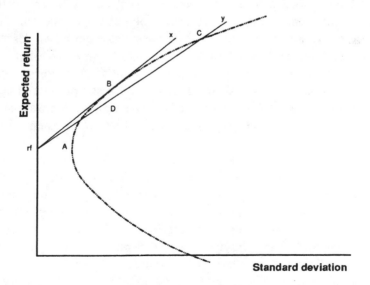

FIGURE 14.8 Efficient frontier.

By drawing a line from the risk-free rate (r_f) to portfolios along the efficient frontier, it is possible to identify respective expected risk/return combinations. For example, line x is tangent to portfolio B, and any point along line x represents a unique combination of Treasury Bills and Treasury Bonds. Since Treasury Bonds are presumably riskier than Treasury Bills, moving to the northeast along line x would suggest that we own fewer Treasury Bills and more Treasury Bonds. Expected risks and returns increase accordingly.

Similarly, line y intersects portfolio C. Any point along line y represents a combination of Treasury Bills and call options. This combination of Treasury Bills and call options is consistent with the Treasury Bills plus call options strategy considered above. Since call options are presumably riskier than Treasury Bills, moving to the northeast along line y would suggest that we own fewer Treasury Bills and more call options. Expected risks and returns increase accordingly.

The reader will now observe that portfolios consisting of Treasury Bills and call options (line y) are inefficient relative to portfolios consisting of Treasury Bills and Treasury Bonds (line x). For example, portfolio D lies below portfolio B. Portfolio D is inefficient because it lies below the efficient frontier.

Recall that only two criteria are required to define an efficient portfolio: mean and variance. A desirable implication of only caring about mean and variance is that these are the only two variables required to describe a normal or log normal distribution. However, the whole idea behind redesigning portfolio returns is that we do not want normal or even log normal distributions. We want distributions that are sharply biased against negative returns and biased in favor of positive returns. We want skewed distributions. We want an expected return distribution consistent with distribution B in Figure 14.6.

In sum, a portfolio of Treasury Bills and call options is inefficient in a MPT framework, partly because the distribution of a Treasury Bill/call option combination is not normal. It is positively skewed and, therefore cannot be described in a mean-variance framework. A higher moment—namely, skewness—is required to describe the distribution adequately. Thus, although MPT may imply that our Treasury Bill/call option combination is inefficient, it may very well be an efficient and desirable strategy for a fixed-income portfolio manager. For this reason, we might say that MPT suffers from its two-dimensional view of the world. Incorporating skewness into portfolio theory is a challenge for future generations of financial theorists and practitioners.

Portfolio Returns Summary

- It is commonly accepted that fixed-income total returns are best characterized with a normal distribution, though rarely if ever does any variable fit neatly into a given distribution in the strictest sense.
- Portfolio returns may be designed in a variety of ways with pros and cons of each methodology.
- An advantage of designing portfolio returns with put options is that delta floats with price changes in the underlying security. A disadvantage of using put options may be that exchange-determined strike prices and/or OTC liquidity constraints may be of concern.
- An advantage of designing portfolio returns with cash/forward or cash/futures combinations is that a flexibility is available that is not afforded by a true option. A disadvantage is that a synthetic option requires constant monitoring.
- Treasury Bills may be combined with call options to replicate a fixed-income portfolio with put protection. Such a strategy may be appropriate for an investor who desires a measured exposure to the fixed-income marketplace.
- MPT suggests that a portfolio of cash securities and options may be inefficient because MPT evaluates portfolios in a mean-variance framework. The whole idea behind adding options to a fixed-income portfolio may very well be to skew total returns. Thus, for portfolio strategies that attempt to go beyond the mean-variance framework consistent with normally distributed variables, MPT will tag these strategies as inefficient.

15

Creating a Synthetic Fixed-Income Portfolio

BETA

Beta is a popular tool among investors in the equity market, and can be a valuable input when creating fixed-income portfolios. Beta is a statistical measure of the expected increase in the value of one variable for a one-unit increase in the value of another variable. The formula for beta is*

$$\beta = cov(a,b) / \sigma^2(b) \tag{15.1}$$

$$cov(a,b) = \rho(a,b) \cdot \sigma(a) \cdot \sigma(b)$$

where: σ^2 = Sigma squared, variance; standard deviation squared
ρ = Rho, correlation coefficient
σ = Sigma, standard deviation; an annualized standard deviation is commonly known as a measure of historical volatility

Since we'll be referring to these variables time and again, let's review them in some detail.

* Calculating a beta can be achieved with an ordinary least squares (OLS) regression. Consistent with the central limit theorem, any OLS regression ought to have a minimum of about 30 observations per series. Further, an investor ought to be aware of the assumptions inherent in any OLS regression analysis. These assumptions—predominantly concerned with randomness—are provided in any basic statistics text.

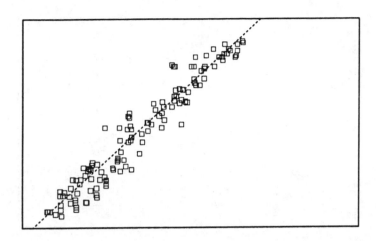

FIGURE 15.1   Positive correlation.

A *correlation coefficient* is a statistical measure of the relationship between two variables. A correlation coefficient can range in value between positive one and negative one. A positive correlation coefficient with a value near one suggests that the two variables are closely related and tend to move in tandem. A negative correlation coefficient with a value near one suggests that two variables are closely related and tend to move opposite one another. A correlation coefficient with a value near zero—regardless of

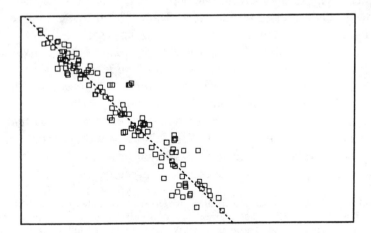

FIGURE 15.2   Negative correlation.

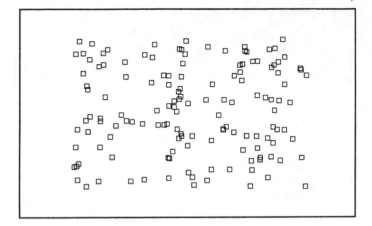

FIGURE 15.3 Zero correlation.

its sign—suggests that the two variables have little in common, and tend to behave independently of one another. Figures 15.1, 15.2, and 15.3 provide graphical representations of positive, negative, and zero correlations.

A *standard deviation* is a measure of a variable's variability or volatility. If a variable takes on a rather wide (narrow) range of values, its standard deviation will probably be relatively large (small).

Finally, *variance* is obtained by simply squaring a standard deviation. Variance is said to be a measure of dispersion.

Now let's consider some examples. Table 15.1 provides two series of data and two beta values that correspond to those series.

A cursory view of the data in Table 15.1 supports the beta values we have calculated. For example, series C and D appear to move in tandem. Further, it seems that series D tends to move by larger amounts than series C. Thus, it is not surprising that the beta is positive for this pair of variables and that the beta is greater than one. This tells us that for a one-unit change in the value of variable C, we would expect a 1.33-unit change in the value of variable D. Statistical tests can be performed to provide some measure of confidence for a given beta's value.*

---

* Confidence intervals, or interval estimates, provide a range of beta values that are likely to contain the true beta value. For a given level of significance, say .05, the confidence intervals are constructed so that the probability that the interval contains the true beta is equal to one minus the level of significance. A significance level of .05 would thus correspond to a probability of 95%. Details of these types of tests are provided in most basic statistic texts.

Table 15.1 Beta Values

A	B	C	D
0.7	21.0	0.3	0.0
1.5	20.3	1.2	1.2
2.3	19.6	2.1	2.4
3.1	18.9	3.0	3.6
3.9	18.2	3.9	4.8
4.7	17.5	4.8	6.0
5.5	16.8	5.7	7.2
6.3	16.1	6.6	8.4
7.1	15.4	7.5	9.6
7.9	14.7	8.4	10.8
8.7	14.0	9.3	12.0
9.5	13.3	10.2	13.2
10.3	12.6	11.1	14.4
11.1	11.9	12.0	15.6
11.9	11.2	12.9	16.8
12.7	10.5	13.8	18.0
13.5	9.8	14.7	19.2
14.3	9.1	15.6	20.4
15.1	8.4	16.5	21.6
15.9	7.7	17.4	22.8
16.7	7.0	18.3	24.0
17.5	6.3	19.2	25.2
18.3	5.6	20.1	26.4
19.1	4.9	21.0	27.6
19.9	4.2	21.9	28.8
20.7	3.5	22.8	30.0
21.5	2.8	23.7	31.2
22.3	2.1	24.6	32.4
23.1	1.4	25.5	33.6
23.9	0.7	26.4	34.8
Beta = −0.875		**Beta = 1.33**	

Conversely, series A and B appear to move opposite one another. Further, it seems that series B tends to move by smaller amounts than series A. Thus, we are not surprised to see that the beta is negative for this pair of variables and that the beta is less than one. This tells us that for a one-unit change in variable A, we expect a −0.875 unit change in the value of variable B.

A popular beta among equity investors is the beta that measures the behavior of price changes in a given equity against changes in a market index such as the Standard and Poor's (S&P) 500. The S&P 500 is a composite of 500 stocks that trade on the New York Stock Exchange. The index is widely regarded as a performance measure of the stock market as a whole. Thus, if a stock's beta is, say 1.75, the stock might be considered to be relatively risky. That is, for a 1 percent change in the S&P 500, the stock's price would be expected to change by 1.75%.

An investor with an interest in comparing betas across stocks will find the comparison is more meaningful if respective betas cover the same period using the same number of observations. For example, if an investor wants to evaluate the beta of the XYZ company relative to the QRS company over a period of one month, then daily data ought to be used for each series against the S&P 500 using the same month's worth of data.

Now that we have an idea of what beta is and how it may be used, we will show how a basket of *stocks* might be used to create a synthetic portfolio of notes and bonds.

CREATING A BASKET

A number of equities are considered to behave much like fixed-income securities. For example, utility stock prices are generally considered to be sensitive to interest rates. The rationale is twofold. First, utilities are generally dependent on debt to finance operations. Thus, if interest rates decline, then the cost of debt financing should also decline; the value of utility equity would be expected to appreciate. Second, utility stocks typically pay out relatively high dividends. Accordingly, many investors will look to utility stocks as an alternative to fixed-income markets for purposes of generating current income. With declining interest rates, prices of utility stocks may be bid higher as investors sell low-yielding fixed-income securities and move into higher-yielding utility stocks.

Once we have identified a basket of equities that may be sensitive to interest rates, we can then calculate respective betas. The betas would be calculated by pairing the log of daily equity price levels against daily yield levels. Since yield is a measure of return, we convert equity price levels into logs so as to express this series as a measure of return as well.

If we assume that the yield curve shifts in a parallel fashion, then it might be argued that it really doesn't matter what interest rate series is used to

Table 15.2   Reasons for Using On-the-Run 10-Year Treasury
Yields for Calculating Utility Stock Betas

1. Treasury yields are "clean"; on-the-run 10-year Treasury yields would not be subject to the exigencies of perceived credit risks, embedded options, or other bells and whistles sometimes associated with corporate securities.

2. Longer-dated yields tend to be much less volatile over time relative to shorter-dated yields, so it would be our *a priori* expectation that the relatively stable sector of utility stocks would more closely pattern a low-volatility yield series.

3. Utility debt issues tend to have longer maturities relative to other industry sectors; a longer-dated yield series would probably be more appropriate to capture the utility industry's debt-financing sensitivities.

4. When investors look to utility stocks as an alternative to fixed-income opportunities, they tend to view them as substitutes for longer-dated issues like a 10-year note as opposed to something like a 3-month Treasury Bill. For example, Treasury Bills do not pay coupons (dividends), but Treasury Notes do.

calculate our betas.* However, the yield curve rarely moves in a parallel fashion. The yield curve tends to bob and weave from one shape to another. Thus, we would presumably do better to allocate equity issues to different interest rate buckets on an *a priori* basis where each bucket represents a sector of the yield curve. For our utility stocks, we would probably want to go with a longer-dated yield series like on-the-run 10-year Treasury yields. Reasons for using this longer-dated yield series are presented in Table 15.2.

Among other things, because utility stocks generally pay dividends on a regular basis (akin to coupon payments) and presumably have a long life (like a note or bond), a longer-dated yield series would appear to be most appropriate.

Figure 15.4, shows the price/yield relationship for the S&P utility stock index against an on-the-run 10-year Treasury yield series and also provides the R-square (R^2) value. R^2 is the square of the correlation coefficient of a given equity and yield series, and it measures the accuracy of a straight line

---

* If the slope of the yield curve has a pronounced slope, then the choice of yield series could be quite important, even with parallel shifts. With parallel shifts in a steep yield curve, relative changes will be greater at the short end of the yield curve relative to the long end of the yield curve.

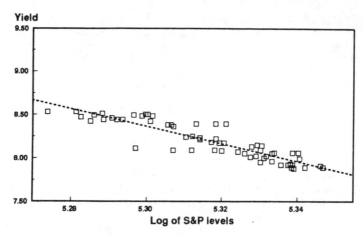

The regression spans July 1991 to October 1991, and daily data are used. R^2 is 0.814, and the standard error is 0.62. Beta is significant at the 0.5% level.

FIGURE 15.4   Yield level versus S&P utility index.

fit as determined by historical regression analysis. As with a correlation coefficient, R^2 may range in value between zero and one. Unlike a correlation coefficient, R^2 is always positive. The closer an R^2's absolute value to one, the tighter the relationship between two series. To discern if our variables of interest have a direct or offsetting relationship, we need to consider the sign of the beta value. If beta is positive, then the two variables have a direct relationship with one another; one variable tends to move in tandem with the other. If beta is negative, then the two variables are offsetting; one variable tends to move opposite the other.

We can see from Figure 15.4 that the R^2 value is reasonably close to a value of one, and the beta is negative. Specifically, R^2 is 0.814. The fact that beta is negative is consistent with the inverse price/yield relationship we would expect for fixed-income securities. The fact that R^2 is close to a value of one suggests that the price/yield relationship is meaningful statistically.

To help demonstrate that there is a unique relationship between utility stocks and interest rates, we also regress the S&P composite index against 10-year yields for the same time period. Results are shown in Figure 15.5.

As we can see from Figure 15.5, the statistical relationship between the S&P composite and interest rates is rather weak. The S&P composite includes equities from every industry sector. Although the composite beta is

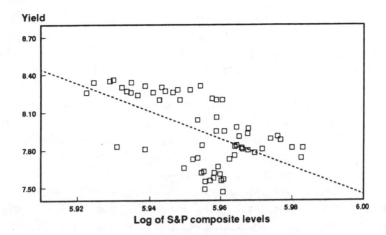

The regression spans July 1991 to October 1991, and daily data are used. R^2 is 0.338, and the standard error is 1.96. Beta is significant at the 0.5% level.

FIGURE 15.5   Yield level versus S&P composite index.

negative, the composite R^2 is but 0.338.* In sum, we demonstrate that there is a statistically significant relationship between utility stocks and yield, and that this relationship does not necessarily hold for a composite of stocks against yield.

Once we have identified a basket of utility and/or other stocks that behave much like fixed-income securities, the question becomes which bundle would an investor prefer to own: A basket of synthetic fixed-income securities created with stocks or a basket of fixed-income securities? The question is deceptively simple. When an investor purchases any fixed-income security, is he or she purchasing it because it's a fixed-income security or because it embodies the desired characteristics of a fixed-income security (i.e., pays periodic coupons, holds capital value, etc.)? If it's because he or she wants a fixed-income security, then there is nothing more to discuss. The investor will buy the bundle of fixed-income securities. However, if he or she simply desires the characteristics of a fixed-

* As further evidence in support of a stronger link between utility stocks and interest rates, the standard error of the utility beta is 0.62. This is in contrast to the standard error of the composite beta of 1.96. Generally speaking, the smaller the standard error of a beta, the stronger the statistical relationship between the two variables.

income security, then we have a great deal more to talk about. Namely, if it is possible to generate fixed-income returns with non-fixed-income products, why not do so? And if it is possible to *outperform* traditional fixed-income products with non-fixed-income securities, why ever buy another note or bond?

Again, if the investor is constrained to hold only fixed-income products, then the choice is clear; he or she may only hold the true fixed-income portfolio. If the investor wants only to create a fixed-income exposure to the marketplace and is indifferent as to how this is achieved, then there are choices to make. How could an investor choose between a true and synthetic fixed-income portfolio? Perhaps on the basis of historical risk/return profiles. If the synthetic fixed-income portfolio is able to outperform the true fixed-income portfolio on a consistent basis at the same or a lower level of risk, then an investor might want seriously to consider owning the synthetic portfolio. A compromise would perhaps be to own a mix of the true and synthetic portfolios.

A theory that may serve as a guide to evaluate risk/return relationships for our true and synthetic portfolios is known as the Capital Asset Pricing Model, or CAPM.

CAPITAL ASSET PRICING MODEL

The CAPM embodies a theory about the way securities are priced relative to their risk. In essence, the theory is based on the premise that all investors use Markowitz portfolio theory to identify efficient portfolios. An investor's choice of a particular efficient portfolio is determined by the risk appetite of that investor.

Markowitz portfolio theory posits that efficient portfolios are defined as those combinations of assets generating the maximum levels of return for a given level of risk. Figure 15.6 shows the well-known Markowitz bullet.

Figure 15.6 suggests that there is a trade-off between risk and reward. For example, as we move from portfolio A to portfolio B, we have a higher expected return but with a greater standard deviation of return. The standard deviation of return is a proxy for risk.

The line or *frontier* that connects portfolios A, B, and C has a special significance. This frontier is called the efficient frontier, and it embodies all combinations of efficient portfolios. The term "efficient portfolio"

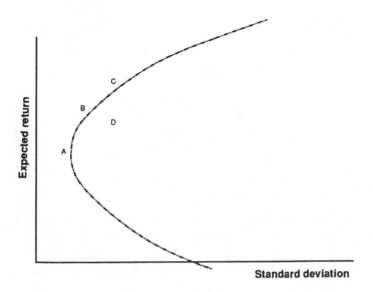

FIGURE 15.6   Efficient frontier.

means that combination of securities generating the maximum possible return for a given level of risk. Portfolio D lies inside the efficient frontier, and it is an inefficient portfolio. Portfolio D is an inefficient portfolio because it has the same level of risk as portfolio C, yet it has a lower expected return. For the same level of risk, an investor could hold portfolio C and earn a higher return.

To generate a frontier of efficient portfolios like the one shown in Figure 15.6, it is necessary to accept a few assumptions.

Assumption One: Investors can choose among portfolios on the basis of expected returns and standard deviations.

Investors can choose among portfolios on the basis of expected returns and standard deviations if either one of two conditions holds. The first condition is that the probability distributions for portfolio returns are all normally distributed. The second condition is that the relationship between an investor's utility and the value of his or her portfolio is quadratic in form. Let's examine these two conditions in greater detail:

Normal Distributions.   Figures 15.7, 15.8, and 15.9 show three probability distributions. Figure 15.7 is normal, Figure 15.8 is positively skewed, and Figure 15.9 is negatively skewed. If we know that a given

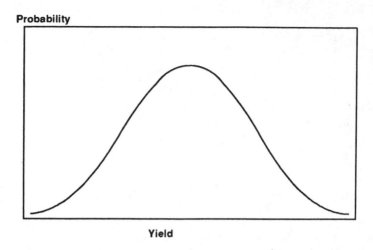

FIGURE 15.7   Normal distribution.

probability distribution is normal, then it is possible to draw the distribution if its expected return (mean) and standard deviation are known.
If a given probability distribution is not normal or log normal, then
more information is required to draw the distribution. A distribution's
mean and variance are known as the first two moments of a distribu-

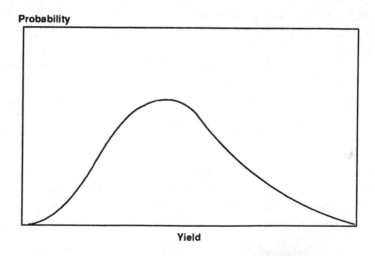

FIGURE 15.8   Positively skewed distribution.

Probability

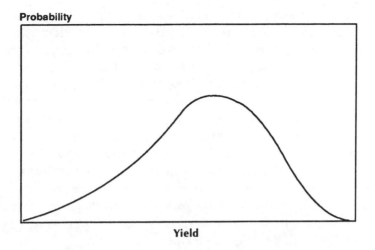

Yield

FIGURE 15.9 Negatively skewed distribution.

tion. To draw a distribution that is not normal, higher moments may be required. That is, the third and fourth moments may be required. The third moment is known as skewness, and the fourth moment is known as kurtosis.

Assuming that investors choose among portfolios on the basis of expected returns and standard deviations alone presumes that investors are indifferent to skewness. This is probably not a realistic assumption if a particular portfolio's returns are skewed (biased toward) positive returns. An investor would presumably prefer to hold a portfolio biased toward positive returns than to hold a portfolio whose returns are normally distributed.

A variety of studies have been done to determine the distribution of security returns. Conclusions generally suggest that returns over short periods of time (daily or weekly) may exhibit some skewness, while returns over long periods of time (monthly or longer) tend to be more normally distributed. Thus, we can generally accept the assumption that returns are normally distributed.

Quadratic Utility Functions. For an investor with a quadratic utility function, the utility that he or she expects to get from a portfolio comes from its expected value and standard deviation. Figure 15.10 shows concentric circles as plotted against expected returns and standard deviations. Each line is called an indifference curve and represents a level of utility. As an investor moves northwest to ever-higher levels of utility, he or she is moving into more desirable portfolios. On any one curve, an investor is indifferent to all risk/return combinations. For example, portfolio A and portfolio B have the same level of utility. Although portfolio B is *riskier* than portfolio A, portfolio B has a *higher* expected return. The higher expected return associated with portfolio B is enough to make our investor indifferent between holding this portfolio at a greater risk relative to portfolio A with a lower risk/return combination.

Assumption Two: All investors plan their investments over a single period of time that is the same for everyone, and all investors agree on the values for inputs used to employ the Markowitz model.

These inputs would include expected returns, standard deviations, and covariances. To calculate the return of a two-asset portfolio, we simply sum across asset returns weighted by an asset's portfolio value. For example, assume that asset A generates a return of 10% while asset B generates a return of 4%. Further, assume that portfolio weights are such that 70% of the portfolio is invested in asset A while 30% of the portfolio is invested in asset B.

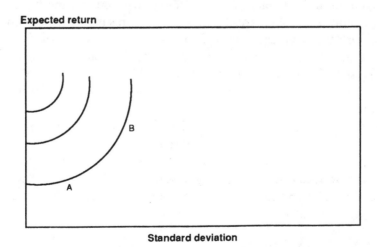

FIGURE 15.10   Quadratic utility.

To calculate the portfolio's return we simply solve for

$$Rp = Ra \cdot Wa + Rb \cdot Wb \qquad\qquad (15.2)$$

$$Rp = 10\% \cdot 0.70 + 4\% \cdot 0.30$$

$$= 8.2\%$$

where: Rp = Return on portfolio
      Ra, Rb = Return on asset a,b
      Wa, Wb = Weight of portfolio in asset a,b

To calculate the standard deviation of a two-asset portfolio, the formula is a bit more complex. A naive approach would be to sum across asset standard deviations weighted by an asset's portfolio value. However, this approach fails to consider any interrelationship among variables. For example, assets A and B may both have high standard deviations suggesting that a portfolio of these two assets would also have a high standard deviation. However, it is possible that the portfolio standard deviation might be less than the standard deviation of either asset A or asset B. How? If the returns of asset A and asset B move opposite one another—that is, if the returns of asset A tend to be offset by the returns of asset B—then combining these assets could actually serve to generate a low portfolio standard deviation. The interrelationship between two assets may be such that respective volatilities are mutually offsetting. Statistically speaking, returns on the two assets may generate a correlation coefficient with a value close to negative one. This phenomenon could serve to generate attractive portfolio returns at relatively low levels of portfolio risk.

In actuality, asset returns across various equities rarely behave in the same way over time. While growth stocks may outperform other equity sectors in times of economic strength, primary services stocks may outperform other equity sectors in times of economic weakness. And the fact that not all assets behave in the same way is a desirable phenomenon. Indeed, the fact that asset returns do not all behave in the same way is a powerful incentive to diversify investments. Rather than just invest in fixed-income securities, it would be appropriate to own some equities as well. And rather than just own growth stocks, it would be appropriate to own blue chip stocks as well. And so it goes.

Now then, to calculate a portfolio standard deviation, we want a formula that considers the standard deviation of individual assets and the interrelationship (or covariance) of asset standard deviations. The standard deviation may be found by taking the square root of the variance as defined below:

$$\sigma^2(p) = \sigma^2(a) \cdot Wa^2 + \sigma^2(b) \cdot Wb^2 + 2 \cdot Wa \cdot Wb \cdot cov(a,b) \qquad (15.3)$$

where: $\sigma^2(p)$ = Variance of portfolio returns
$\sigma^2(a,b)$ = Variance of returns for asset a,b
Wa, Wb = Weight of portfolio in asset a,b
cov(a,b) = Covariance of returns for assets a and b
cov(a,b) = $\rho(a,b) \cdot \sigma(a) \cdot \sigma(b)$

Assumption Three: There are no frictions in the capital market.

Frictions are any impediments to the free flow of capital and information in the marketplace. The assumption of frictionless markets generally means that there are no transactions costs, no taxes, and information is freely available. Clearly, there are frictions in markets, and these ought to be considered with any CAPM analysis.

In sum, CAPM is presently the most commonly accepted theoretical basis for evaluating portfolios. To answer the question of whether our portfolio manager ought to purchase the bundle of synthetic fixed-income securities (utility stocks) or true fixed-income securities, it would be instructive to see how respective risk/return profiles evolve over time in a CAPM risk/reward framework.

Many investment advisors are in the business of identifying the most appropriate portfolio bundles to own over time. One such investment advisor, NISA, Inc., is actively involved with identifying opportunities related to true versus synthetic portfolios. NISA has found that synthetic bundles often do indeed outperform true portfolios on a CAPM risk/reward basis.

Creating a Synthetic Fixed-Income Portfolio: Summary

- It may be possible to create a synthetic fixed-income portfolio with equities. This can be achieved with betas to identify equities that exhibit fixed-income characteristics. Once a portfolio of equities has been created, a CAPM framework may be applied to evaluate risks and returns of respective portfolios over time.

16
Creating an International Fixed-Income Portfolio

MODERN PORTFOLIO THEORY

A considerable amount of research has been offered in support of international portfolio diversification. Much of that research incorporates Modern Portfolio Theory (MPT) and the notion that efficient portfolios can be identified in a mean-variance framework. The most powerful argument behind international diversification is that it may serve to reduce portfolio risk and increase portfolio returns. To see how, consider Equation 16.1.

Equation 16.1 provides the formula to calculate variance for a two-asset portfolio. This is the same equation for portfolio variance as presented in Chapter 15.

$$\sigma^2(p) = \sigma^2(a) \cdot Wa^2 + \sigma^2(b) \cdot Wb^2 + 2 \cdot Wa \cdot Wb \cdot cov(a,b) \quad (16.1)$$

where: $\sigma^2(p)$ = Variance of portfolio returns
$\sigma^2(a,b)$ = Variance of return for asset a,b
Wa, Wb = Weight of portfolio in asset a,b
cov(a,b) = Covariance of returns for assets a and b
cov(a,b) = $\rho(a,b) \cdot \sigma(a) \cdot \sigma(b)$

One variable in Equation 16.1—the correlation coefficient, ρ—is particularly worthy of consideration. In Chapter 15, we stated that a correlation coefficient is a measure of correlation between two variables. It may be positive or negative and may range in value between negative one and positive one. A correlation coefficient that is positive and close to a value of one implies a direct relationship between two variables. As variable A rises (falls), variable B tends to rise (fall) as well. A negative correlation coefficient close to an absolute value of one implies an inverse relationship between two variables. As variable A rises (falls), variable B tends to fall (rise). A correlation of zero implies no correlation between two variables.

As the value of ρ goes from positive one to negative one in Equation 16.1, portfolio variance declines. The intuition behind this is straightforward. As ρ moves from positive one to negative one, this implies that the correlation between two variables is moving from a direct relationship (positive one) to an inverse relationship (negative one). A correlation coefficient of negative one suggests that the two variables are mutually offsetting.

Thus, the more two variables tend to offset one another, the lower the correlation coefficient and the lower the portfolio variance. Therefore, a powerful motivation for building a diversified portfolio is that different asset classes may behave differently over time. If all of an investor's funds are invested in the stock market, then he or she will be quite happy as long as the stock market generates positive returns. But as soon as the stock market begins to suffer, an investor may wish he or she had put away some eggs in another basket or two.

Table 16.1 provides correlation coefficients for a variety of U.S. fixed-income securities and global fixed-income securities.

The table shows that correlation coefficients among U.S. fixed-income securities tend to be positive and close to one. For example, the correlation coefficient between the on-the-run 30-year Treasury Bond and the on-the-run 10-year Treasury Note is 0.95. Conversely, the correlation coefficients among global fixed-income securities are more apt to be less than 0.5 than above 0.5. For example, the correlation coefficient between the front-month U.S. Treasury Note future and the Italian Treasury Note future is −0.85.

Now that we have a sense of why a portfolio manager would be motivated to invest at least a portion of his or her assets in international securities, how could he or she do it? One way would be to build portfolios selectively with the fixed-income securities of interest. This could be a real challenge. Every country may have its own unique way of transacting in fixed-income

Table 16.1 Correlations among U.S. and International Fixed-Income Products

	Correlation Coefficients for U.S. Securities				
	30-Year	10-Year	5-Year	2-Year	3-Month
30-year	1.00				
10-year	0.95	1.00			
5-year	0.88	0.98	1.00		
2-year	0.82	0.95	0.99	1.00	
3-month	0.63	0.81	0.90	0.94	1.00

	Correlation Coefficients for 10-Year Global Financial Futures			
	USA	Italy	Australia	UK
United States	1.00			
Italy	−0.85	1.00		
Australia	0.54	0.20	1.00	
United Kingdom	0.70	−0.57	0.35	1.00

securities. There may be appreciable differences in day-count basis, liquidity, tax law, and so forth. In short, going global could be a big headache. Alternatively, instead of going to cash fixed-income markets, an investor might create synthetic cash portfolios with money market securities and futures contracts. Futures contracts are standardized instruments that trade on exchanges all over the world. Table 16.2 provides a partial listing of exchanges and the longer-dated fixed-income futures contracts that trade there.

Table 16.2 International Financial Futures

Exchange	Longer-Dated Futures Contracts
CBOT	U.S. long bond, 10-, 5-, and 2-year notes
LIFFE	U.K. long gilt
MATIF	French 10-year OAT
SYDNEY	Australian 3- and 10-year notes
MONTREAL	Canadian 10-year note
DTB	German 5- and 10-year notes
TOKYO	Japanese 10-year note and 20-year bond
NZFE	New Zealand 10-year note

In Part Three we discuss how to create synthetic notes and bonds with money market securities and futures contracts. That methodology is appropriate for the international arena as well.

Modern Portfolio Theory Summary

- Modern portfolio theory suggests that there can be significant advantages to portfolio diversification.
- Correlation coefficients are an important factor when evaluating the benefits of a diversified portfolio. In particular, low and/or negative correlations among assets may serve to lower a portfolio's expected variance while increasing a portfolio's expected returns.
- U.S. fixed-income securities tend to exhibit low-to negative correlation coefficients with international fixed-income securities. Thus, it may be prudent for U.S. fixed-income investors to own at least some nondollar assets in their fixed-income portfolios.
- Given the complications of building an international portfolio with cash securities, international futures contracts may provide a clean and standardized way to achieve diversification.

ECU OPPORTUNITIES

An ECU is an European Currency Unit. Our interest in the ECU is twofold. First, its significance as a currency will increase dramatically in the next few years. Second, it makes for an attractive product for creating synthetic assets.

The ECU is a mix of all currencies of those countries that make up the Exchange Rate Mechanism (ERM) of the European Monetary System (EMS). Membership in the EMS does not require membership in the ERM. Table 16.3 provides a list of member countries of the ERM and shows the percentage weighting for each member's currency in the ECU.

We can see from Table 16.3 that the Deutschemark carries the greatest weight in the ECU. That is, the Deutschemark makes up 30.4% of the ECU's value. It is a generally accepted rule-of-thumb among ERM analysts that the Deutschemark has a strong, positive correlation with the Dutch kroner. As shown in Table 16.3, both Germany and the Netherlands are members of the ERM.

Table 16.3   ECU Weightings

ERM Country	Percentage in ECU
Belgium	7.90
Luxembourg	2.45
France	19.40
Germany	30.40
Ireland	1.10
Netherlands	9.50
Britain	12.60
Greece	0.75
Spain	5.20
Portugal	0.80
Italy	9.90

One reason these two currencies tend to trade in tandem is that respective governments have traditionally pursued comparable monetary policies. To the extent that domestic monetary policy influences a national currency, the Deutschemark and Dutch kroner have generally traded in line with one another. Of course, this historical relationship may change as Germany grows increasingly involved with the integration of former East and West Germany and former Eastern and Western Europe.

Another factor that argues for the Deutschemark and Danish kroner to trade close in line is that membership in the ERM imposes an upper and lower bound of where one currency may trade relative to another and/or relative to the ECU. In particular, most ERM currencies may not diverge from one another or from the ECU's central parity by more than plus or minus 2.25%.

Let's assume that we accept the notion that the Deutschemark and Danish kroner trade closely over time and that this relationship may continue over the near term. If we combine the ECU weightings of the Deutschemark and Danish kroner, we find that these total 39.9%. That's almost half of the ECU's total value. Why is that of interest? Well, if we ever wanted to create an ECU, it might be less expensive to create a *demi*-ECU with a *subset* of currencies that comprise a major part of the ECU. However, if we were to use only a subset, we would run the risk that the synthetic would not perform in precisely the same way as the ECU itself.

A variety of ECU-denominated assets are in the marketplace. For example, both the United Kingdom and Italy have issued ECU-denominated

Treasury Bills, and a variety of ERM member governments have issued ECU-denominated securities across the yield curve. Moreover, a number of entities have issued ECU-denominated Eurobonds. The term "entities" means both governmental and nongovernmental issuers.

If a Eurobond or any other asset is denominated in ECUs, an incentive may exist to create a synthetic version of that security. For example, an ECU-denominated Eurobond ought to trade at a yield that reflects—among other things—the ECU-weighted yield levels of all ERM member countries.

Let's say that the World Bank issues an ECU-denominated 10-year Eurobond. The World Bank has been rated AAA/Aaa by Moody's and Standard & Poors. The World Bank's debt generally is not regarded as equivalent to a sovereign credit, but is rather viewed as carrying the risk of a supranational organization. Now then, if we wanted to evaluate whether or not this World Bank issue were fairly priced, how might we go about the task? We would want to determine the World Bank's "credit spread," and we would want to identify an appropriate "ECU yield."

"Credit spread," refers to the number of basis points required to compensate for the fact that the World Bank is not a sovereign credit. For example, say that a dollar-denominated 10-year World Bank security trades at a yield of 21 basis points over 10-year Treasury Note yields in the United States, and a Deutschemark-denominated 10-year World Bank security trades at a yield of 23 basis points over 10-year government bond yields in Germany. Accordingly, we might say that the World Bank's credit spread to a sovereign issuer is worth a little more than 20 basis points. One reason the World Bank security yields more may be that a sovereign entity has the ability to tax as a means of generating revenues. The financial standing of a supranational organization is usually dependent on the contributions of its member countries.

To calculate an "ECU yield," we might simply take the 10-year yield of each EMS member's government debt and weight those yields by respective weightings within the ECU. Assume that we do this and find that the World Bank's 10-year security is actually trading 50 basis points less than where it ought to trade. That is, the World Bank's 10-year security is trading 50 basis points rich to its theoretical yield level. Certainly, 50 basis points allows for considerable leeway to account for such things as different perceptions of credit risk and/or appropriate government yield levels. If it is our view that investors will eventually recognize the discrepancy between the World Bank's yield in the market versus its theoretical value, we might have an incentive to enter into a special strategy. We might have an incentive to go short the true 10-year World Bank Eurobond, and go long a synthetic 10-year World Bank Eurobond.

If the market recognizes that the World Bank issue is priced rich, its yield would be likely to rise. For this reason, we would want to be short the true World Bank security. The rationale for wanting to be long the synthetic World Bank issue is that the market may rise and fall from the time a mispricing is recognized until such time that the mispricing is corrected. Thus, if the true World Bank issue were to be sold short with no offsetting trade, the market might rally before the World Bank's yield were to rise. In short, we may make the correct call with rising World Bank yield levels, but we may get hammered along the way in a bull market. However, if we were to buy a synthetic World Bank issue at the same time that we were to sell the true, then we protect ourselves from at least a portion of any market risk. In the end, we want to capture a perceived opportunity with yield spreads, not market direction.

So how would we create our synthetic ECU-denominated 10-year World Bank Eurobond? Perhaps we would buy a bundle of World Bank and/or sovereign 10-year securities denominated in those currencies that make up the ECU. And as discussed in the very early part of this chapter, the strength of correlations across respective currencies might allow us to cut some corners with respect to just how many different securities we purchase. Since a bid/ask spread exists for every security we would seek to include in the synthetic basket, an incentive exists to keep the number to a minimum. However, the investor must bear in mind that the fewer the number of securities included, the greater the risk of a mispriced synthetic asset over time. That risk may be more manageable the shorter the investment horizon, and the better the selected assets are able to proxy the true ECU-denominated securities.

Finally, some interesting currency plays may be made with the ECU and non-EMS member countries. For example, both Sweden and Finland have linked their currencies to the ECU. Thus, trading strategies may be created for a variety of synthetic combinations involving the financial instruments of these countries as well.

ECU Opportunities Summary

- Innovative investment strategies may be created with ECU-denominated financial instruments and synthetic assets created with a subset of ECU components. These opportunities may exist not only among the financial instruments of countries belonging to the ERM, but for those countries that have linked their currency to the ECU.

PART FIVE
VARIATIONS ON A THEME

The products discussed in the following pages embody an amalgamation of securities and strategies discussed thus far. Many of these products carry the characteristics of other securities such as options and futures. Sometimes these other security-types are embedded—not detachable from the security as a whole—and in other instances they may be separable and traded in other markets.

17

Equity- and Commodity-Linked Securities

CONVERTIBLES AND EXCHANGEABLES

Convertible debt may be exchanged for the equity of the entity issuing the debt. Exchangeable debt may be exchanged for the equity of an entity other than the issuer. For example, if the XYZ company were to issue debt that could be traded for equity in the XYZ company, then this would be convertible debt. However, if the XYZ company were to issue debt that could be traded for equity in the QRS company, then this would be exchangeable debt.

Why issue convertible and/or exchangeable debt? First, there is the possibility of issuing an overvalued asset. That is, if investors do not accurately identify the fair market value of a convertible or exchangeable issue, then they may pay more than the asset's theoretical value. Second, there may be tax and/or balance sheet incentives. For example, equity-linked debt tends to carry a lower coupon since investors have the potential to own an equity stake in the issuer. This lower coupon may translate into a lower net interest expense for the issuer.* Third, if a given issuer is

---

* For further consideration of tax issues on these securities, see "The Case for Issuing Synthetic Convertible Bonds," by John D. Finnerty in the *Midland Corporate Finance Journal* (Vol. 4, No. 3, 1986), and "Equity-Linked Debt," by E. Phillip Jones and Scott P. Mason, in the *Midland Corporate Finance Journal* (Vol. 3, No. 4, 1986).

not highly regarded in the marketplace, a convertible or exchangeable may serve as a sweetener to entice investors.

The largest issuers of these securities tend to be manufacturing companies followed by commercial concerns, and offerings tend to be greatest in rallying equity markets.

Two important considerations when evaluating a convertible or exchangeable security are the characteristics of the issuer and the issue. As to the issuer, important considerations include the firm's business risk, financial risk, and dividend policy. Since convertibles and exchangeables combine elements of senior securities with junior equity, these products are particularly vulnerable to industry-specific events in addition to traditional interest rate sensitivities. By industry-specific events, we mean such things as corporate earnings, consumer demand, and business climate. Rating agencies have tended to rate these securities one risk class below a straight debenture. As such, these products are generally regarded as subordinated debt.

As to the issue itself, important considerations include its maturity, coupon, and redemption provisions. Let's examine each of these factors in turn.

Maturity

Maturity can be a double-edged sword. On the one hand, the longer the maturity of the issue, the greater the likelihood of default. This is particularly relevant if the issue carries a lower credit rating. Convertible and exchangeable debt tend to be issued by entities with less than top-tier credit ratings. Indeed, one reason these firms often choose to issue exchangeable or convertible debt is that it makes their debt more marketable relative to traditional debt offerings. Another reason is that the longer the maturity of a convertible or exchangeable security, the longer an issuer enjoys paying out relatively low-coupon streams. This lower coupon opportunity cost is all the more disconcerting to investors as yields rise in the marketplace.

On the other hand, the longer the maturity, the more time available potentially to make an attractive conversion or exchange. In an attempt to quantify just how long an investor would have to hold a convertible or exchangeable to break even, Equation 17.1 is often used. Anything in excess of a 5-year breakeven time is generally considered to be excessive.

$$Bt = Cs \,/\, Is \qquad\qquad\qquad (17.1)$$

where: Bt = Time to breakeven
 Cs = Conversion (or exchange) premium per share
 Is = Income differential per share

Let's consider the terms of Equation 17.1 in greater detail. The conversion premium per share is simply the difference between the prevailing price per share of the stock and the price per share of the stock where the conversion or exchange may be made. Thus, if the current market price of the stock is $5 per share and a conversion or exchange may be made at $7 per share, then the conversion premium per share is $2. This conversion premium might be viewed as the cost of an out-of-the-money call option on the price of the convertible or exchangeable.

Conversion prices are usually 15% to 25% above the price of a firm's common stock at the closing of the market on the day an offering is priced. Further, exchangeables or convertibles generally carry antidilution provisions. For example, if the stock splits over the life of the exchangeable or convertible, the conversion or exchange price is adjusted accordingly. For example, assume that a stock makes a 3-for-1 split. This means that for every share of stock owned by an investor, he or she now owns three shares of stock in its place. And if the price per share of stock were $30 before the 3-for-1 split, the price per share of stock would be $10 per share after the 3-for-1 split.

While some issues have delayed conversion or exchange premiums where an investor must give advance notice of intent to convert or exchange, most are immediate. Moreover, most rights to convert or exchange expire at or just before the maturity or redemption date of the convertible or exchangeable.

Finally, there may be a scenario where an issuer would find it desirable to call a convertible or exchangeable issue so as to force conversion or exchange. The conversion or exchange may be forced because the after-tax interest expense per bond exceeds the amount of dividends on the underlying stock.

The Is term in Equation 17.2 is the income differential per share. The income differential per share is calculated by solving for Equation 17.2:

$$\frac{C - (Rc \cdot Ds)}{Rc} \tag{17.2}$$

where: C = Coupon of convertible or exchangeable
          Rc = Conversion (or exchange) ratio
          Ds = Dividend per share

The conversion ratio is the dirty price of the security (price plus accrued interest) divided by the conversion price. Thus, if the security is trading at a dirty price of $120 and the conversion price is $30, then the conversion ratio is 4. If we want to be more precise with our calculation of Equation 17.2, we would calculate the present value of every expected cashflow over the investment horizon.

Coupon Rate

As we have stated, the coupon on a convertible or exchangeable tends to be lower than coupons on traditional debt. This is explained by the option component of the issues. Specifically, a convertible or exchangeable embodies a long call option on a stock. Because this long call is held by the investor, a lower coupon is paid by the issuer. The strike price of the call option is the price at which the stock may be obtained with the convertible or exchangeable.

Even if the price of the relevant stock has appreciated such that it would be profitable to exercise the option embedded in a convertible or exchangeable, an investor may wisely choose not to exercise the option. If the coupon income being received on the convertible or exchangeable exceeds the expected dividend on the stock, then the investor may put off exercising the option.

When a convertible or exchangeable is sold prior to exercise, the seller is entitled to any accrued interest. However, when a convertible or exchangeable is exercised, any accrual is generally lost.

Redemption Provisions

Redemption provisions detail the terms for obtaining the relevant equity. These terms would include special instructions for making the trade, the date(s) for making the trade, and the conversion premium.

Convertibles and Exchangeables Summary

- Convertibles and exchangeables offer an unique opportunity for an investor to own both equity and fixed-income securities in one product.
- Before purchasing the stock of a particular company, an investor may find it profitable to see first if any convertible or exchangeable securities trade to that equity. In short, the equity may trade to something more or less than its fair market value across various products.

WARRANTS

Fixed-income warrants are generally issued with a debt offering, and are separable from that offering. That is, the warrant may be stripped from the offering to trade independently. This is in contrast to a convertible or exchangeable where the option to convert or exchange is embedded in the security.

A warrant is very much like an option. For example, a warrant trades to an underlying security, embodies a strike price (or sometimes, a series of strike prices), and exercise may be European or American. If the underlying security is equity, then a standard Black–Scholes pricing model is generally appropriate to value the warrant.

An incentive to issue warrants may be to achieve a lower effective cost of capital. The lower effective cost of capital may be realized by selling the warrant at a price above fair market value, by capturing a particular tax incentive, and/or by saving on the costs otherwise incurred with traditional offerings.

Many times a warrant may trade for more than fair market value because a comparable option does not exist. For example, warrants tend to be issued with a longer time to expiration, and warrants tend to be offered on many different types of investments. Warrants have been issued on just about everything from the price appreciation of the Japanese stock market to the yield differential of French versus German government bonds.

If a warrant trades to an underlying equity, then new equity is created at the time the warrant is exercised. This is in contrast to an option, convertible, or exchangeable, which is traded for equity that already exists.

Since a warrant is traded for new equity, dilution is an important factor to consider when valuing a given warrant. Dilution means that the newly created equity adds to the supply of existing equity. As a result, earnings per share are less because the number of shares has increased with no offsetting change in expected earnings.* Thus, while warrants are often priced with option models, the fair market value for a warrant ought to be less than that of a comparable option because of the potential for dilution.

The value of a warrant might be calculated as

$$W = (1 - n / (n + m)) \cdot Vbs \qquad\qquad (17.3)$$

where: n = The number of new issues to be created
           m = The number of outstanding shares
           W = The value of the warrant
           Vbs = The Black-Scholes value of a call option

Because warrants tend to have a longer life relative to options, the risk-free rate in an options formula takes on greater importance. Moreover, the stable volatility assumption of the Black–Scholes model may not be as appropriate for a longer-dated warrant.

Unlike a convertible or exchangeable, which is typically exchanged for the relevant equity, a warrant may stipulate that the associated debt, cash, or a combination of the two be traded for the equity. A bond that can be used instead of cash at exercise is known as a usable security, and demand for the issue generally increases as an in-the-money warrant approaches its expiration date.

---

* It may not be entirely true to say that the earnings per share becomes less because there is no offsetting change in expected earnings. The warrant may require an exchange of outstanding debt. Thus, if it is perceived that a reduction in the debt burden will improve future earnings, then there may be some positive effect on earnings per share. However, the effect might be negligible, and it might already be discounted by the marketplace.

Similar to convertibles and exchangeables, a bond is surrendered without valuation for accrued interest when tendered for the exercise of a warrant. And like convertibles and exchangeables, warrants are often issued by firms with less than stellar credit ratings. Accordingly, an investor will want to consider carefully the credit risks of the security.

In contrast to convertibles and exchangeables, coupons of debt instruments linked to warrants are generally not substantially different from comparable traditional debt securities. Further, warrants tend to carry a higher conversion premium relative to convertibles and exchangeables.

Generally speaking, a warrant's maturity is significantly less than the maturity of the related debt, the warrant and related debt are separately redeemable, and the size of the related debt is generally more than enough to cover the exercise of all the warrants.

When would an entity prefer to issue debt with warrants instead of a convertible or exchangeable? When the structure of the former is somehow more advantageous. For example, the issuer would want to consider comparative merits on tax liabilities, earnings per share, early redemption opportunities, and ability to mold the balance sheet in the desired way—that is, creating the desired debt/equity mix.

For the investor, choosing among extendibles, exchangeables, or debt with or without warrants can involve trade-offs with coupon income, maturity structures, and tax implications. For example, an unexercised expiration of the option embedded in a convertible or exchangeable has no tax consequences for either the issuer or investor. The expiration of an unexercised warrant gives rise to a capital loss for the investor. Finally, if the universe of convertibles and exchangeables does not appeal to an investor, one might be created synthetically with warrants. That is, a convertible or exchangeable may be thought of as a combination of a straight bond and a warrant.

Warrants Summary

- When choosing among exchangeables, convertibles, and warrants, there are many important factors to consider for both issuers and investors. These factors would include tax issues, total return profiles, and the effective cost of capital.
- An investor with an interest in a particular stock could find it worthwhile to see if that stock has any associated exchangeables,

convertibles, or warrants. Aside from the possibility that the exchangeable or convertible is undervalued, the exchangeable or convertible may offer a higher current return for less of a credit risk.

- Given the comparable features of convertibles, exchangeables, and warrants, synthetic securities may be created for investment or arbitrage opportunities. For example, a warrant might be viewed as a synthetic relative to options, convertibles, or exchangeables.

ADJUSTABLE RATE PREFERRED STOCK

Another example of a security with a mix of equity and fixed-income characteristics is an adjustable rate preferred stock (ARPS). An ARPS was first introduced in May 1982.

The idea behind an ARPS is that the stock's dividend is linked to an index. In this way, an ARPS is not dramatically different from a floating rate note (FRN). The index for an ARPS might be linked to a short-term rate such as 3-month Treasury Bills, or a longer-term rate such as the yield of a 10-year Treasury Note. And as with FRNs, an ARPS generally pays the index rate plus or minus a spread. For example, each quarter an ARPS's dividend may be based on the appropriate 10-year Treasury Note yield plus 50 basis points paid in arrears. The term "in arrears" means that the dividend is determined one period before it is actually paid.

An ARPS may also have a cap and/or floor. A cap is a ceiling on how high a dividend payment may go, and a floor is a lower bound on how small a dividend payment may be.

Among corporate money managers, ARPS and ARPS-like products are popular because dividends enjoy an 85% exclusion from federal income taxes. For equity investors, ARPS are desirable because they are considered to be less volatile than standard preferred equity. The fact that dividends are adjusted quarterly is said to reduce the price volatility of an ARPS relative to the "fixed" dividend of a preferred stock. The term "fixed" is in quotes because although preferred dividend payments tend to stay fairly constant over time, they may change.

ARPS have been popular among issuers for many reasons. First, pretax yields on ARPS tend to be below pretax yields on comparable debt securities. Second, an ARPS provides an issuer with a source of equity capital without the dilution that might accompany a common stock issue. Third, call provisions for ARPS have generally been less costly to an issuer relative to fixed-dividend preferred issues.

ARPS and other floating-rate assets serve to transfer interest rate risk from the investor to the issuer. For the investor who desires this type of risk, ARPS may make for attractive asset substitutes relative to FRNs. Respective differences in tax law may be a particularly important consideration when evaluating such a strategy.

Finally, since the inception of ARPS, comparable products have been introduced. For example, MMPs, or Money Market Preferreds, have grown in popularity. Although structures vary from issue to issue, MMPs are generally distinguished from ARPS by the way in which the rate on the dividend is determined. Namely, rates on MMPs are set by Dutch auction, and minimum and maximum rate levels are established (also known as collars). Such features help to reduce the price volatility of these bank-dominated securities during times of uncertainty.

Adjustable Rate Preferred Stock Summary

- ARPS are like FRNs and may offer an investor the opportunity to own a money market-type security yet with a preferable return profile.
- Since equities may be taxed differently than fixed-income securities, pre- and posttax returns ought to be considered.

COMMODITY-LINKED PRODUCTS

It is important to state that many developments in the area of commodity-linked structures have evolved as a response to tax and/or regulatory motivations. While this is not the appropriate forum to delve into the minutiae of tax codes and regulatory procedures, it is appropriate to consider that many financial innovations have been born out of creative responses to otherwise limiting impositions of a free market. Thomas Edison said that necessity is the mother of invention, and perhaps limitation is the mother of innovation.

In 1989, the Commodity Futures Trade Commission (CFTC) issued a statutory interpretation recognizing a jurisdictional exclusion for two broad categories of hybrid instruments. Broadly defined, for purposes of

CFTC considerations, a hybrid instrument involves combining a futures contract with some other security. The two categories recognized for jurisdictional exclusion are (a) debt securities within the meaning of Section 2.(1) of the Securities Act of 1933, and (b) time deposits within the meaning of 12 C.F.R. 204.2.(c)(1) offered by a bank whose deposits are insured by the Federal Deposit Insurance Corporation, and marketed and sold directly to a customer. Table 17.1 provides a list of the criteria that must be met for a new product to be excluded from regulation by the Commodities Exchange Act (CEA). These new products are often referred to as "hybrid instruments."

Table 17.1 Qualifications for Exclusion of a Hybrid Instrument from Regulation under the CEA

There may not be more than a one-to-one relationship between the value of the hybrid instrument and the value of its underlying commodity. For example, if the hybrid instrument is indexed to the Deutschemark, then the value of the hybrid instrument may not appreciate in value by more than one dollar if the value of the Deutschemark increases by one dollar.

The maximum loss on the security may not be greater than the commodity-independent face value and/or coupon value of the security. For example, if the hybrid instrument links a zero coupon bond with the value of gold, the maximum loss on the security may not exceed the value of the hybrid instrument with the gold stripped out. That is, the maximum loss may not exceed the face value of the zero coupon bond.

The commodity-independent yield must be at least 50% but no more than 150% of the yield on a comparable nonhybrid instrument. For example, if the yield on a comparable nonhybrid security is 10%, then the commodity-independent yield of a hybrid security must be at least 5% but no more than 15%.

The commodity component of a hybrid instrument may not be severable. For example, with our gold-linked zero coupon bond security, the gold component may not be stripped from the hybrid instrument and sold off as a separate and distinct product.

The hybrid instrument may not call for delivery of a commodity by means of an instrument specified in the rules of a futures exchange. A gold-linked hybrid instrument may not call for delivery of gold.

The hybrid instrument may not be marked as being or having the characteristics of a futures contract or commodity option.

In July 1989, the CFTC approved rules providing for exemption on certain optionlike hybrid products. The exemption applies to debt securities, preferred equity securities, and bank deposits. Both securities registered in accordance with the Securities Act of 1933 and those qualifying for specified exemptions from such registration are included. Also exempt are most demand deposits and transactions accounts offered by financial institutions whose deposits are insured by a U.S. government agency or government chartered corporation, or securities offered by a foreign bank in the U.S. if supervised by federal banking authorities. Table 17.2 lists the qualifications that must be met for these securities to be exempt from CEA regulations.

To provide the reader with a flavor of innovative structures available in the fixed-income marketplace, the following case studies represent a random sampling of some recent issues. By no means is this sampling

Table 17.2   Qualifications for Jurisdictional Exclusion

The value of the implied option premium must be no greater than 40% of the price of the hybrid instrument.

Any one of the following requirements must be satisfied:

1. The hybrid instrument has been rated in one of the four highest categories by a nationally recognized rating organization, or if not rated, other comparable instruments of the issuer have been so rated.
2. The issuer maintains at least $100 million in net worth.
3. The issuer maintains cover equal to the amount of its commodity-related commitments.
4. The hybrid instrument is eligible for insurance by a U.S. government agency or government-chartered agency.

Section 4c (7 U.S.C. 6c) as amended by section 203(a) of the act was again amended. The amendment states that nothing in the act shall be considered to govern or in any way be applicable to any transaction in or involving an instrument that meets the following requirements:

The hybrid instrument may not derive more than 50% of its value from the value of the option at the date of issuance.

It is expected that less than 50% of the value gained from and payable on the hybrid instrument will be due to movement in the price of the option or options embedded in that hybrid instrument.

exhaustive, nor can it be. A complete survey of innovative commodity-linked products could well be a book in and of itself. Rather, the case studies show how a given structure may be broken into its various pieces; thus, the reader will be able to appreciate how *any* asset may be built with a basic understanding of the fundamental building blocks. To this end, the reader should not view these case studies as isolated, self-contained products, but as instructive exercises about how securities may be put together.

Case Studies

CAC 40-Linked Zero Coupon Bond. Interfinance Credit National issued a 6-year 500 million French franc zero coupon bond linked to the CAC 40. The CAC 40 is an index of 40 stocks on the Paris stock exchange. Put and call options are attached to the zero coupon bond, and the put options may be exercised at the end of years three, four, and five. The call option may be exercised at the end of year three.

The maturity date of the zero coupon bond is July 24, 1996. It may be redeemed at par plus the maximum of either zero or 115% of the appreciation of the CAC 40 over the life of the bond.

The maturity date of the call option is August 18, 1993, and its strike price is par plus 144% of any appreciation in the CAC 40. To calculate the appreciation of the CAC 40, we solve for

$$100 \cdot \frac{((\text{CAC 40 in year 3}) - (\text{CAC 40 at issue date}))}{\text{CAC 40 at issue date}}$$

The maturity dates of the put options are August 23 in years 1993, 1994, and 1995, respectively. The strike prices of the put options are par plus the maximum of either zero or 103%, 107%, and 111%, respectively, of any appreciation in the CAC 40. At the time of issue the CAC-40 stood at 2053.

If the bond were held to maturity, an investor's payoff profile would resemble a long synthetic call. The synthetic call would be equivalent to holding the CAC 40 stocks and buying a put on the CAC 40. The holder of this synthetic call receives the benefits of the dividends on the stocks. These dividends might be expected to produce revenues of about 15%

over six years. This return is the same as the final payoff of the zero coupon bond; namely, par plus the maximum of zero or 115% of the appreciation of the CAC 40 over the life of the bond. If the security is indeed held to maturity—and unless the CAC 40 drops to very low levels, there is no incentive to exercise before maturity—the investor will have paid about FFr 55 for the zero coupon bond and FFr 45 for a six-year at-the-money European call option on 1.15 CAC 40 indices.

If the bond is called after three years, the investor will have invested in a 3-year zero coupon bond with a return of 13%. At the time of issue, 13% represented a 300-basis-point spread over yields on French government bonds (so-called OATs, or Obligation Assimilation du Trésor).

The payout structure for an investor at year three looks like a call spread with strike prices of 2053 and 2930. The payout profile of this structure is shown in Figure 17.1.

Assuming the security will expire in three years, then the premium paid for a 3-year call spread on the CAC 40 is the difference between par and a 3-year zero coupon bond, or

FFr 100 – FFr 74.5 = FFr 25.5

If the issue were completely sold and the bond were called or put in year three, this would represent a profit potential of at least FFr 5 per FFr 100 face.

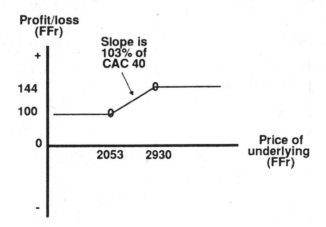

FIGURE 17.1 CAC 40.
Payoff in year three.

Before continuing on, it's worth commenting on an issuer's choice of reference price when forward transactions are involved. The current spot price is a typical reference price when the market forward price is not used. In certain markets, the forward price typically exceeds the spot price. This is known as cotango. In other markets, the spot price typically exceeds the market forward price. This is known as backwardation.

Trading Range Gold Warrants. Shearson Lehman Hutton Capital (London) issued Trading Range Warrants. These warrants enable investors to benefit from a limited move in the price of gold. Each warrant was sold at a price of $71.40 with a maturity of two years and a European exercise.

If the price of gold at maturity is less than $360/oz., then the warrant entitles the investor to receive $(100/360) \cdot$ (price of gold). If the price of gold at maturity is between $360/oz. and $400/oz., then the investor receives 100. And if the price of gold is greater than 400/oz., the investor receives $(100/360) \cdot$ (760-price of gold). A payout profile of this strategy is shown in Figure 17.2.

For the price of $71.40 per warrant, an investor purchases a 2-year zero coupon bond, sells 1/3.6 put options on the price of gold struck at $360/oz., and sells 1/3.6 call spreads on the price of gold struck at $400/oz. on the short call leg and $760/oz. on the long call leg.

By assuming a yield level for the 2-year zero coupon bond, it is an easy matter to back out an implied price and volatility for the option components

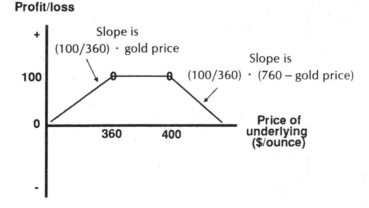

FIGURE 17.2   Trading range gold warrants.

of the trade. In fact, the implied volatility on the structure was significantly below prevailing market levels. Thus, Shearson was able to obtain some rather low-cost options, and investors were able to buy into an investment offering a potential 40% return over two years.

Yield Differential Warrants. Mitsubishi Finance International issued 100,000 call and 100,000 put warrants on the implied yield difference between the near-month U.S. Treasury Bond futures contract and the near-month U.S. Treasury Bill futures contract. The warrants were exercisable from September 2, 1991, to May 22, 1992, with each basis point move in the yield curve worth $1.00. The strike price of 284.3 was set at the implied closing spread on the issue date.

The methodology employed by Mitsubishi to calculate the rate of discount on the Treasury Bill future is the same used by the futures exchange. Namely, the rate of discount is calculated as $D = 100 - Pf$, where Pf is the price of the Treasury Bill future. To calculate the yield of the Treasury Bond future, the following formula is used:

$$\sum_{n=1}^{40} \frac{F \cdot C/2}{(1 + Y/2)^n} + \frac{F}{(1 + Y/2)^{40}} \tag{17.4}$$

where: P = Price of the Treasury Bond future
  Σ = Summation over 40 semiannual periods
    A Treasury Bond future trades to a notional 20-year bond, so 40 semiannual periods are used
  F = Face value of the bond, 100
  C = Coupon
    A Treasury Bond future trades to a notional 8% coupon bond, so C is equal to 8%
  Y = Bond-equivalent yield

Thus, to calculate the spread between the Treasury Bill and Treasury Bond futures, Mitsubishi solves for $Y - D$. However, we know from Part One that a rate of discount (D) is not the same as a bond-equivalent yield (Y). For starters, these measures of return assume different day-count bases. In particular, Y is calculated assuming an Actual/Actual day-count basis, and D is calculated assuming an Actual/360 day-count basis. Therefore, if we were interested in calculating the yield spread on an "apples-to-apples" basis, we might want to convert D into Y.

For an investor interested in hedging either the call or put warrants on a delta-equivalent basis, a weighted combination of Treasury Bill and Treasury Bond futures contracts would have to be used. The reason for this is that Treasury Bill futures contracts trade to an underlying value of $1 million per contract, and Treasury Bond futures contracts trade to an underlying value of $100,000 per contract. Further, a one-basis-point move on a Treasury Bill future is worth $25, and a one-basis-point move on a Treasury Bond future is a function of the duration of the cheapest-to-deliver security. Calculating the duration of a futures contract is discussed in Part Three.

USD/DM GROI Warrants. Swiss Bank Corporation (SBC) issued Guaranteed Return on Investment (GROI) warrants on the U.S. dollar/Deutschemark (USD/DM) exchange rate. One million warrants were issued at a price of DM100, and the exercise period was to be from October 15, 1991, to December 30, 1993. The minimum redemption price was set at DM108 and the maximum redemption price was to be unlimited. With a redemption price of DM108, a minimum guaranteed annualized return of 3.542% is earned.

The minimum guaranteed return is structured with four options in a strategy commonly known as a "box." When a box is held to maturity, an investor keeps all of the up-front premium received at the time the box is created. For example, assume that an investor (a) buys a USD call and sells a USD put at a strike price of 1.50, and (b) buys a USD put and sells a USD call at a strike price of 2.00. Each option will expire in December 1993, and has a face value of USD216. Figure 17.3 shows that the combination of these options will give an investor DM108 at maturity, regardless of the value of the USD/DM exchange rate.

As shown in Figure 17.3, if the exchange rate at maturity is above DM2.00, the two calls create a long call spread with a maximum payout of DM0.50. If the exchange rate at maturity were below 1.50, the two puts create a long put spread with a maximum payout of DM0.50. If the rate is between 1.50 and 2.00, the call spread and put spread will combine to generate a payout of DM0.50. Thus, regardless of the exchange rate at maturity, the box generates a payout of USD216 · DM0.50 = USD108.

The fact that SBC structured the "Guaranteed" portion of the GROI with options was a unique twist. Up to that time, the "Guaranteed" portion of a GROI was generally structured with money market securities. By using options instead of a money market securities, SBC was able

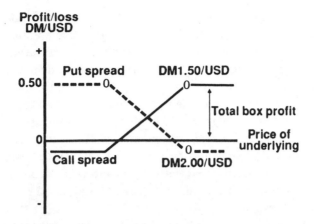

FIGURE 17.3   Payout of the 1.50–2.00 USD/DM box.

to capitalize on German tax law that provided for tax-free treatment of capital gains on options with maturities greater than six months.

As to the unlimited upside component of the GROI, the structure provides for three tiers of call options on the USD with strike prices of DM1.65, DM1.85, and DM2.00. The payout profile is provided in Table 17.3.

Dual Currency Bonds.   Swedish Export Capital (SEK) launched a 5-year reverse dual currency bond with Nomura Securities. The market convention for defining a dual currency bond is that the coupon is paid in the

Table 17.3   Payout of the 1.50–2.00 USD/DM Box*

Exchange Rate at Maturity	Box Payout	Payout of 1.65 Call	Payout of 1.85 Call	Payout of 2.00 Call	Total Payout/ Total Return (%)
1.25	DM 108				DM 108/3.542
1.50	DM 108				DM 108/3.542
1.65	DM 108				DM 108/3.542
1.85	DM 108	DM 6.0			DM 114/6.099
2.00	DM 108	DM 10.5	DM 4.5		DM 123/9.792
2.10	DM 108	DM 13.5	DM 7.5	DM 3.0	DM 132/13.330
2.20	DM 108	DM 16.5	DM 10.5	DM 6.0	DM 141/16.728

* Above 2.00 DM per USD, the GROI pays off on a linear basis at 9 DM for every 0.10 increase in the exchange rate.

base currency of the issuer, and the principal is paid in a nonbase currency. For example, for a Japanese issuer, coupons would be denominated in yen, but the principal would be denominated in say, Deutschemarks.

For a *reverse* dual currency bond, the coupon is denominated in a nonbase currency, and the principal is denominated in the base currency. Again, for a Japanese issuer, coupons would be denominated in, say, Deutschemarks, and coupons would be denominated in yen.

A dual or reverse dual currency bond allows a fixed-income investor to play both the fixed-income and currency markets. Since some portfolio managers may be restricted from buying or selling foreign exchange as a separate asset class, buying a currency-linked fixed-income product may be the next best thing.

Just how much of a currency bet an investor is making depends, in part, on the coupon and maturity of the security. For a dual currency bond, the only currency risk is the currency risk associated with the principal payment. This assumes that the base currency of the dual currency bond is the base currency of the investor as well. For a reverse dual currency bond, currency risk is present with every coupon payment. Again, we assume that the base currency of the reverse dual currency bond is also the base currency of the investor. The currency risk of the coupon payments may or may not outweigh the safety of the base currency principal payment. It depends on the realized value of the cashflows over the investment horizon. Clearly, the longer the maturity of the reverse dual currency bond, the more important the coupon cashflows in determining the security's realized total return. Accordingly, an investor will want to value a dual or reverse dual currency bond with a variety of currency scenarios to better assess the risks of the trade.

In the mid-1980s, Japanese investors were fond of yen/U.S. dollar reverse dual currency bonds. Coupons were paid at a rate above Japanese securities, and cashflows were denominated in the U.S. dollar, which appreciated against the yen over much of the investment horizon.

Dual and reverse dual currency bonds have been popular with issuers for generally two reasons. First, with investor appetite on the part of the Japanese and others, an issuer may be reasonably assured that an offering will be fully sold. Second, the issuer can fully hedge any currency risk exposure in the base currency, often with an arbitraged profit. The arbitraged profit is a result of investors paying more than fair market value for the innovative securities. As alluded to above, one reason an investor may pay up for such a structure is that he or she is otherwise prohibited from investing in other types of foreign exchange products.

There are other products with the look and feel of dual and reverse dual currency bonds. For example, Morgan Stanley has underwritten a variety of so-called PERLS and reverse PERLS. PERLS stands for Principal Exchange Rate Linked Security. A standard PERLS pays both coupon and principal in the base currency, but the principal is paid according to some redemption formula linking it to movements in exchange rates. For example, a PERLS may be denominated in dollars, yet be linked to the Australian dollar. Thus, as the Australian dollar appreciates (depreciates) against the dollar, the value of the principal grows. In this way, a PERLS is analogous to a dual currency bond, yet without the actual payment of the nonbase currency.

A reverse PERLS is not analogous to a reverse dual currency bond. A reverse PERLS pays the principal based on a redemption formula that benefits the investor when the nonbase currency *depreciates* against the base currency. This is in contrast to a reverse dual currency bond, which is characterized by coupon payments in a nonbase currency with the principal payment in the base currency.

There are also multicurrency PERLS. These securities pay the principal based on a redemption formula using two or more currencies. It is then up to the investor to decide which of the two formulas he or she will use at the maturity of the security. Oftentimes the investor is forced to choose the redemption formula several months before the maturity date.

Finally, another type of currency product may be an indexed medium-term note. Although under a different name, this security basically carries the same structure of a PERLS.

Commodity-Linked Products Summary

- An investor who is knowledgeable of the basic building blocks can easily identify the pieces of a given structure.
- Since tax laws and regulatory constraints often play an important role with product innovations, investors who have a clear understanding of regulatory codes are better equipped to understand commodity-linked instruments. Furthermore, they are better able to create synthetic assets.

18

Synthetic Option Strategies

EXTENDIBLES AND RETRACTABLES

As the name implies, an extendible issue is an asset that may be converted into a security with a longer maturity. An example would be an investor's right to convert a 10-year note into a 30-year bond at some predetermined date. Conversely, a retractable issue is an asset that may be converted into a security with a shorter maturity. An example would be an investor's right to convert a 30-year bond into a 10-year note at some predetermined date.

An investor will exercise his or her right to extend or retract an issue when it is in his or her best interests to do so. That is, when there is an opportunity to gain from lengthening or shortening the maturity of an issue given the dynamics of the marketplace.

To value extendibles and retractables, many investors use an option-type model. For example, to identify the fair market value of an extendible, it would be appropriate to value the option of creating a longer-dated asset relative to an already existing longer-dated issue. If the extendible would allow for the creation of a longer-dated asset under terms more favorable than an outright purchase of a comparable security, then the extendible would be an attractive investment.

Components of an option model such as volatility, current market price, and strike price would all lend themselves to valuing an extendible or retractable. Whether an extendible is trading in-, at-, or out-of-the-money depends on the extended coupon relative to prevailing market yields on alternative assets. If the extended coupon were higher than the yield on alternative assets, it would be advantageous to extend into a security trading at a premium rather than retire the issue at par. In this way an extendible is viewed as a having an embedded call option.

Whether a retractable is trading in-, at-, or out-of-the-money depends on its retracted coupon relative to prevailing market yields on alternative assets. If the retracted coupon were lower than yields on alternative assets, it would be advantageous to retract and receive par rather than continue to hold the security at a discount. In this way, a retractable is viewed as having an embedded put option.

All else being equal, the yield on a retractable or extendible issue will tend to be lower than yields on standard securities. The reason for this is that the choice of whether to extend or retract resides with the investor. Because it is the investor who may choose to exercise the option, he or she is presumably willing to pay up for this with a yield slightly below that of standard securities with comparable features.

Finally, extendibles and retractables may be combined with short call or put options respectively, to create synthetic traditional fixed-income securities. Swaptions may also be appropriate products for these synthetic strategies.

CALLABLES AND PUTTABLES

Up to this point, we have considered callable bonds in some detail. The reader is referred to Part Three for a detailed overview.

From an investor's perspective, a puttable bond may be thought of as a long position in a bond and a put option. In contrast to a callable bond, the *investor* is the one who owns the option with a puttable bond.

A puttable bond gives an investor the right to sell back (to put) an issue prior to its maturity date at some predetermined price. Since a put option takes on value when yields rise, it may be profitable to exercise the embedded put option in a bearish market environment. The investor will receive par while comparable securities are trading at a discount owing to higher yield levels.

Figure 18.1 shows the price/yield profile for a puttable bond. In contrast to a callable bond, a puttable bond experiences price compression when yields rise rather than when yields fall.

Just as it is possible to create synthetic noncall securities with callable issues (see "Creating Noncall Securities with Callable Issues and Swaptions," in Chapter 12), it is possible to create synthetic nonput securities with puttable issues. For example, a puttable issue might be combined with a short put swaption to create a synthetic nonput security that is somehow more attractive than a traditional note or bond.

Callables and Puttables Summary

- While it may be said that callable bonds suffer from price compression when yields fall, puttable bonds enjoy price support when yields rise.
- This price support has value for an investor who is long a puttable bond, and for this reason puttable securities tend to trade at a lower yield relative to other security types.
- It is possible to create synthetic nonput securities that may outperform traditional fixed-income issues.

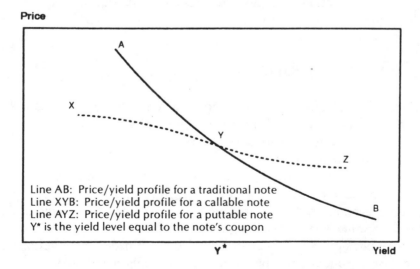

FIGURE 18.1   Price/yield profiles for callables and puttables.

SINKING FUNDS

With a sinking fund,* the issuer may be obliged to buy back bonds over time. A sinking fund bond differs from a callable bond in many ways. First, with a sinking fund bond, the issuer may be obligated to buy back bonds. With a callable bond, the issuer has the right but not the obligation to buy back bonds. Second, with a sinking fund bond, only a portion of the bonds might be bought back at any one time. With a callable bond, the issuer usually buys back all of the bonds at one time. Third, a callable bond may only have one strike price. Although terms may vary considerably from issue to issue, there are generally different prices at which sinking fund issues are retired over time. For example, a sinking fund may retire the first 10% of outstanding issues at a price of 100, the second 10% of outstanding issues at a price of 102, and so forth. The precise terms of a sinking fund issue would be spelled out in its prospectus.

To value a sinking fund issue, an investor might make use of a probability-based option-type model. The probability component of such a model would attempt to quantify the likelihood of early redemption for a given investor's holdings of sinking fund securities. Clearly, the more of a sinking fund issue held by an investor, the greater the value of the sinking fund provision. By owning a significant amount of securities, an investor may be better positioned to frustrate an issuer's attempt to buy back bonds in the marketplace.

The option component of a sinking fund model would attempt to quantify the value of early redemptions at the prices detailed in the prospectus. When trading at a discount, the owner of a significant stake of a sinking fund issue may be thought of a holding a traditional fixed-income security and a series of put options. Depending on the exact structure of the issue (the percentage of the issue subject to sink, the strike prices, the sink horizon, etc.) the series of options may help to provide some price support in an environment of rising yields. That is, the lower value of the fixed-income security may be compensated, in part, by the greater value of the series of options. While other securities

*An excellent overview of sinking funds is provided in "The Valuation and Management of Bonds with Sinking Fund Provisions," *Financial Analysts Journal,* March/April 1992, Andrew J. Kalotay and George O. Williams.

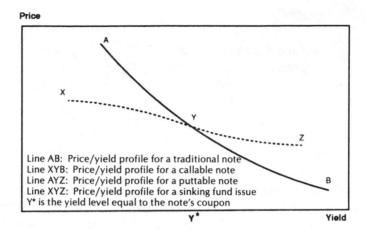

FIGURE 18.2   Price/yield profile for a sinking fund issue.

are trading at a discount, the prospect of getting hit on a sink at a price above the market looks rather attractive. In this respect, a sinking fund issue may be seen as embodying properties of a puttable bond.

At the same time, sinking fund securities tend to be issued with an embedded short call. The short call serves to dampen price appreciation as yields fall. Figure 18.2 shows how the price/yield profile of a sinking fund issue might appear.

If a sinking fund issue can be appropriately valued, it may be all the easier to devise synthetic and other strategies with this product. For example, it may prove profitable to combine call and/or short put options with a sinking fund issue to create a nonsinking fund security that is somehow more attractive than a traditional note or bond.

Sinking Funds Summary

- Sinking fund bonds have optionlike features and may offer investors a unique investment opportunity when bought or sold separately or in combination with other products. It is important that an investor own a significant portion of a sinking fund issue to capture the effect of a series of put options.

A FINAL NOTE

In a sense, there is no "end of the story" because new financial products will continue to be introduced. For this reason, the notion of an "all-inclusive" text is rather elusive by design.

Yet, while market opportunities will come and go, the fundamentals will never change. It is my hope that this book provides the reader with a solid foundation in the basics, and a taste of the more exotic.

To the future investors and issuers of fixed-income synthetic assets, I wish you every success.

Appendix A

Identifying Investment Opportunities among Treasury Bills and Short Coupons

---

EXAMPLE 1

On May 4, 1990, the Treasury Bill of 5/31/90 had 24 days from settlement to maturity and traded at a 7.360%/7.310% rate of discount. The "bid/offer" (or market quote) for the Treasury Bill of 5/31/90 was 7.360%/7.310%. Fixed-income securities are generally purchased at the offer rate and are sold at the bid rate. Since prices have an inverse relationship to the level of yields, we see that fixed-income securities are generally purchased (offer-side) at a price that is higher than where they are sold (bid-side).

All market examples provided throughout the text used appropriate bid/offer rates.

On the same day, the 8.125% Treasury Note of 5/31/90 traded at a bond-equivalent yield of 8.147%/7.408%. An investor who wanted to purchase a 4-week security would have been interested in knowing whether the Treasury Bill or Treasury Note provided the better investment opportunity. To have made this judgment, the Treasury Bill and Treasury Note would have had to be evaluated on an apples-to-apples basis. To convert the Treasury

Bill and Treasury Note into comparable measures of return, we calculate respective money market yields.

Treasury Bill of 5/31/90

From rate of discount (D) to money market yield (M)

$$\text{Bid } 7.397\% = \left(\frac{100 - 99.5093}{99.5093}\right)\left(\frac{360}{24}\right)$$

$$\text{Offer } 7.345\% = \left(\frac{100 - 99.5127}{99.5127}\right)\left(\frac{360}{24}\right)$$

8.125% Treasury Note of 5/31/90

From bond-equivalent yield (Y) to money market yield (M)

$$\text{Bid } 7.762\% = \left(\frac{100\,(1 + 0.08125/2) - (100 + 3.52679)}{100 + 3.52679}\right)\left(\frac{360}{24}\right)$$

$$\text{Offer } 7.307\% = \left(\frac{100\,(1 + 0.08125/2) - (100.03125 + 3.52679)}{100 + 3.52679}\right)\left(\frac{360}{24}\right)$$

We see that an investor would not have been indifferent between owning the Treasury Bill or Treasury Note. The Treasury Bill would have allowed an investor to pick up 3.8 basis points (7.345% vs. 7.307%) over the Treasury Note.

Since it is more often the case that Treasury Bills and coupon securities mature on different dates, let's consider another example.

EXAMPLE 2

On May 4, 1990, the Treasury Bill of 6/28/90 had 52 days from settlement to maturity and traded at a 7.570%/7.520% rate of discount. On the same day, the 7.25% Treasury Note of 6/30/90 had 54 days from settlement to maturity and traded at a bond-equivalent yield of 8.380%/ 8.171%. To evaluate the Treasury Bill and Treasury Note on an apples-to-apples basis, we convert respective securities into money market yields.

Treasury Bill of 6/28/90

From rate of discount (D) to money market yield (M)

$$\text{Bid } 7.654\% = \left(\frac{100 - 98.90656}{98.90656}\right)\left(\frac{360}{52}\right)$$

$$\text{Offer } 7.603\% = \left(\frac{100 - 98.91378}{98.91378}\right)\left(\frac{360}{52}\right)$$

7.25% Treasury Note of 6/30/90

From bond-equivalent yield (Y) to money market yield (M)

$$\text{Bid } 8.265\% = \left(\frac{100(1 + 0.0725/2) - (99.8125 + 2.543508)}{99.8125 + 2.543508}\right)\left(\frac{360}{54}\right)$$

$$\text{Offer } 8.059\% = \left(\frac{100(1 + 0.0725/2) - (99.84375 + 2.543508)}{99.84375 + 2.543508}\right)\left(\frac{360}{54}\right)$$

If an investor owned the Treasury Bill, we see that it would have been enticing to sell (bid-side) the Treasury Bill at a 7.654% money market yield and buy (offer-side) the Treasury Note at a 8.059% money market yield. With two simple transactions, investors could have picked up more than 40 basis points (8.059% vs. 7.654%) for a trade-off of committing funds over two extra days (6/30/90 vs. 6/28/90). Too good to be true? Well, yes.

For one thing, 6/30/90 was a Saturday, and this meant that an investor holding the Treasury Note would not have actually received good funds until the following Monday. Coupon and principal payments are not made on weekends or national holidays. Because both 6/30/90 and 7/1/90 were "bad days," this served to add another two days to the Treasury Note's holding period. Accordingly, the Treasury Note's money market yield drops to 7.771% when adjusted for two bad days. The adjustment is accomplished by changing the 54 to 56 in the denominator of the Treasury Note's second term. However, 7.771% does represent a pickup of 11.7 basis points (7.771% vs. 7.654%) over the Treasury Bill of 6/28/90.

So would it have been worthwhile to sell the Treasury Bill and buy the Treasury Note after all? One way to answer this question is to calculate a hypothetical value for the Treasury Note. If the Treasury Note could have been purchased for a price less than that suggested by the market, then we may indeed say we identified a bargain.

The Treasury Bill of 7/5/90 would have been the next Treasury Bill to mature following the Treasury Bill of 6/28/90. Since the 7.25% Treasury Note of 6/30/90 was to mature between the maturity dates of 6/28/90 and 7/5/90, let's calculate a hypothetical yield for the Treasury Note with a simple averaging technique. Figure A.1 helps to provide a context for our problem.

To calculate a hypothetical offer-side money market yield for the Treasury Note, we solve

$$X = 7.654\% + 4/7 \ (7.819\% - 7.654\%).$$

$$X = 7.748\%$$

Thus, the Treasury Note could have been purchased for a pickup of 11.7 basis points over the Treasury Bill of 6/28/90, *and* with a pickup of 2.3 basis points (7.771% vs. 7.748%) over a hypothetical market value. It may have made for a good trade.

The methodology used to calculate the Treasury Notes' hypothetical value implicitly assumes a *linear* relationship among yield levels and maturities. While this assumption may not always be appropriate—yield

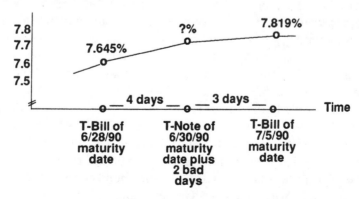

FIGURE A.1   Identifying a hypothetical money market yield
                 for the 7.25% Treasury Note.

curves often exhibit a "bend"—the relevant time span of only seven days serves to minimize any serious consequence of a linear calculation.

The preceding examples have shown that two securities with similar cashflows and maturity dates may have very different values. Financial theory suggests that this ought not to be possible. All else being equal, two securities with comparable profiles ought to be valued such that one security does not provide an appreciable price advantage over another. However, in the preceding examples, factors other than cashflows and maturity dates had an effect on respective prices. Liquidity, for instance, is an important consideration when valuing fixed-income securities. Liquidity, which refers to how actively a security is traded, can be influenced by such things as a security's size and maturity, and investor preferences. One good measure of an issue's liquidity is its bid/offer spread, also known as a bid/ask spread. The narrower or "tighter" the difference between a given bid and offer, the more liquid the issue and the more likely the issue will trade expensive to securities with wider bid/ask spreads. Wide bid/ask spreads are sometimes said to reflect a "liquidity premium."

In our first Treasury Note/Treasury Bill example, the issue size of the Treasury Note was $8.037 billion, and the issue size of the Treasury Bill was $15.2 billion. In this instance, the issue size of the "cheap" security (Treasury Note) was slightly more than half the issue size of the "rich" security (Treasury Bill), but the Treasury Bills were much more actively traded; they were more liquid.

The original term-to-maturity of a coupon security can also affect its present value. An original term-to-maturity 2-year Treasury Note may be more likely to trade when it becomes a short coupon than when an original term-to-maturity 30-year Treasury Bond becomes a short coupon. Longer-dated securities tend to get tucked away into investment portfolios and are not as apt to be candidates for swaps when they become short coupons. On May 4, 1990, the 8.25% Treasury Bond of 5/15/90 and 7.875% Treasury Note of 5/15/90 both had eight days from settlement to delivery. The bond-equivalent yield for the Treasury Note was 7.589%/6.224%, and the bond-equivalent yield for the Treasury Bond was 9.300%/6.574%. Bid/offer spreads were 137 basis points and 273 basis points, respectively. The longer original term-to-maturity of the Treasury Bond contributed to a bid/offer spread nearly *twice* that of the Treasury Note.

As further evidence in support of widening bid/offer spreads as maturity dates draw near, Figure A.2 shows Treasury Note and Bond prices for

TREASURY BONDS, NOTES & BILLS

Monday, June 15, 1992

Representative Over-the-Counter quotations based on transactions of $1 million or more.

Treasury bond, note and bill quotes are as of mid-afternoon. Colons in bid-and-asked quotes represent 32nds; 101:01 means 101 1/32. Net changes in 32nds. n-Treasury note. Treasury bill quotes in hundredths, quoted on terms of a rate of discount. Days to maturity calculated from settlement date. All yields are to maturity and based on the asked quote. Latest 13-week and 26-week bills are boldfaced. For bonds callable prior to maturity, yields are computed to the earliest call date for issues quoted above par and to the maturity date for issues below par. *-When issued.

Source: Federal Reserve Bank of New York.

U.S. Treasury strips as of 3 p.m. Eastern time, also based on transactions of $1 million or more. Colons in bid-and-asked quotes represent 32nds; 101:01 means 101 1/32. Net changes in 32nds. Yields calculated on the asked quotation. ci-stripped coupon interest. bp-Treasury bond, stripped principal. np-Treasury note, stripped principal. For bonds callable prior to maturity, yields are computed to the earliest call date for issues quoted above par and to the maturity date for issues below par.

Source: Bear, Stearns & Co. via Street Software Technology Inc.

GOVT. BONDS & NOTES

Rate	Maturity Mo/Yr	Bid	Asked	Chg.	Ask Yld.
8 1/4	Jun 92n	100:06	100:08	− 1	1.20
8 3/8	Jun 92n	100:07	100:09	....	0.48
10 3/8	Jul 92n	100:17	100:19	− 1	2.53
8	Jul 92n	100:17	100:19	....	2.98
4 1/4	Aug 87-92	98:09	98:25	+ 2	11.74
7 1/4	Aug 92	100:17	100:19	....	3.48
7 7/8	Aug 92n	100:21	100:23	....	3.33
8 1/4	Aug 92n	100:23	100:25	....	3.31
8 1/8	Aug 92n	100:28	100:30	....	3.41
8 1/8	Sep 92n	101:07	101:09	....	3.55
8 3/4	Sep 92n	101:13	101:15	....	3.51
9 3/4	Oct 92n	101:30	102:00	....	3.52
7 3/4	Oct 92n	101:13	101:15	....	3.68
7 3/4	Nov 92n	101:17	101:19	− 1	3.78
8 3/8	Nov 92n	101:26	101:28	....	3.71
10 1/2	Nov 92n	102:22	102:24	− 1	3.66
7 3/8	Nov 92n	101:18	101:20	....	3.72
7 1/4	Dec 92n	101:24	101:26	....	3.80
9 1/8	Dec 92n	102:24	102:26	....	3.78
8 3/4	Jan 93n	102:23	102:25	....	3.83
7	Jan 93n	101:26	101:28	....	3.92
4	Feb 88-93	95:13	95:29	....	10.54
10 1/8	Nov 94	110:23	110:25	....	5.30
11 5/8	Nov 94n	114:03	114:05	+ 1	5.29
7 5/8	Dec 94n	105:11	105:13	....	5.32
8 5/8	Jan 95n	107:19	107:21	+ 1	5.40
3	Feb 95	94:27	95:27	− 1	4.68
5 1/2	Feb 95	100:04	100:06	....	5.42
7 3/4	Feb 95n	105:21	105:23	....	5.42
10 1/2	Feb 95	112:11	112:13	+ 1	5.43
11 1/4	Feb 95n	114:04	114:06	+ 1	5.45
8 3/8	Apr 95n	107:08	107:10	+ 1	5.55
5 7/8	May 95n	100:27	100:29	+ 1	5.53
8 1/2	May 95n	107:22	107:24	....	5.58
10 3/8	May 95	112:22	112:24	....	5.57
11 1/4	May 95n	114:30	115:00	+ 1	5.60
12 5/8	May 95	118:30	119:02	+ 1	5.45
8 7/8	Jul 95n	108:27	108:29	....	5.60
8 1/2	Aug 95n	107:28	107:30	+ 1	5.72
10 1/2	Aug 95n	113:18	113:20	+ 1	5.73
8 5/8	Oct 95n	108:09	108:11	+ 1	5.83
8 1/2	Nov 95n	107:31	108:01	+ 1	5.87
9 1/2	Nov 95n	111:00	111:02	....	5.87
11 1/2	Nov 95	117:04	117:08	+ 1	5.85
9 1/4	Jan 96n	110:10	110:12	....	5.99
7 1/2	Jan 96n	104:26	104:28	+ 1	5.98
7 7/8	Feb 96n	105:30	106:00	....	6.03
8 7/8	Feb 96n	109:06	109:08	+ 1	6.02
7 1/2	Feb 96n	104:23	104:25	....	6.04
7 3/4	Mar 96n	105:15	105:17	− 1	6.09
9 3/8	Apr 96n	110:30	111:00	+ 1	6.11
7 5/8	Apr 96n	105:02	105:04	....	6.12

Rate	Maturity Mo/Yr	Bid	Asked	Chg.	Ask Yld.
7 7/8	Jan 98n	105:20	105:22	+ 2	6.64
8 1/8	Feb 98n	106:24	106:26	+ 2	6.66
7 7/8	Apr 98n	105:16	105:18	+ 2	6.71
7	May 93-98	101:06	101:14	− 3	5.36
9	May 98n	110:28	110:30	+ 3	6.73
8 1/4	Jul 98n	107:07	107:09	+ 2	6.77
9 1/4	Aug 98n	112:03	112:05	+ 2	6.80
7 1/8	Oct 98n	101:18	101:20	+ 2	6.80
3 1/2	Nov 98n	93:26	94:26	+ 5	4.44
8 7/8	Nov 98n	110:08	110:10	+ 3	6.86
6 3/8	Jan 99n	97:12	97:14	+ 3	6.87
8 7/8	Feb 99n	110:09	110:11	+ 3	6.91
7	Apr 99n	100:16	100:18	+ 1	6.90
8 1/2	May 94-99	105:03	105:11	− 4	5.52
9 1/8	May 99n	111:19	111:21	+ 1	6.97
8	Aug 99n	105:17	105:19	+ 2	6.99
7 7/8	Nov 99n	104:25	104:27	+ 2	7.03
7 7/8	Feb 95-00	103:15	103:19	+ 1	6.39
8 1/2	Feb 00n	108:06	108:08	+ 2	7.09
8 7/8	May 00n	110:12	110:14	+ 2	7.13
8 3/8	Aug 95-00	105:23	105:27	....	6.31
8 3/4	Aug 00n	109:20	109:22	+ 1	7.16
8 1/2	Nov 00n	108:02	108:04	+ 1	7.20

U.S. TREASURY STRIPS

Mat.	Type	Bid	Asked	Chg.	Ask Yld.
Aug 92	ci	99:13	99:13	....	3.68
Nov 92	ci	98:13	98:13	....	3.91
Feb 93	ci	97:14	97:15	....	3.92
May 93	ci	96:13	96:14	....	4.04
Aug 93	ci	95:05	95:06	....	4.29
Nov 93	ci	93:22	93:23	....	4.65
Feb 94	ci	92:14	92:15	....	4.76
May 94	ci	90:31	91:01	....	4.98
Aug 94	ci	89:14	89:16	− 2	5.20
Nov 94	ci	87:29	87:31	+ 1	5.39
Nov 94	np	87:26	87:28	....	5.43
Feb 95	ci	86:13	86:15	....	5.53
Feb 95	np	86:10	86:12	+ 1	5.58
May 95	ci	84:30	85:00	+ 1	5.66
May 95	np	84:25	84:28	....	5.72
Aug 95	ci	83:14	83:16	+ 1	5.78
Aug 95	np	83:07	83:10	....	5.86
Nov 95	ci	82:00	82:02	+ 1	5.88
Nov 95	np	81:23	81:25	+ 1	5.98
Feb 96	ci	80:01	80:03	+ 1	6.15
Feb 96	np	79:27	79:30	+ 1	6.21
May 96	ci	78:15	78:18	+ 1	6.27
May 96	np	78:09	78:12	+ 1	6.33
Aug 96	ci	76:31	77:02	+ 1	6.36
Aug 96	ci	75:24	75:27	+ 1	6.37
Nov 96	np	75:15	75:19	+ 1	6.45

Mat.	Type	Bid	Asked	Chg.	Ask Yld.
Feb 00	np	57:11	57:15	+ 1	7.36
May 00	ci	55:27	55:31	+ 1	7.47
May 00	np	56:02	56:06	+ 1	7.42
Aug 00	ci	54:21	54:25	+ 1	7.51
Aug 00	np	55:01	55:06	+ 1	7.42
Nov 00	ci	53:21	53:25	+ 1	7.51
Nov 00	np	53:30	54:02	+ 2	7.45
Feb 01	ci	52:09	52:13	+ 2	7.60
Feb 01	np	52:26	52:30	+ 2	7.48
May 01	ci	51:06	51:10	+ 2	7.63
May 01	np	51:23	51:27	+ 2	7.51
Aug 01	ci	50:04	50:09	+ 1	7.65
Aug 01	np	50:21	50:26	+ 1	7.53
Nov 01	ci	49:01	49:05	....	7.69
Nov 01	np	49:19	49:24	+ 1	7.56
Feb 02	ci	47:25	47:30	+ 4	7.76
May 02	ci	46:27	46:31	+ 6	7.77
Aug 02	ci	45:29	46:01	+ 6	7.78
Nov 02	ci	44:30	45:03	+ 5	7.80
Feb 03	ci	43:25	43:29	+ 6	7.87
May 03	ci	42:29	43:01	+ 6	7.88
Aug 03	ci	41:31	42:04	+ 6	7.90
Nov 03	ci	41:04	41:08	+ 4	7.91
Feb 04	ci	40:00	40:05	+ 1	7.98
May 04	ci	39:06	39:11	+ 1	7.99
Aug 04	ci	38:12	38:17	+ 1	8.00
Nov 04	ci	37:15	37:19	+ 2	8.04
Jul 04	bp	37:26	37:31	+ 1	7.96
Feb 05	ci	36:22	36:26	+ 2	8.05
May 05	ci	35:29	36:02	+ 1	8.06
May 05	bp	36:09	36:13	+ 2	7.98
Aug 05	ci	35:05	35:10	+ 1	8.07
Aug 05	bp	35:17	35:21	+ 2	7.99
Nov 05	ci	34:15	34:20	+ 1	8.07
Feb 06	ci	33:17	33:21	+ 1	8.13
Feb 06	bp	34:03	34:08	+ 1	8.00
May 06	ci	32:27	32:31	+ 2	8.14
Aug 06	ci	32:06	32:10	+ 2	8.14
Nov 06	ci	31:16	31:20	....	8.15
Feb 07	ci	30:25	30:29	+ 1	8.17
May 07	ci	30:04	30:08	+ 1	8.18
Aug 07	ci	29:17	29:21	+ 2	8.18
Nov 07	ci	28:30	29:02	+ 1	8.18
Feb 08	ci	28:03	28:07	+ 1	8.24
May 08	ci	27:17	27:22	+ 1	8.24
Feb 21	ci	9:30	10:01	− 1	8.19
Feb 21	bp	10:11	10:14	....	8.04
May 21	ci	9:25	9:27	....	8.18
May 21	bp	10:07	10:10	....	8.02
Aug 21	ci	9:19	9:22	− 1	8.17
Aug 21	bp	10:03	10:06	....	7.99
Nov 21	ci	9:30	10:00	− 1	7.98
Nov 21	bp	10:04	10:07	− 1	7.91

TREASURY BILLS

Maturity	Days to Mat.	Bid	Asked	Chg.	Ask Yld.
Jun 18 '92	1	3.73	3.63	+ 0.04	3.69
Jun 25 '92	8	3.28	3.18	− 0.04	3.24
Jul 02 '92	15	3.47	3.37	− 0.01	3.43
Jul 09 '92	22	3.47	3.37	− 0.03	3.43
Jul 16 '92	29	3.43	3.39	− 0.01	3.46
Jul 23 '92	36	3.51	3.47	− 0.01	3.54
Jul 30 '92	43	3.52	3.48	− 0.04	3.55
Aug 06 '92	50	3.55	3.51	− 0.01	3.59
Aug 13 '92	57	3.55	3.51	....	3.59
Aug 20 '92	64	3.58	3.56	....	3.64
Aug 27 '92	71	3.61	3.59	− 0.01	3.68
Sep 03 '92	78	3.63	3.61	− 0.01	3.69
Sep 10 '92	85	3.65	3.63	− 0.01	3.71
Sep 17 '92	92	3.66	3.64	− 0.01	3.73
Sep 24 '92	99	3.67	3.65	....	3.75
Oct 01 '92	106	3.69	3.67	+ 0.01	3.76

FIGURE A.2 U.S. Treasury Bills. Source *The Wall Street Journal,* June 15, 1992. Reprinted by permission of *The Wall Street Journal,* © Dow Jones & Company, Inc. All Rights Reserved Worldwide.

June 15, 1992 as reprinted from the *Wall Street Journal*. While a bid/offer price spread of 2/32 looks to be the norm across most issues, investors should bear in mind that a 2/32 spread for a shorter-dated security translates into many more basis points relative to a 2/32 spread for a longer-dated security.

Another factor affecting a security's present value is that investors may simply have a preference for one security over another (Treasury Bills versus short coupon securities) and/or particular maturity targets. Many investment funds are constrained by the type of securities they may buy and sell. Respective bid/offer spreads will reflect this.

In sum, the larger an issue's size, the shorter an issue's original term-to-maturity, and the more active a security is traded, then the more liquid an issue is likely to be over time.

Among newly auctioned Treasury securities, bid/offer spreads may be about one basis point. Among older, so-called off-the-run Treasury issues, the bid/offer spread can be several basis points.

Finally, another explanation for the price differential between the Treasury Bill and Treasury Note may lie with respective differences in modified durations. The Treasury Note had a higher modified duration than the Treasury Bill. Thus, it may be argued that the Treasury Note traded cheaper than the Treasury Bill to compensate, in part, for the Treasury Note's greater risk as implied by its greater sensitivity to changes in yield. The Treasury Note's higher modified duration may seem counterintuitive. After all, both securities matured on the same day, and the Treasury Note was a coupon security while the Treasury Bill was a discount (or zero coupon) security.

The Treasury Note's higher modified duration is explained by the fact that modified duration has a direct relationship with price. Because the Treasury Note had the higher price (owing to accrued interest that had to be paid along with the clean price), its modified duration was higher.

Appendix B

Credit Ratings

CREDIT RATINGS

Moody's	S&P	Fitch	D&P	
Aaa	AAA	AAA	AAA	Highest quality
Aa1	AA+	AA+	AA+	
Aa2	AA	AA	AA	High quality
Aa3	AA−	AA−	AA−	
A1	A+	A+	A+	
A2	A	A	A	Upper medium quality
A3	A−	A−	A−	
Baa1	BBB+	BBB+	BBB+	
Baa2	BBB	BBB	BBB	Lower medium quality
Baa3	BBB−	BBB−	BBB−	
Ba1	BB+	BB+	BB+	
Ba2	BB	BB	BB	Low quality
Ba3	BB−	BB−	BB−	
B1	B+	B+	B+	
B2	B	B	B	Highly speculative
B3	B−	B−	B−	
		CCC+		
Caa	CCC	CCC	CCC	Substantial risk
		CCC−		
Ca	CC	CC		
C	C	C		Extremely speculative
		C1		
			DDD	Default
			DD	
		D	D	

Appendix C

Money Market Profiles

MONEY MARKET PROFILES

Commercial Paper

Issuers Issuers are primarily major corporations including industry, manufacturing, and finance. While the former tend to issue through dealers, finance companies tend to sell their issues directly into the market.

Maturity Most paper has a maturity of 30 days or less. Paper can have a maturity of up to 270 days, but paper with more than 270 days to maturity must be registered with the SEC and is considered to be a medium-term note.

Credit Ratings Moody's, S&P's, and Fitch.

Interest Calculation Actual/360, discount basis.

Settlement Same day (cash).

Clearing Physical delivery.

Tax Considerations Fully taxable.

Miscellaneous CP is an unsecured promissory note that corporations issue as an alternative to bank financing. All CP is negotiable, but most is held to maturity. CP is generally rolled over by issuers, and the paper is usually backed by lines of credit from banks either in whole or in part. Eurodollar CDs trade cheaper to Domestic CDs and generally follow

Eurodollar deposits. Maturities tend to be longer than Domestic CDs, and settlement is next day with clearing generally through Euroclear.

Bankers' Acceptances

Issuers Banks.

Maturity 1 to 6 months.

Trading Characteristics BA yields generally track Eurodollar deposit rates, and tend to trade at a premium to CP.

Credit Ratings Unrated; credit risk of the underlying bank's paper.

Interest Calculation Actual/360, discount basis.

Settlement Same day (cash).

Clearing Physical delivery.

Tax Considerations Fully taxable.

Miscellaneous BAs are short-term, non-interest-bearing securities. Although BAs may arise in a variety of ways, they are trade-related securities backed by the issuer's pledge, the guarantee of the accepting bank, and any underlying goods. Most BA investors consist of money managers; other investors include foreign central banks, corporations, and institutional investors. BAs are generally spread against Eurodollar deposit rates, and Japanese BAs tend to trade with Eurodollar deposit CDs. Eurodollar deposit CDs tend to trade a little cheaper to Domestic BAs.

Negotiable Certificates of Deposit

Issuers Banks.

Maturity Although maturities range between 14 days and 7 years, most paper has a maturity of 1 to 3 months.

Trading Characteristics CDs are generally issued at face value and typically pay interest at maturity. Yields are influenced by Fed Funds, Libor, and Eurodollar futures.

Credit Ratings Unrated; credit risk of the underlying bank's paper.

Interest Calculation Actual/360, simple interest.

Settlement   Same day (cash).

Clearing   Physical.

Tax Considerations   Fully taxable.

Miscellaneous   New issuance is a function of a bank's loan demand. Although most CDs are sold directly by banks to investors, some dealer business is done. Aside from the type of CD described above, there are also Eurodollar CDs and Yankee CDs. Eurodollar CDs are purchased by money managers, Euromarket banks, U.S. corporations, and institutional investors. Many Eurodollar CDs are issued through dealers and brokers who maintain secondary markets, and these issues are more liquid than domestic CDs. Yankee CDs trade close in yield to Eurodollar CDs, but new issuance has declined. Major buyers include corporations seeking greater yield and those who fund to date. Finally, floating rate CDs exist that reset at 30-day or 3-month intervals. Eurodollar CDs are generally spread off of Eurodollar deposit rates and tend to trade in line with Japanese BAs.

Treasury Bills

Issuer   The U.S. Treasury.

Maturity   3, 6, and 12 months.

Trading Characteristics   Generally trades against Eurodollar rates, appropriate repo rates, and short-term Treasuries of maturities at 2 years or less.

Credit Ratings   Backed by the full faith and credit of the U.S. government.

Interest Calculation   Actual/360, discount basis.

Settlement   One business day (regular).

Clearing   Fedwire.

Tax Considerations   Exempt from state and local taxes.

Agencies

Issuers   FHLB, FNMA, FFCB, SLMA, FHLMC, and World Bank among others.

Trading Characteristics   Agencies generally trade with Fed Funds, U.S. Treasury Bills, and the repo rate appropriate for agency issues.

Credit Ratings   These shorter-term securities are viewed as AAA/Aaa equivalents because their credit risk is considered to be analogous to that of longer-term issues.

Interest Calculation   Actual/360 for money market securities, and 30/360 for notes and bonds.

Settlement   Same day, one business day, or two business days (cash regular or skip).

Clearing   Fedwire.

Tax Considerations   FHLB, FFCB, AND SLMA issues are exempt from state and local taxes. Other issues are fully taxable.

Miscellaneous   Short-term agency issues vary considerably in terms of size, new issue cycles, and maturities. A few agencies have been known to issue floating rate notes.

Eurodollar Floating Rate Notes as Cash Substitutes

Issuers   Primarily banks, although corporations, sovereigns, and others have also issued FRNs.

Maturity   Maturities generally range between 2 and 10 years, with most issues falling in a 2- to 5-year maturity.

Trading Characteristics   Eurodollar FRNs generally trade in line with Libor.

Credit Ratings   FRNs carry a broad range of credit ratings; many issues are unrated.

Interest Calculation   Actual/360.

Settlement   Five business days (Corporate).

Clearing   Primarily Euroclear.

Tax Considerations   Fully taxable.

Miscellaneous   As with other longer-term issues, FRNs may be callable and may have such features as sinking funds, caps, or floors. And while many FRNs may trade close to par over time, other issues, particularly subordinate debt, may trade at a discount over the life of the issue.

Appendix D

U.S. Treasury Futures Contracts

2-Year Treasury Note

Exchange   Chicago Board of Trade.

Contract Unit   U.S. Treasury notes having a face value at maturity of $200,000 or multiple thereof.

Price Quotation   Points ($2,000) and one quarter of $1/32$ of a point.

Minimum Price Change   One quarter of $1/32$ of a point ($15.625 per tick) rounded up to the nearest cent per contract. Par is on the basis of 100 points.

Daily Price Change Limit   1 point ($2,000 per contract) above or below the previous day's settlement price, expandable to $1 1/2$ points.

Delivery   Delivery months include March, June, September, and December. Delivery to satisfy a "sold" position in the expiring contract may be made on any business day, at the seller's discretion, during the delivery month. Delivery is a three-day process: seller's notice of intention (day 1), notice to buyer (day 2), delivery and payment calculated from day 1 settlement price (day 3).

Good Delivery   Generally, the three most recently auctioned 2-year U.S. Treasury Notes (as of the first day of the delivery month) can be delivered into the 2-year futures contract. Also eligible for delivery are those seasoned 3-, 4-, and 5-year Treasury Notes whose remaining time to maturity is no less than 1 year 9 months from the first day of the delivery month. The 2-year note issued at the end of a delivery month will not be eligible for delivery in that month because its issuance, and sometimes even its auction, follows contract expiration.

A cash-settled 2-year Treasury Note future trades on the Financial Instrument Exchange with a contract size of $500,000, and tick value of $50.

5-Year Treasury Note

Exchange Chicago Board of Trade.

Contract Unit U.S. Treasury Notes with a face value of $100,000 bearing stated interest rate of 8% with an original issue maturity of 5 years.

Price Quotation U.S. Treasury Note Futures Contract prices are quoted as a percentage of par (100) with fractions in 32nds and one-half 32nds of a point. A price of 88-025 means 88 and $2\frac{1}{2}$ 32nds, or 88.078125.

Minimum Price Change One-half of $\frac{1}{32}$ of a point or $15.625 per contract.

Daily Price Change Limit $\frac{96}{32}$ (three points) or $3,000 per contract unit above or below the previous day's settlement price.

Delivery Delivery months include March, June, September, and December. Delivery to satisfy a "sold" position in the expiring contract may be made on any business day, at the seller's discretion, during the delivery month. Delivery is a three-day process: seller's notice of intention (day 1), notice to buyer (day 2), delivery and payment calculated from day 1 settlement price (day 3).

Contract Trading Termination Trading in the expiring contract ends at 12:00 noon (Chicago) on the eighth-to-last business day of the delivery month. There is no trading in this contract during the last seven business days of the delivery month.

Good Delivery Delivery may be made with any U.S. Treasury Note having a face value of $100,000 with an original maturity of not more than 5 years and with a maturity as of the first day of the delivery month of not less than 4 years. That is, only notes that are issued as 5-year Treasury Notes are deliverable. The settlement price of the contract unit will be adjusted by a factor for the delivery of non-8% notes to provide a yield equivalent to that of an 8% note at the futures settlement price.

A cash-settled 5-year Treasury Note future trades on the Financial Instrument Exchange with a contract size of $250,000, and a tick value of $50.

10-Year U.S. Treasury Note Futures

Exchange   Chicago Board of Trade.

Contract Unit   U.S. Treasury Notes with a face value of $100,000 bearing a stated interest rate of 8%, which have an actual maturity of not less than $6^{1}/_{2}$ years and not greater than 10 years.

Price Quotations   U.S. Treasury Note Futures Contract prices are quoted as a percentage of par (100) with fractions in 32nds of a point.

Minimum Price Change $^{1}/_{32}$ of one point or $31.25 per contract unit.

Daily Price Change Limit $^{96}/_{32}$ (three points) or $3,000 per contract unit above or below the previous day's settlement price.

Delivery   Delivery months include March, June, September, and December. Delivery to satisfy a "sold" position in the expiring contract may be made on any business day of the expiring month. Notice of intention to sell must be given 2 business days prior to delivery.

Contract Trading Termination   Trading in the expiring contract ends at 12:00 noon (Chicago) on the eighth-to-last business day of the delivery month. There is no trading in this contract during the last seven business days of the delivery month.

Good Delivery   Any U.S. Treasury Note with a face value of $100,000 maturing not less than $6^{1}/_{2}$ years or more than 10 years from date of delivery is good delivery for the futures contract. The settlement price of the contract will be adjusted by a factor for the delivery of non-8% notes to provide a yield equivalent to that of an 8% note at the futures settlement price.

U.S Treasury Bond Futures

Exchange   Chicago Board of Trade.

Price Quotations   U.S. Treasury Bond Futures Contract prices are quoted as a percentage of par (100) with fractions in 32nds of a point.

Minimum Price Change $\frac{1}{32}$ of one point or $31.25 per contract unit.

Daily Price Change Limit $\frac{96}{32}$ (three points) or $3,000 per contract unit above or below the previous day's settlement price.

Delivery   Delivery months include March, June, September, and December and as permitted by the exchange. Additional months may be February, May, August, and November. Delivery to satisfy a "sold" position in the expiring contract may be made on any business day, at the seller's discretion, during the delivery month. Delivery is a three-day process: seller's notice of intention (day 1), notice to buyer (day 2), delivery and payment calculated from day 1 settlement price (day 3).

Contract Trading Termination   Trading in the expiring contract ends at 12:00 noon (Chicago) on the eighth-to-last business day of the delivery month. There is no trading in this contract during the last seven business days of the delivery month.

Good Delivery   Any U.S. Treasury Bond issue with a face value of $100,000 maturing at least 15 years from the first day of the futures delivery month, or if callable, not subject to call for at least 15 years following the first day of the delivery month, is good delivery for the futures contract. The settlement price of the contract will be adjusted by a factor for the delivery of non-8% notes to provide a yield equivalent to that of an 8% note at the futures settlement price.

U.S. Treasury Bond futures also trade on the London International Financial Futures Exchange, the Mid-America Commodity Exchange, and the Tokyo Stock Exchange.

Glossary

Accrued Interest   The current dollar value of the next coupon payment.

Agency   An especially empowered body of the U.S. government, where the full faith and credit of the government may or may not back the security.

American Option   An option that may be exercised at any time in the life of the option.

Arbitrage   A riskless trade where an investor simultaneously buys and sells a security to generate a positive return.

Backwardation   The circumstance of the spot price typically exceeding the forward price.

Bankers' Acceptances (BAs)   A money market-type security issued by a bank for purposes of generating short-term cash.

Basis   The difference in price between a cash fixed-income security and the relevant futures contract. When this is expressed as an annualized Actual/360 return, it is often known as an implied repo rate.

Basis Trade   See Cash-and-Carry.

Bear Floater   A floating rate note whose coupon payments increase as yields rise.

Beta   A measure of the statistical relationship between two series. A positive (negative) beta suggests a direct (indirect) relationship between two series. The larger (smaller) the value for beta, the larger (smaller) the expected change in one series relative to a one-unit change in the other series.

Bond   A cash fixed-income security with 10 years or more to maturity.

Bond-Equivalent Yield   A measure of return typically applied to Treasury coupon securities or Treasury issues with a maturity of more than one year. The day-count basis for this calculation is Actual/Actual. If all of the security's cashflows are invested at the purchase bond-equivalent yield over the life of the security, and if the security or strategy is held to maturity, then the bond-equivalent yield will also be equal to the security's return. If the Treasury issue is a STRIPS, then the bond-equivalent yield will be equal to the security's return if the security is held to maturity.

BP01   The basis point value of a one dollar change in the price of a fixed-income security. Mathematically, a BP01 is generally calculated with a security's dirty price and modified duration.

Bull Floater   A floating rate note whose coupon payments increase as yields decline.

Cap   A swap structured such that the trade has the return profile of a long put option.

Capital Asset Pricing Model (CAPM)   A finance model used to identify efficient portfolios in a risk/return context.

Caption   A product which gives the bearer the right to own a cap.

Cash-and-Carry   A strategy whereby an investor purchases a cash security and sells the relevant number and type of futures contracts against that cash position.

Cashflow   A cash payment associated with a security. A cashflow may be cash paid as when an investor purchases a security, or cash received as when an investor receives a coupon or principal payment.

Clean Price   Price without accrued interest. Also, flat price.

Collateralized Mortgage Obligation (CMO)   A mortgage-backed security (MBS) that has been packaged into various tranches with unique interest rate sensitivities associated with each tranche.

Commercial Paper (CP)   A money market-type security with a maturity of no more than 180 days.

Compound Interest   A measure of return that considers the value of investing a security's cashflows (if any) over the investment horizon.

Convexity   A measure of a fixed-income security's price support when yields rise, and price enhancement when yields fall. Mathematically, convexity can be expressed as the second derivative of price with respect to yield using a standard price/yield equation and a Taylor series expansion. Another method to calculate convexity is with a few enhancements to a duration's time-weighted calculation.

Correlation Coefficient   A measure of the strength of correlation between two series. A correlation coefficient may range in value between one and negative one. A value near one suggests a strong, direct relationship between two series. A value near negative one suggests a strong, indirect relationship between two series. A value near zero suggests no correlation between two series.

Cost-of-Carry   The difference between the rate of return on a security and the cost of financing that security. There is a positive (negative) cost-of-carry when the rate of return on a security is greater (less) than the cost to finance.

Cotango   The circumstance of the forward price typically exceeding the market price.

Coupon   An interest payment from the issuer of a cash fixed-income security to the holder of that fixed-income security.

Covariance   A measure of the covariability of two series.

Cross Rate   The value of a nondollar currency relative to another nondollar currency.

Current Yield   A measure of return calculated by dividing the annual coupon of a fixed-income security by its dirty price.

Day Count Basis   The convention used to annualize a yield or rate of return. For example, the rate of discount for a Treasury Bill annualizes on the basis of a 360-day year, and a bond-equivalent yield calculation annualizes on the basis of a semiannual Actual/Actual calculation from one coupon payment period to the next.

Delivery   The terms by which an investor satisfies a forward or futures trade.

Delta   A measure of the relationship between a change in price of the option relative to a change in the underlying's price.

Dirty Price   Price plus accrued interest, if any. Also, full price.

Discounted Margin   A value in basis points added to or subtracted from the index rate of a floating rate note to determine the security's yield.

Dollar Roll   A trade whereby an investor loans mortgage-backed securities in exchange for cash. Comparable to a reverse repo.

Duration   A measure of a fixed-income security's price sensitivity to a given change in yield.

DV01   The dollar value of a one-basis-point change in the yield of a fixed-income security. Mathematically, a DV01 is generally calculated with a security's dirty price and modified duration.

ECU   A currency that comprises the individual currencies of ERM members.

ERM   Exchange Rate Mechanism of the EMS. Requires that members of the ERM keep exchange rate values within a specified band against a fixed central rate.

EMS   European Monetary System.

Eurodollar Strip   A series of 3-month Eurodollar futures contracts that an investor would go long or short all at one time.

European Option   An option that may be exercised only at the maturity of the option.

Exchange Rate   The value of a nondollar currency relative to the U.S. dollar.

Face Value   The final principal value of a cash fixed-income security.

FHLB   Federal Home Loan Bank; an agency of the U.S. government.

Flex Repo   The placement of a bundle of cash proceeds in the repo market for drawdown over an anticipated horizon.

Floating Rate Note (FRN)   A fixed-income security that pays variable coupons linked to a specified index rate.

Floor   A swap structured such that the trade has the return profile of a long call option.

Floortion   A product that gives the bearer the right to own a floor.

FNMA   Federal National Mortgage Association; an agency of the U.S. government.

Forward   An obligation to satisfy a future purchase or sale of a security. No up-front cash is paid or received.

Forward Rate   The implied or breakeven rate derived from a given term structure of spot rates.

Forward Rate Agreement (FRA)   A trade whereby an investor agrees to exchange a payment linked to a fixed (floating) rate for a payment linked to a floating (fixed) rate at some point in the future.

Full Price   See *Dirty Price.*

Future   An obligation marked-to-market on a daily basis where an investor is required to satisfy a future purchase or sale of a security. There is theoretical and intuitive support for viewing a futures contract as a series of daily forward contracts.

Going Long   Generally used with forward-type instruments where no up-front premium is paid. Since no up-front premium is paid, going long may be a more appropriate term than "purchase."

Going Short   Generally used with forward-type instruments where no up-front premium is received. Since no up-front premium is received, going short may be a more appropriate term than "selling."

Historical Volatility   An annualized standard deviation derived from market observations of a security's price or yield. Generally annualized with a 250-day year.

Holding Period Return   The expected return on a security or strategy assumed to be held to maturity.

Implied Repo Rate   The holding period return earned on a cash-and-carry trade held until maturity. See Basis.

Implied Volatility   An annualized standard deviation derived from an option pricing formula.

Interest Only MBS (IO)   The coupon strip component of a MBS that has been stripped. Technically speaking, an interest-only security of a federal agency may not consist of 100% coupon payments, but must carry a minimum of 1% of the principal of the underlying loans to be accepted by the book-entry system of the Federal Reserve Bank of New York.

Interest Rate Parity   A theory of interest rate/currency behavior. The theory states that it ought to be possible to have comparable yields for any two interest rate securities of different currencies if the securities have the same maturity and denomination (for example, if 90-day Canadian and U.S. Treasury Bills are both valued in U.S. dollar terms.

Interest Rate Swap   A trade whereby an investor agrees to exchange payments linked to a fixed (floating) interest rate for payments linked to a floating (fixed) interest rate. Payments are based on a notional principal value and are exchanged at regular intervals over a predetermined horizon. There is no payment or receipt of principal.

Inverted Yield Curve   A negatively sloped yield curve where interest rates at very short maturities are above interest rates at very long maturities.

Kurtosis   A measure of a distribution's peakedness. Kurtosis is required to define a distribution if the distribution is neither normal nor log-normal.

Log Normal Distribution   A distribution that is asymmetrical on either side of the distribution's mean. A property of this distribution is that it may be defined with a mean and a standard deviation.

Macaulay's Duration   A measure of duration that may be calculated in one of two ways. First, it may be calculated as the first derivative of price with respect to yield using a standard price/yield equation and a Taylor series expansion. Second, it may be calculated with a simple modification to a standard price/yield equation. Namely, in the numerator of a standard price/yield equation, a time value is multiplied against the particular cashflow being discounted. This second methodology is sometimes described as a time-weighted average value of cashflows over the investment horizon.

Maturity Date   The date on which a security ceases to exist.

Mean   A measure of the average value of a series or distribution.

Mismatched Floating Rate Note   A floating rate note whose coupons are determined on one basis (say, weekly) and paid on another basis (say, quarterly).

Modified Duration   A measure of duration which attempts to adjust for the fact that coupon investment is done on a discrete rather than on a continuous basis. Mathematically, modified duration is obtained by dividing Macaulay's duration by (1 + Y/N) where Y is yield and N is the number of coupon payments per year.

Money Market Yield   A measure of return typically applied to money market securities but also relevant for fixed-income securities held for less than one year. The day-count basis for this calculation is Actual/360.

   If a money market yield is calculated for a security or strategy with only one cashflow from the time of purchase until maturity (as with a Treasury Bill), and if the security or strategy is held until maturity, then the security's money market yield will be equal to the security's return.

Mortgage-Backed Security (MBS)   A fixed-income security with principal and coupon payments linked to one or more underlying mortgages. A MBS linked to one underlying mortgage is often referred to as a whole loan MBS.

Negative Skewness   The narrowing tail on the left side of a non-normal distribution. If the skewness is such that the distribution is non-normal, then the distribution cannot be defined with only a mean and a standard deviation.

Non-Normal Distribution   Any distribution that cannot be defined with a mean and a standard deviation alone.

Normal Distribution   A distribution that is symmetrical on either side of the distribution's mean. A property of this distribution is that it may be defined with only a mean and a standard deviation.

Normal Volatility Curve   For a volatility curve created with prices of fixed-income securities, a normal curve has a positive slope. That is, volatilities at the short-end of the volatility curve are lower than volatilities at the long-end of the volatility curve. For a given change in yield, prices of shorter-dated securities tend to change by less than prices of longer-dated securities. This is what we would intuitively expect from the properties of duration. Thus, the normal slope of a volatility price curve is positive.

For a volatility curve created with yields of fixed-income securities, a normal curve has an inverted slope. That is, volatilities at the short end of the volatility curve are higher than volatilities at the long end of the volatility curve. For a given change in price, yields of shorter-dated securities tend to change by more than yields of longer-dated securities. This is what we would intuitively expect from the properties of duration. Thus, the normal slope of a volatility yield curve is negative.

Normal Yield Curve   A positively sloped yield curve where interest rates at very short maturities are below interest rates at very long maturities.

Note   A cash fixed-income security with 10 years or less to maturity.

Notional Value   The benchmark or reference value of a trade as with a notional principal value for an interest rate swap.

Option   An instrument that embodies the right to take a long (with a call) or a short (with a put) position in the underlying security.

Par   100% of the original face value of a cash fixed-income security.

Perpetual Floating Rate Note   A floating rate note with no specified maturity date.

Positive Skewness   The narrowing tail on the right side of a non-normal distribution. If the skewness is such that the distribution is non-normal, then the distribution cannot be defined with only a mean and a standard deviation.

Premium   The up-front payment received (paid) when an option is sold short (purchased).

Present Value   Today's price of one or more future cashflows.

Principal   The final cashflow of a cash fixed-income security less the final coupon payment.

Principal Only MBS (PO)   The principal component of a MBS that has been stripped.

Rate of Discount   1. The measure of a U.S. Treasury Bill's rate of return if held to maturity. The day count basis for a rate of discount on a U.S. Treasury Bill is Actual/360.

2. The rate at which cashflows are discounted over an investment horizon. For example, for a bond-equivalent yield calculation, the cashflows of a Treasury Note or Bond are all discounted at the same rate; that is, the bond-equivalent yield.

Reconstitution   Combining stripped coupon and principal cashflows to create a traditional coupon security.

Repo   A transaction whereby an investor agrees to lend securities over a predetermined period of time in exchange for a loan of cash.

Repo Rate   The rate of interest paid (bid side) or received (offer side) in a repo (reverse repo) transaction. Day count basis is Actual/360.

Reverse Repo   A transaction whereby an investor agrees to lend cash over a predetermined period of time in exchange for securities.

Risk-Free Rate   The rate of return expected for a riskless asset such as a Treasury Bill. In many instances an overnight repo rate is used as a riskless rate—even if the trade is to be held for longer than one day.

Settlement   The day on which cashflows are exchanged for a cash security trade, and the reference date for accrued interest calculations, if any.

Short Coupons   A coupon Treasury security with one or two coupon payments until maturity.

Sinking Fund Issue   A fixed-income security is retired a piece at a time at predetermined dates and prices.

Simple Interest   A measure of a security's return. Generally, simple interest is reserved for securities with one year or less to maturity. Although there is no standard day count basis for calculating a simple interest value, the most common practice is to use Actual/360.

Simple Margin   A measure of return in basis points that is either added to or subtracted from an index rate to derive a yield.

Spot Rate   The yield on a security with a single cashflow.

Standard Deviation   A measure of the volatility or variability of a series or distribution.

Standstill Return   The expected return on a security or strategy assuming that all variables are held constant until the security or strategy is reversed. This return is commonly used for option strategies since an option's value is critically dependent on more than one variable.

STRIPS Separate Trading of Registered Interest and Principal Securities. A single cashflow security.

Stripping Creating single cashflow securities from a coupon-bearing security.

Swap Spread The value in basis points over a benchmark yield to be paid on the fixed-rate side of an interest rate swap. The benchmark yield for the U.S. and Canadian markets would be the appropriate Treasury yield.

Swaption A trade that gives an investor the right to enter into an interest rate swap at a future date. An investor who purchases a call (put) swaption has the right to exchange fixed- (floating-) rate cashflows for floating- (fixed-) rate cashflows over time.

Synthetic A product created with a combination of securities for the purpose of replicating or creating an asset.

Term Repo A repo rate of any period of time longer than overnight.

Term Structure of Interest Rates A curve created by plotting interest rates against respective maturities.

Term Structure of Volatility A curve created by plotting volatilities against respective maturities.

Treasury Bill An obligation of the U.S. government with one year or less to maturity. Yield is calculated with a rate of discount with Actual/360 day-count basis.

Variance Standard deviation squared. A measure of the dispersion of a series.

Volatility An annualized standard deviation. A measure of the expected trading range for a security. Sometimes viewed as a measure of a security's risk.

Yield-to-Maturity A measure of a fixed-income security's return.

Z-Tranche Generally, the tranche of a collateralized mortgage obligation (CMO) that has been reserved for paying out the very last of any cashflows.

Index